I0793341

IMAGES
of America

GALLATIN COUNTY

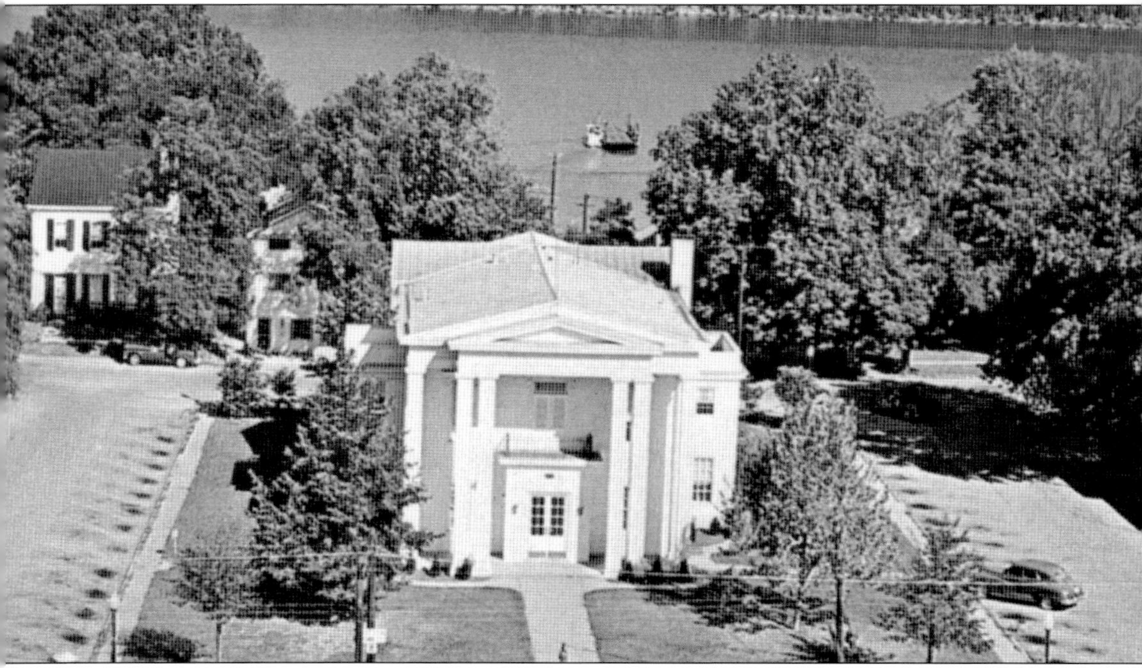

Pulse of the County. This 1940s aerial photograph shows the location of the county courthouse in Warsaw and its proximity to the Ohio River. Built in 1837, the building faced the river from the hill directly above the ferry landing (note the ferry on the river). It was remodeled in 1939 by the Works Progress Administration (WPA) to have the main entrance face Main Street and remove the bell tower. The county clerk's office (back left) was built in the 19th century and is known to local residents as the Craig House. (Courtesy of Darrell Maines.)

On the Cover: Harold Brown (left) and Whitney Payne ride their carriage away from the Warsaw riverfront in this 1910 photograph. Behind them docked at the landing are a wharf boat and the *City of Cincinnati* steamboat. Warsaw was a regular stop for the steamer on its route between Cincinnati and Louisville. (Courtesy of Robert and Alexandra Weldon.)

IMAGES
of America

GALLATIN COUNTY

Melinda Sartwell and Rebecca Riesenberg

ARCADIA
PUBLISHING

ISBN 978-1-4671-1430-1

Published by Arcadia Publishing
Charleston, South Carolina

Printed in the United States of America

Library of Congress Control Number: 2015930636

For all general information, please contact Arcadia Publishing:
Telephone 843-853-2070
Fax 843-853-0044
E-mail sales@arcadiapublishing.com
For customer service and orders:
Toll-Free 1-888-313-2665

Visit us on the Internet at www.arcadiapublishing.com

Contents

Acknowledgments

We would like to thank the following people for their help and encouragement throughout this endeavor: Darrell Maines, Robert and Alexandra Weldon, Dale Samuel, Russell Hall, Jacqueline Mylor of the Gallatin County Historical Society, Dana Benne, JC and Mary Spencer Noel, Brad Noel, Len Glockner of the Kentucky Speedway, Dan Fuehner, Bernie Spencer, nkyviews.com for the wealth of information provided on the site, and the Gallatin County Free Public Library for the use of their facilities and local history materials that were invaluable to the writing of this book. We also want to thank our family members Michael Riesenberg and Greg and Amy Dickerson for their help and support during this endeavor.

We would also like to thank our editor, Jesse Darland, for his guidance and patience throughout the process of creating a book out of the vast array of photographs and information that was gathered for this project.

INTRODUCTION

Founded in 1798, Gallatin County lies along the banks of the Ohio River approximately halfway between Cincinnati and Louisville. Early settlers traveling down the Ohio River in search of new land found the fertile river bottom a perfect site to put down roots.

Settled by pioneer Col. Robert Johnson about 1800, the tiny hamlet named Great Landing was clustered around the river port. As the village grew, the name was changed to Fredericksburg in 1815, thought to be named after Colonel Johnson's hometown of Fredericksburg, Virginia. By 1831, the population had grown enough for the residents to request their own post office. It was thought that since another town in Kentucky was named Fredericksville, the names were too similar, and the village was forced to change its name. While there are different theories about the origins of the name Warsaw, the likeliest version is that the name was chosen as a tribute to the revolutions occurring in Poland at the time. Though nearby Port William (now Carrollton) was the county seat, Warsaw quickly became an important stop for steamboats traveling between Cincinnati and Louisville, eventually connecting with the Mississippi River on their way to New Orleans. This provided an economic base for both businesses and farms that dotted rolling hills surrounding the town and throughout the county. Warsaw became the county seat in 1837, when Port William was included in the newly created Carroll County. The courthouse was erected the same year and is still in use today.

The river was not the only economic factor to benefit the county. With the advent of rail travel, the Louisville & Nashville Railroad built a line through the county to connect Cincinnati and Louisville. Crossing through both Sparta and Glencoe on the southern border of the county, the railroad provided another layer of economic opportunity for the more rural residents. The highway system that was built in the early 1940s increased the usage of trucks for the delivery of goods and passenger vehicles for travel, resulting in the railroad system fading away in importance. Gallatin remained a vital artery, as US Highway 42 crosses the county directly through Warsaw.

At its founding, Gallatin County was one of the largest counties in Kentucky. As the population grew, the county was divided several times and eventually reached its status as the commonwealth's smallest county, with a current population of approximately 8,600 people and just under 100 square miles. The riverfront area around the original landing known as "under the hill" largely disappeared under the river after years of being ravaged by floods and as the pool level of the river rose with the construction of the dam system. Most of the remaining area is now the city park.

Today, Gallatin County is still largely rural, and Warsaw retains its small-town charm, with numerous National Register historic buildings still in use as businesses and residences. Boating is a popular activity, and the marina at Warsaw draws numerous visitors from the surrounding area. Directly across the river from the marina in Indiana is the Belterra Casino, which also brings in tourists who frequent local businesses. Two major businesses located their operations in Warsaw: Gallatin Steel, a major steel manufacturer, and Dorman Products, an automotive parts supplier.

The big draw for Gallatin County is the Kentucky Speedway. Located by Interstate 71 in Sparta, the racetrack opened in 2000 with a seating capacity of 110,000. In 2011, the speedway hosted its first NASCAR Sprint Series Quaker State 400. Thousands of tourists come to the speedway not only for this race but also for other smaller races, concerts, and tours of the enormous facility. These tourists also visit Warsaw to eat, visit the marina, take the historical walking tour, and enjoy other activities that have provided a boon to the local economy.

Gallatin County is a unique combination of history and modern amenities, a rural retreat close to the city life of both Cincinnati and Louisville. The continued growth of the large businesses and the resurgence of the downtown district of Warsaw with quaint shops and restaurants make Gallatin County a desirable place to live.

One

THE EARLY YEARS

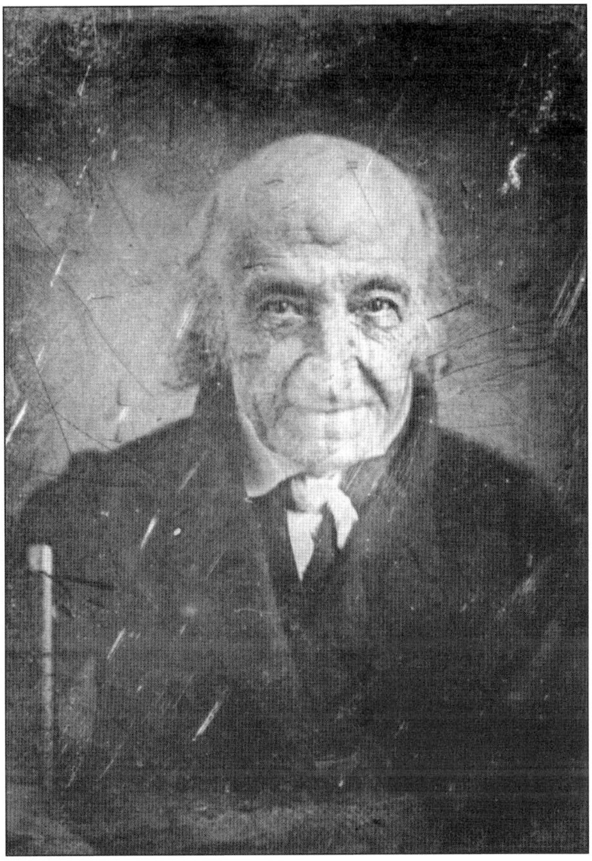

A DISTINGUISHED STATESMAN. Gallatin County was named for Swiss-born statesman Albert Gallatin. Born in 1761, Gallatin forged a long career as a financier, Pennsylvania legislator, diplomat, and secretary of the treasury for Thomas Jefferson and James Madison. His statue can be seen in front of the US Treasury Building in Washington, DC. He died in 1849 and is buried in New York City. He is not known to have ever visited the Kentucky county that was named in his honor. (Courtesy of the Library of Congress.)

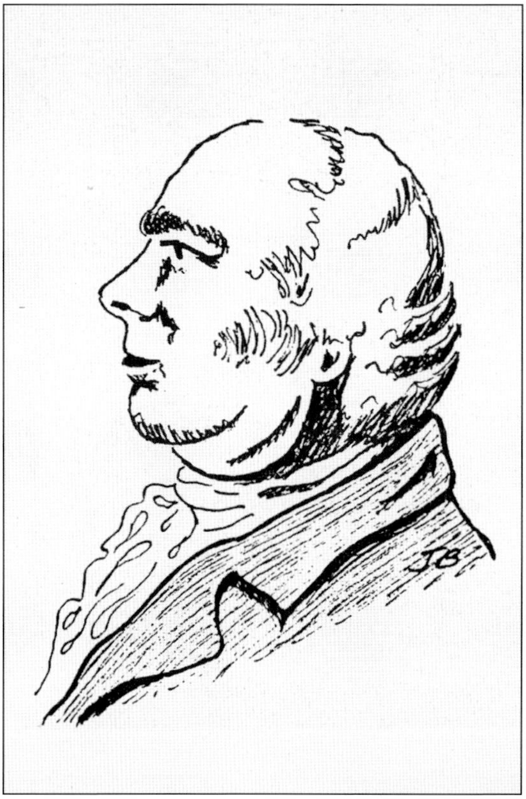

Founding Fathers. Col. Robert Johnson was an early settler and wealthy landowner in Scott County, Kentucky, who purchased large acreage on the riverbank, creating a tiny settlement called Great Landing about 1800. By 1814, more settlers began arriving, so Johnson and his partner, Henry Yates, platted a village of 172 lots to be divided evenly between them and sold. Colonel Johnson constructed a large two-story brick home on the outskirts of the platted town (now known as High School Court), which was torn down in 1918. Fredericksburg was recorded in 1815, but Johnson died before the sale of lots began. His son Richard Mentor Johnson later became vice president under Martin Van Buren, from 1836 to 1841. Henry Yates chose to build a simple log house on the corner of High Street across from the courthouse. His son Richard Yates later became the governor of Illinois. The house is still in use as a private residence. (Left, courtesy of the Gallatin County Free Public Library; below, courtesy of Darrell Maines.)

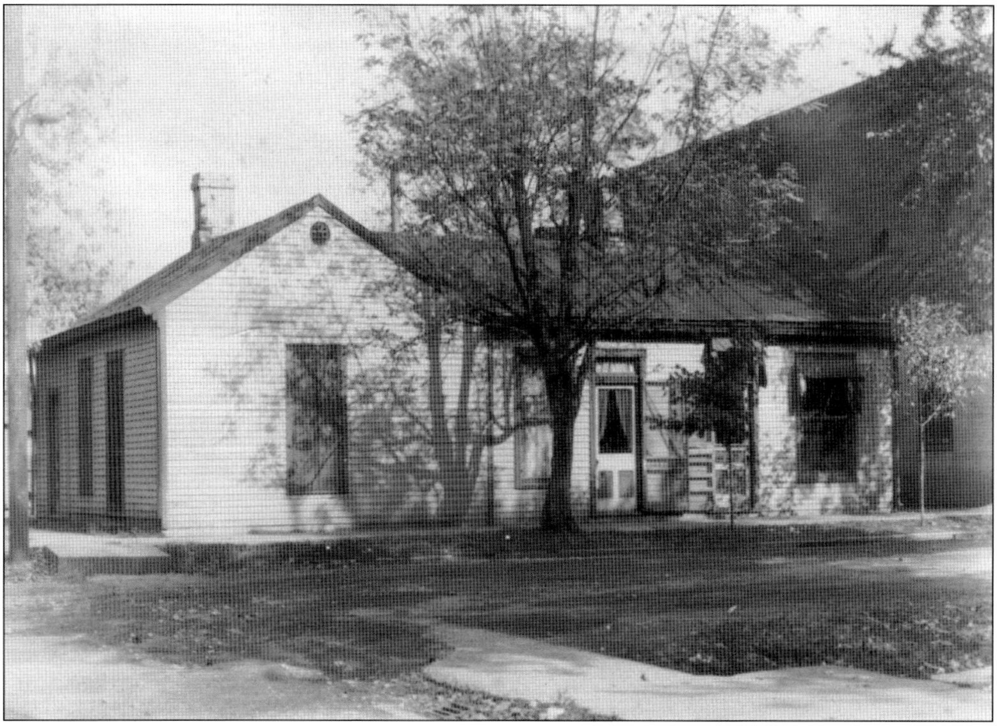

The Governor. Born in Fredericksburg in 1815, Richard Yates was the son of early settler Henry Yates. After his mother died, the family moved to Springfield, Illinois, where Yates later practiced law and served as a state senator. He was then elected as a US representative during the 1850s and served as governor of Illinois from 1861 to 1865. He was a close friend and advisor to Pres. Abraham Lincoln while Lincoln was in Illinois and remained close during the tumultuous years of the Civil War. After the war, he was a US senator, dying suddenly in 1873. His son Richard Yates Jr. also served as governor of Illinois. (Courtesy of the Library of Congress.)

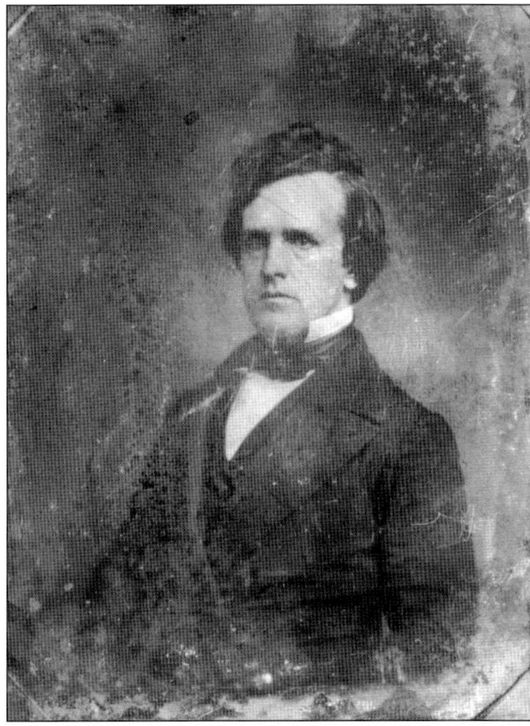

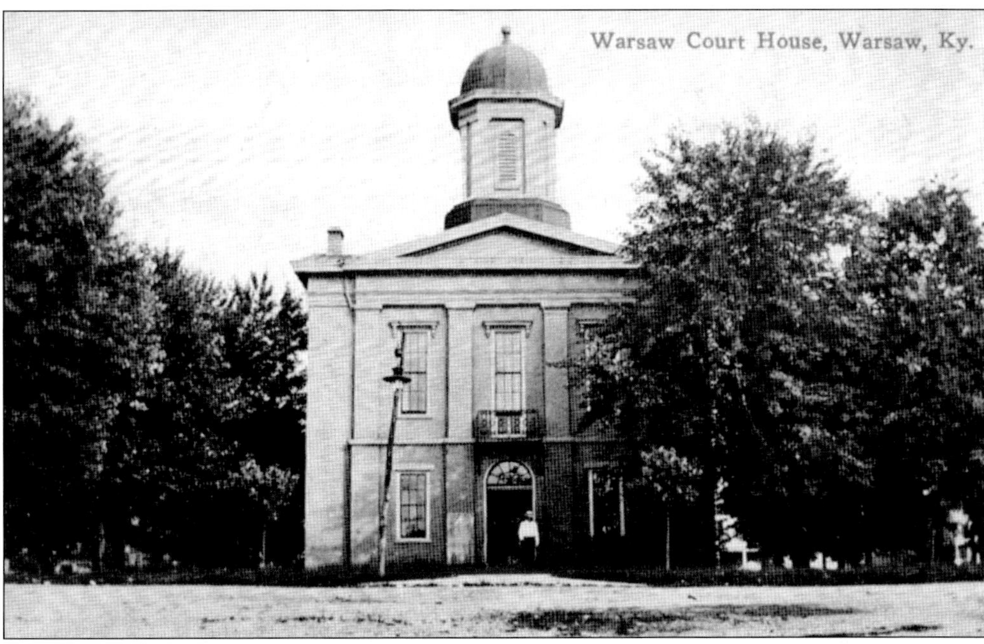

The Old Courthouse. This photograph, taken about 1900, shows the courthouse as it stood facing the river. The bell tower was added in 1868. It was remodeled in 1938, fashioned in the Greek Revival style, and now faces Main Street (US 42). The building had the good fortune to not suffer the fate of fire that many early structures encountered. The courthouse is the oldest still in use in Kentucky. (Courtesy of Darrell Maines.)

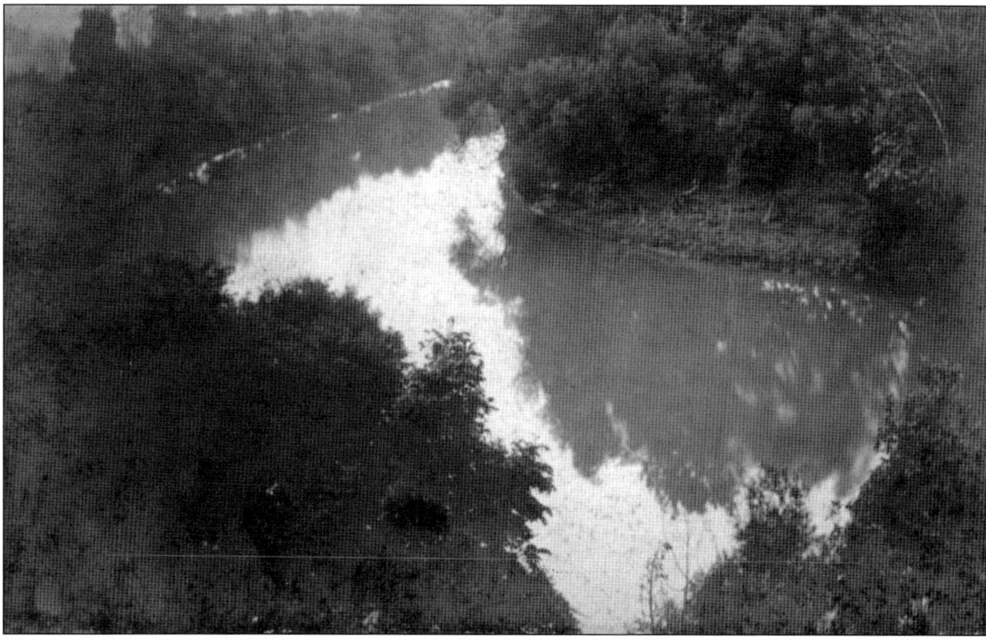

Inland Communities. This early 20th-century view of the Eagle Creek Valley shows the sprawling family farms that dotted the rolling landscape. While the county largely depended on the river trade, settlers found the rolling hills and fertile soil ideal for establishing family farms and small communities away from the bustle of the river traffic. Numerous creeks provided plenty of water, and gristmills arose along the Eagle Creek corridor. The inner corridor population further multiplied when the Louisville & Nashville Railroad route cut through the southern border of the county. Depots erected in Sparta and Glencoe kept busy with shipments of goods and travelers between Cincinnati, Ohio, and Louisville. (Both, courtesy of Darrell Maines.)

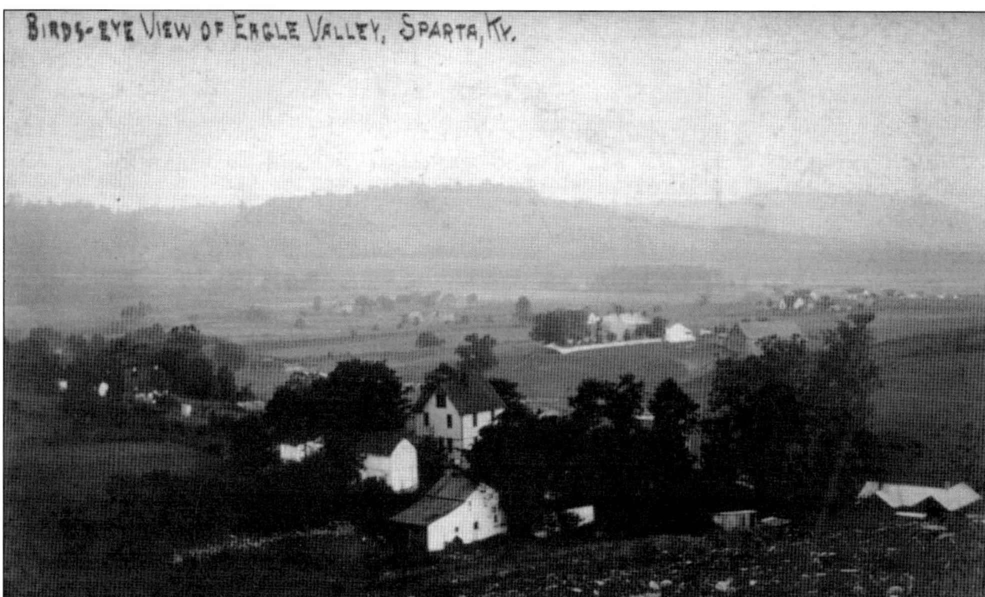

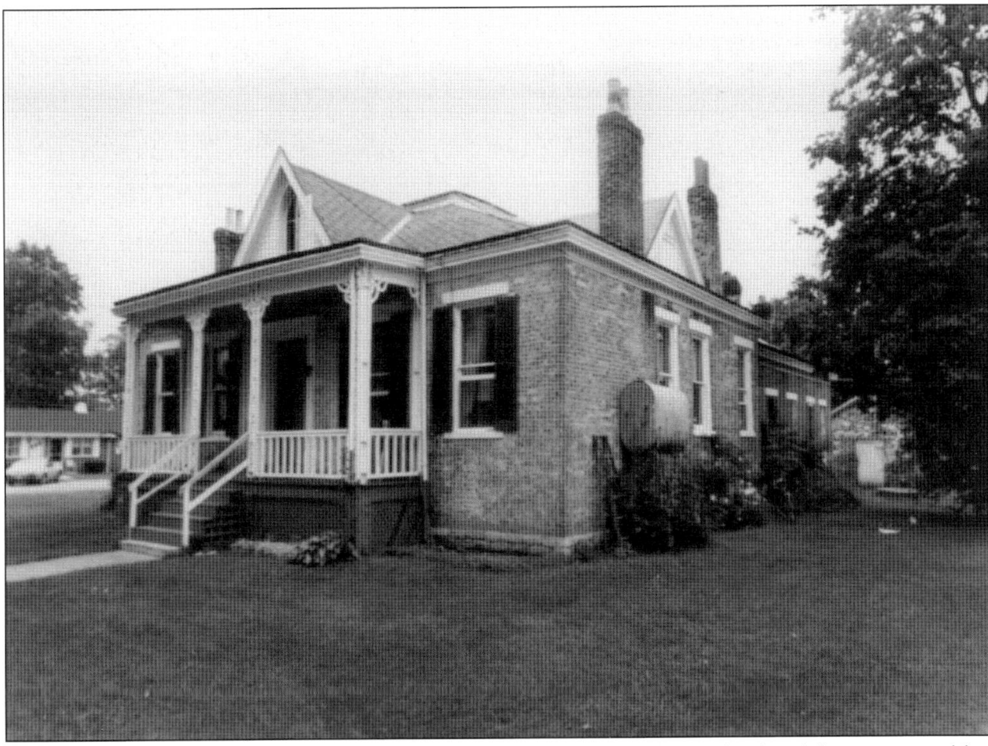

Hawkins-Kirby House. Built in 1843 by lawyer Edmund Hawkins, this brick house was sold to Capt. William Kirby, a longtime steamboat captain. Located on the southwest corner of Second and Market Streets, the building is now the home of the Gallatin County Historical Society. (Courtesy of Darrell Maines.)

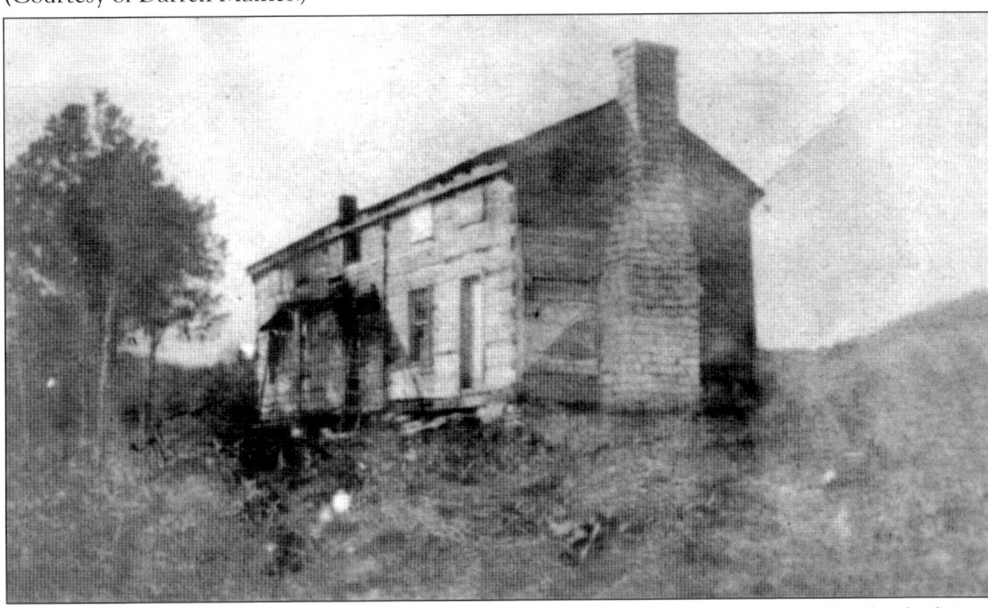

Early Home. The Mort Riblin house on Sparta Pike was typical of log houses built during early settlement. The Riblin family are longtime residents of Gallatin County. (Courtesy of Dale Samuel.)

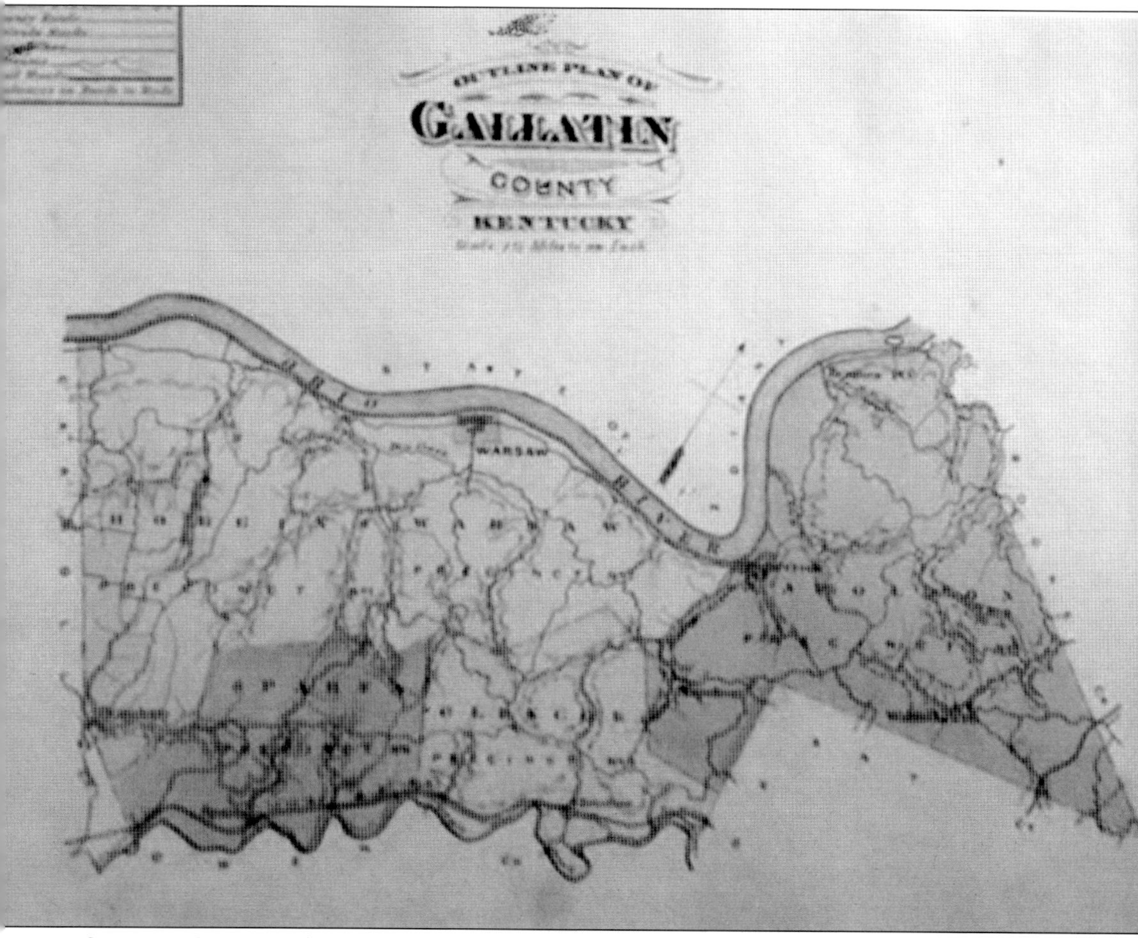

Smallest County. This image from the 1883 D.J. Lake Carroll and Gallatin County Atlas shows Gallatin in its final configuration. Originally one of the largest counties in the commonwealth, its boundaries were changed when Carroll County was formed out of the western half of the county. Later pieces were added to Trimble, Owen, Grant, and Boone Counties, resulting in a landscape of approximately 100 square miles, making it the smallest county in Kentucky. (Courtesy of the Gallatin County Free Public Library.)

Two

THE OHIO RIVER

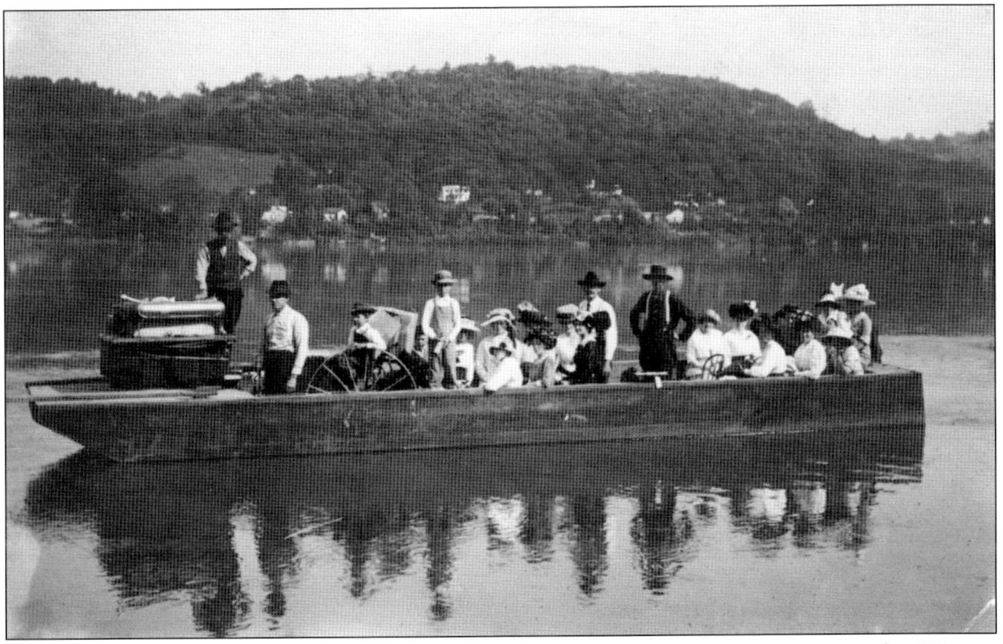

MUSIC BOAT. A group of boaters take a break from their river cruise to pose near the Warsaw ferry landing around 1890. The equipment on the bow of the boat is thought to house an unknown musical instrument. The hills of Indiana can be seen in the background. (Courtesy of Darrell Maines.)

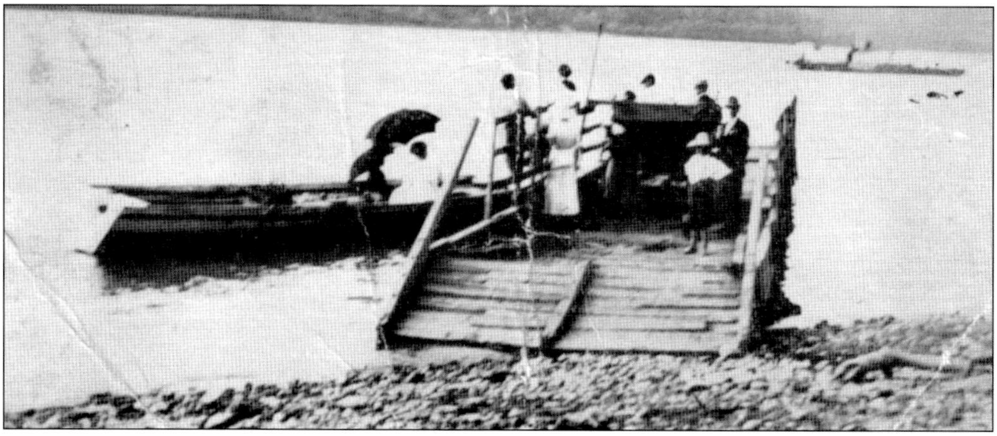

EARLY TRANSPORTATION. Warsaw was built around the early river landing, depending on the riverboats to transport goods and people. The ferry was also important for business and residents wishing to cross the river to Indiana. The Warsaw ferry, pictured above around 1916, shows passengers waiting to leave the landing toward Indiana. Ice was often a problem during the winter months, resulting in boats being frozen in place. The 1930s *Everett Lee* ferryboat (below) was immobile until the river thawed. The boat was named for owner Jeff Webb's son Everett Lee, who was killed in an explosion. (Both, courtesy of Darrell Maines.)

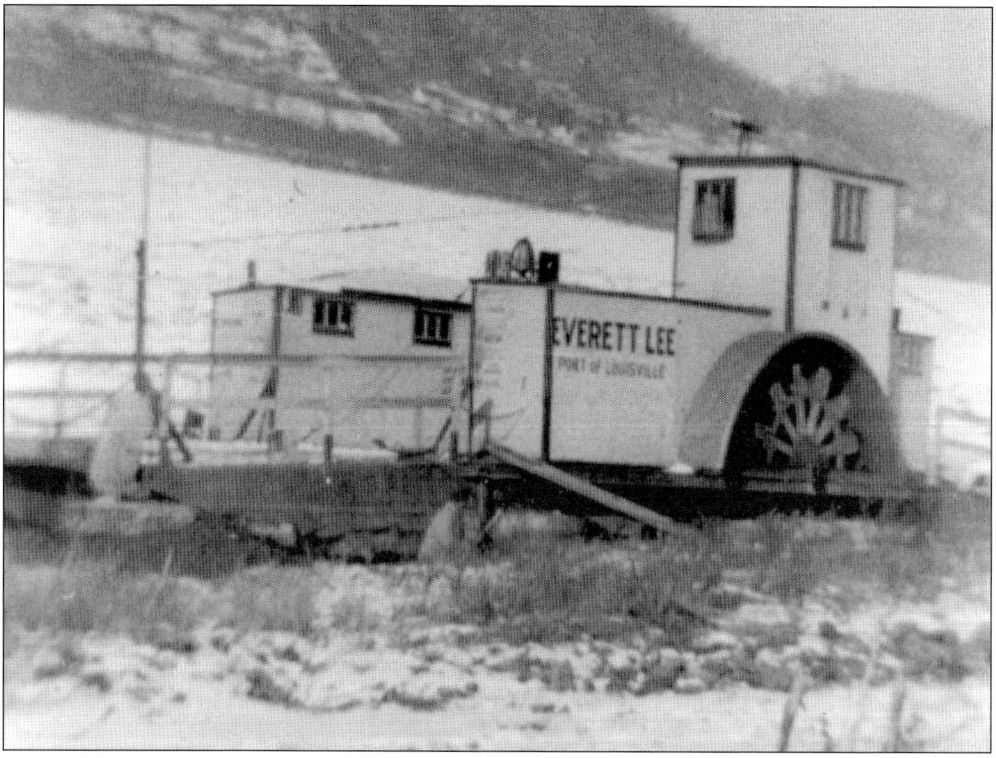

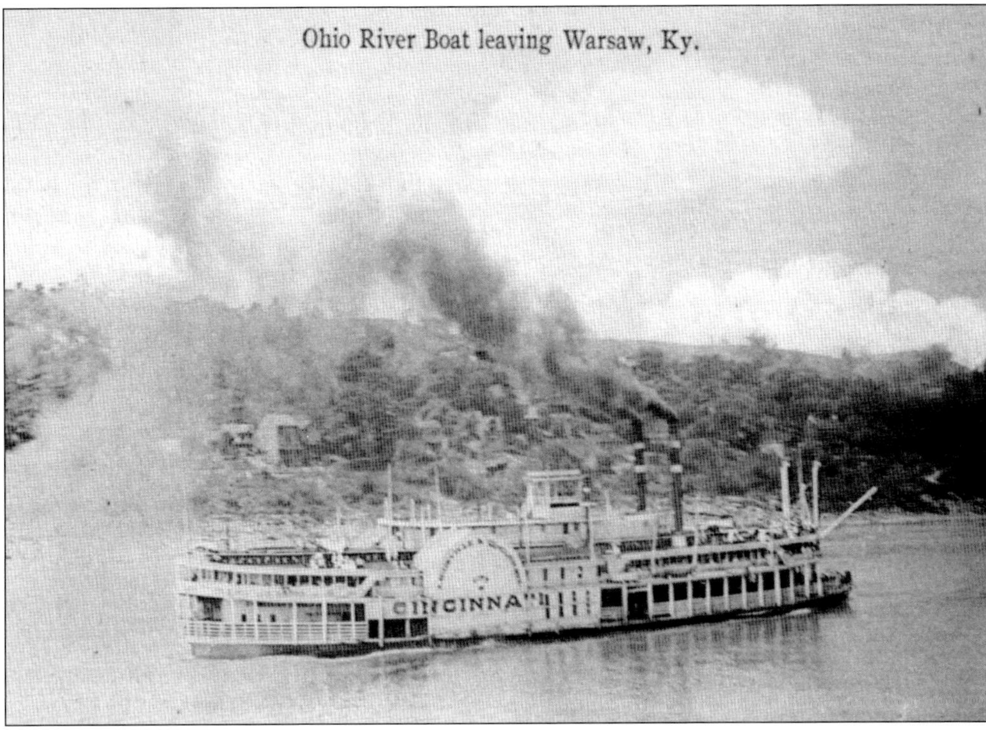

SIDE-WHEELING. Large side-wheel steamboats had the ability to travel long distances on the Ohio and Mississippi Rivers, making them vital to the economic success of river towns such as Warsaw. This image of the *Cincinnati* from about 1910 shows a typical view of river traffic in that era. The steamer stopped at the Warsaw landing on her many regular trips between Cincinnati and Louisville. She was destroyed by ice in 1918. Below, three unidentified men relax under the trees near the riverbank while a steamer makes its way on the Ohio River around 1920. (Both, courtesy of Darrell Maines.)

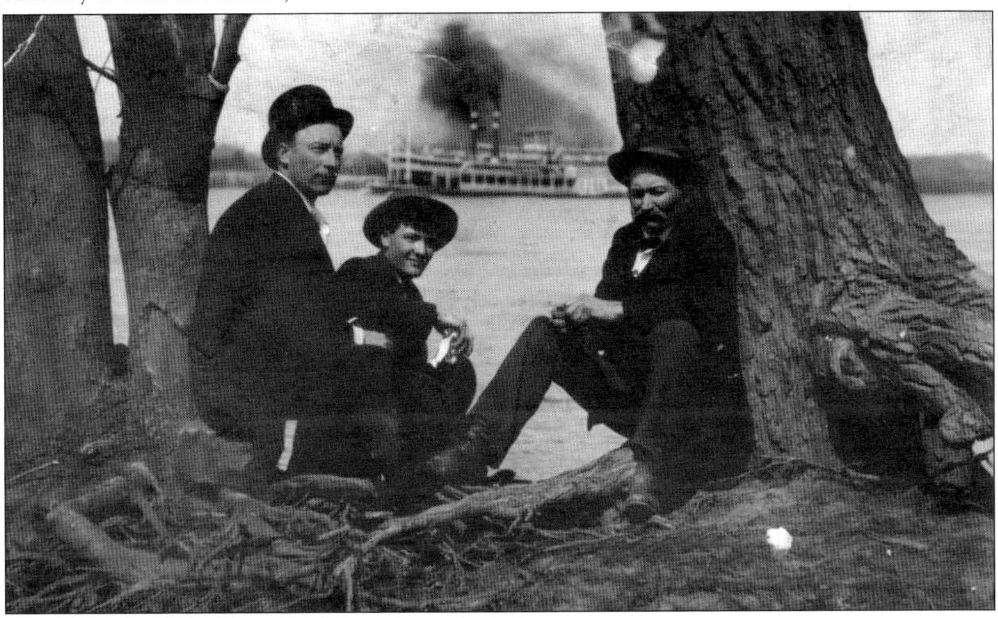

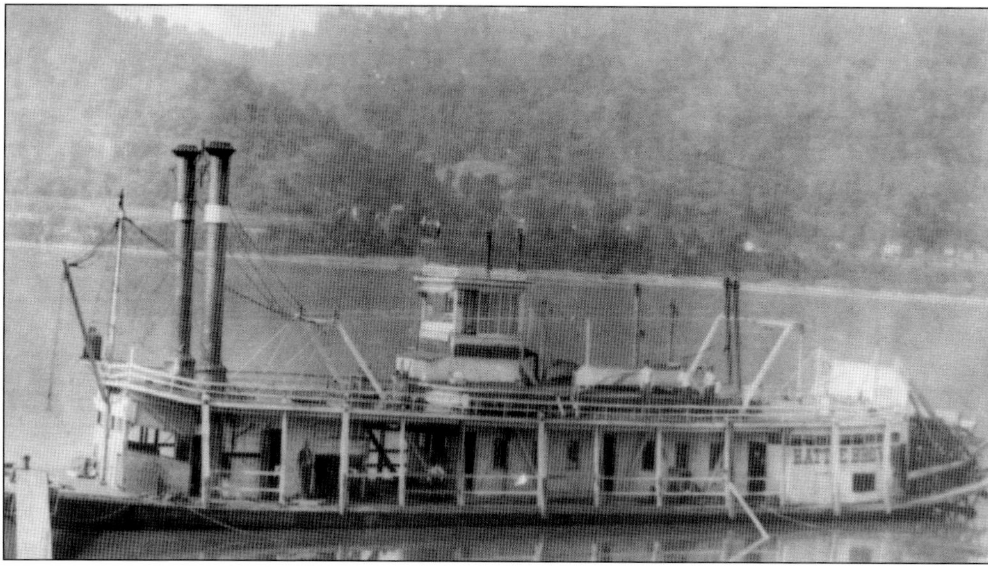

The *Hattie Brown*. Packet boats provided an economical means of local travel. Much smaller than the side-wheelers, these unglamorous boats ran the routes between the smaller river towns, often the only type of travel available before the advent of the railroad and reliable roads for automobiles. The *Hattie Brown* was a favorite of residents and traveled between Warsaw, Carrollton, and Madison, Indiana. She was destroyed by ice in 1918. Her engine and whistle were salvaged for use on a new packet, the *Vim*, but the *Hattie Brown* was sorely missed by all. (Courtesy of Darrell Maines.)

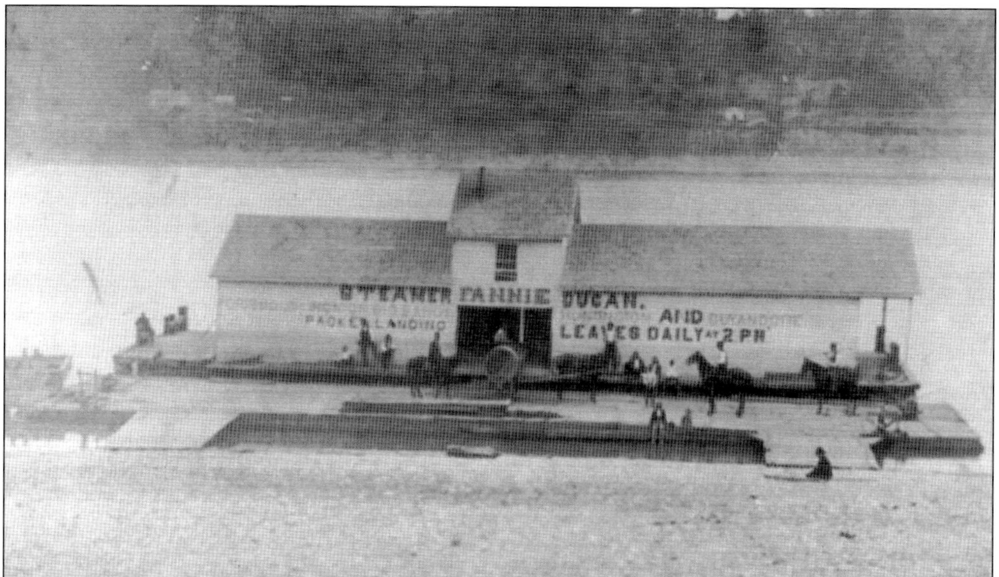

Busy Wharf Boat. The *Fanny Dugan* was a side-wheeler that ran between Warsaw, Carrollton, and Madison, Indiana. The larger steamers frequently had their own wharf boats that were permanently attached to the shore. Steamboats pulled up to load and unload cargo. The wharf boats also were used for storage of incoming and outgoing goods. Built in 1872, this wharf boat was originally stationed at Madison, Indiana, before being moved to the Warsaw landing. (Courtesy of Darrell Maines.)

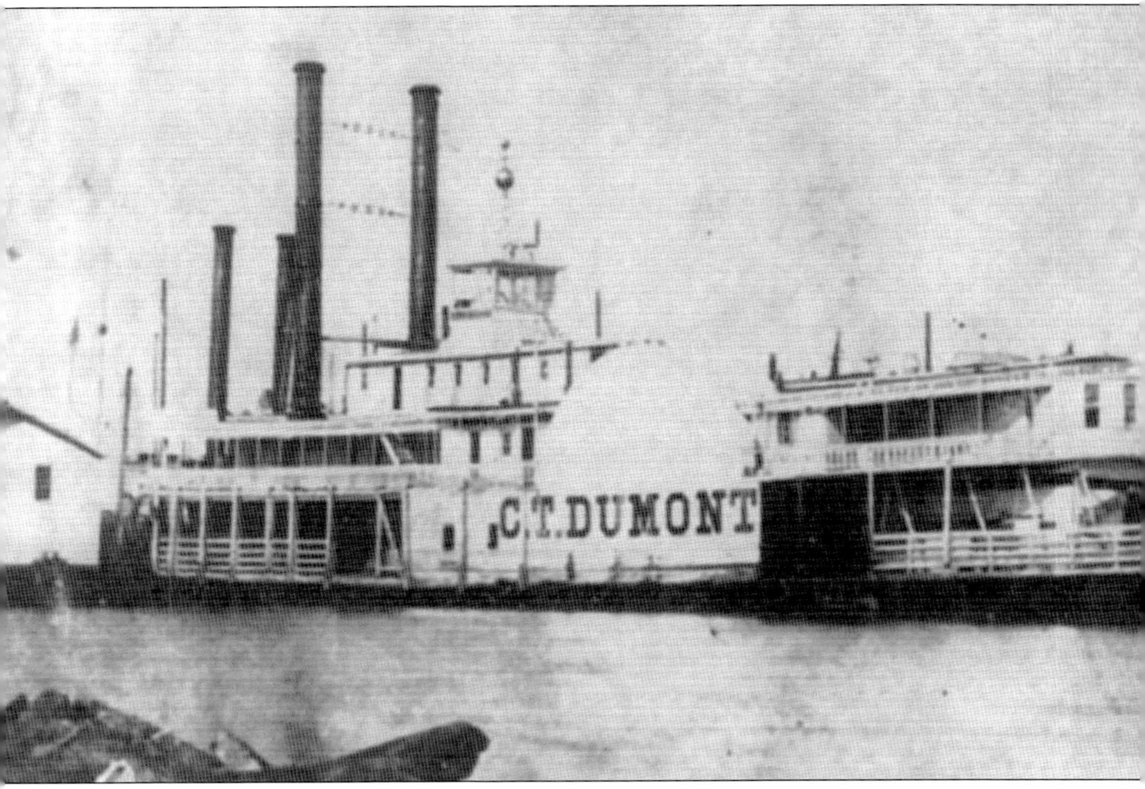

A Busy Riverboat. Built in Cincinnati in 1864, the *C.T. Dumont* ran the mail route between Cincinnati and Madison, Indiana. In 1865, it crashed at nearby Big Bone Island, but the craft was repaired. In 1867, while docked at Warsaw, a tornado hit the boat and pushed it across the river to the Indiana side. Severely damaged, the boat was again repaired and put into trade service between Cincinnati and Louisville. The *C.T. Dumont* also transported Gen. Ulysses S. Grant, his family, and Gen. Kirby Smith to Cincinnati. (Courtesy of Darrell Maines.)

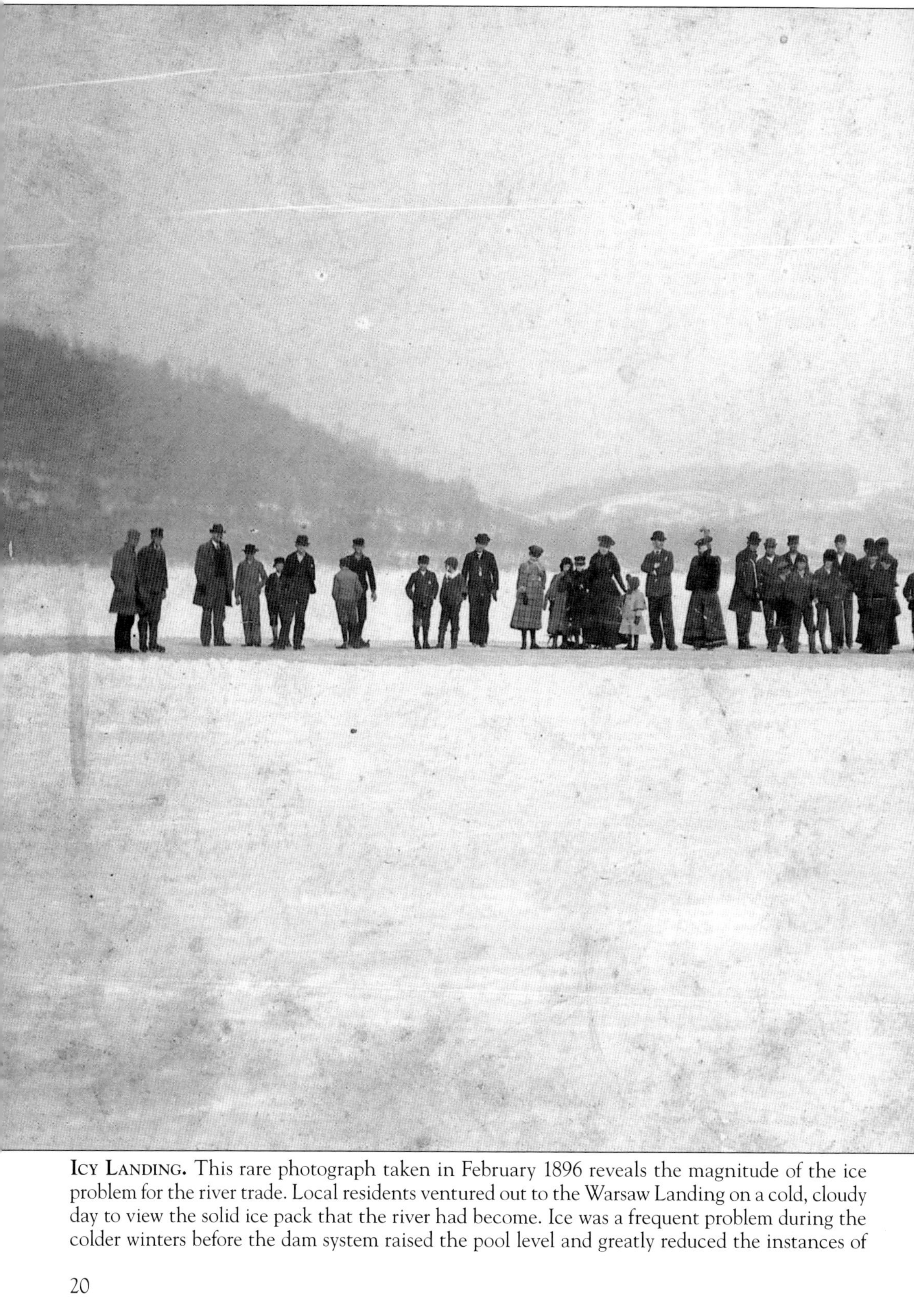

Icy Landing. This rare photograph taken in February 1896 reveals the magnitude of the ice problem for the river trade. Local residents ventured out to the Warsaw Landing on a cold, cloudy day to view the solid ice pack that the river had become. Ice was a frequent problem during the colder winters before the dam system raised the pool level and greatly reduced the instances of

the river freezing over. The ice prevented boats from traveling and greatly impacted economic activity for the river towns. Steamboats often fell victim to the heavy ice and were destroyed or severely damaged. (Courtesy of Darrell Maines.)

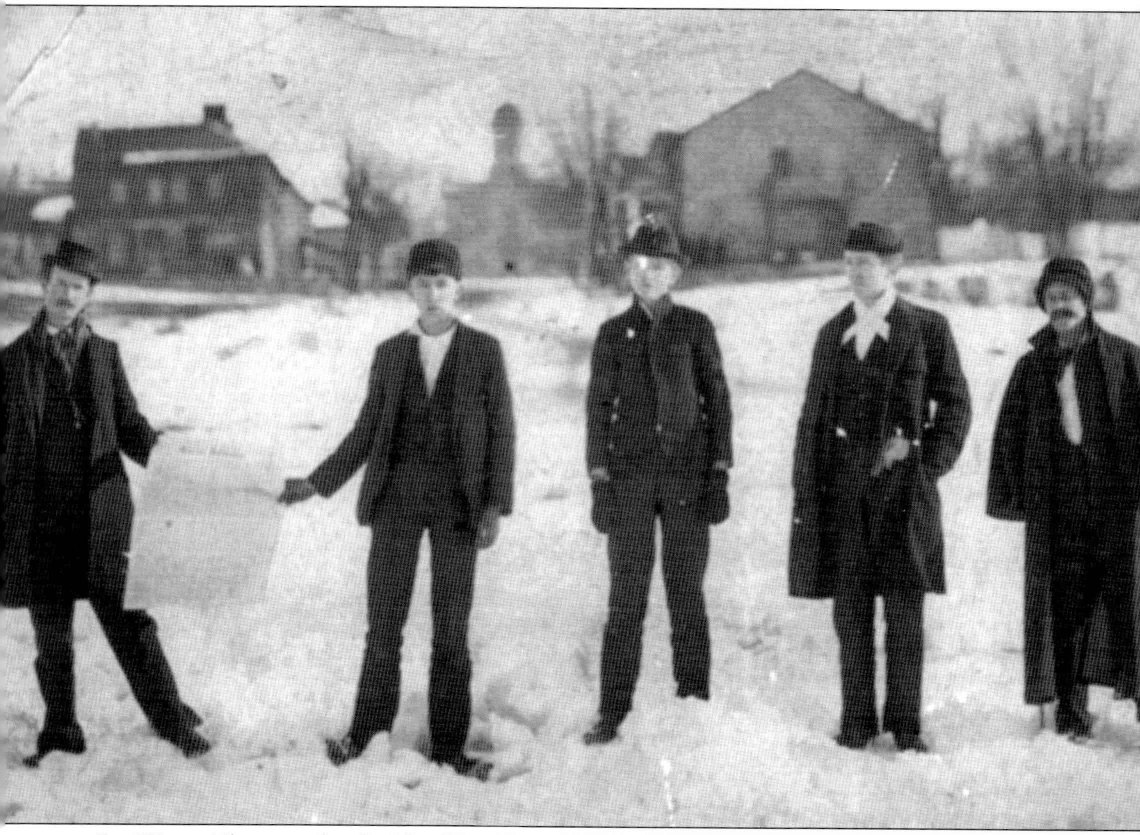

ICE WALK. The water level of the Ohio River was much lower before the modern dams were built. As this photograph from 1918 shows, the shallow waters were subject to freezing solid during unusually cold winters. The identifiable men are Don Ethol Vanice and Arthur Vanice (second and third from left); the other individuals are, in no particular order, D.B. Wallace (owner of the *Warsaw Independent*), Joe Taylor, and Tom Kirby. The two men on the left are holding a copy of the *Warsaw Independent*. (Courtesy of Darrell Maines.)

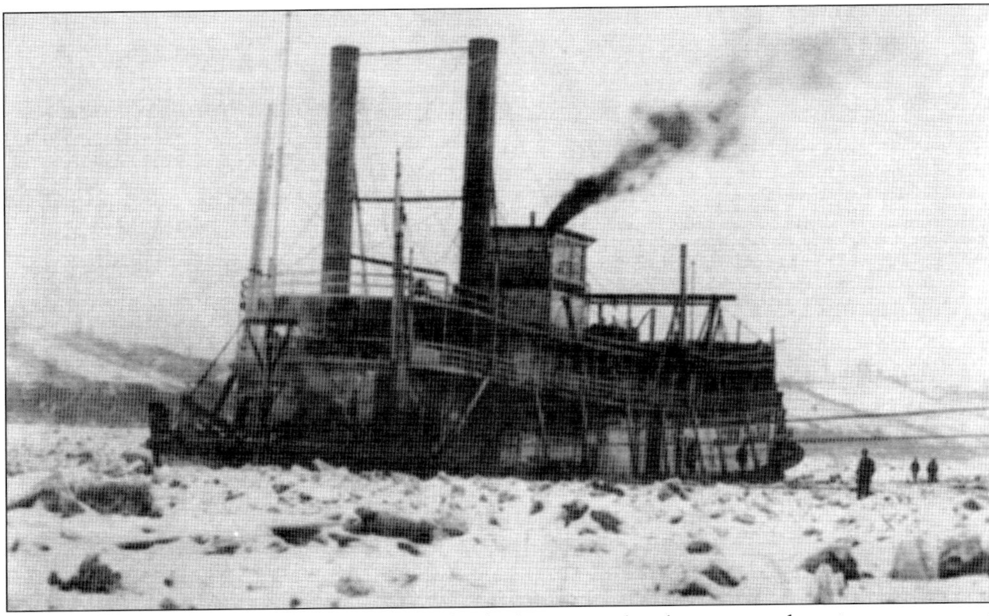

Stuck in the Ice. Before the dams were built, low water level or ice in the winter prevented riverboats from running their routes. This 1892 photograph of the *John Dana* frozen at Sugar Creek depicts one of the hazards faced by tradesmen and travelers on the river before the advent of the dam system. While low water levels prevented boats from running, a frozen river destroyed boats unlucky enough to be in the way when the ice dam broke. (Courtesy of Darrell Maines.)

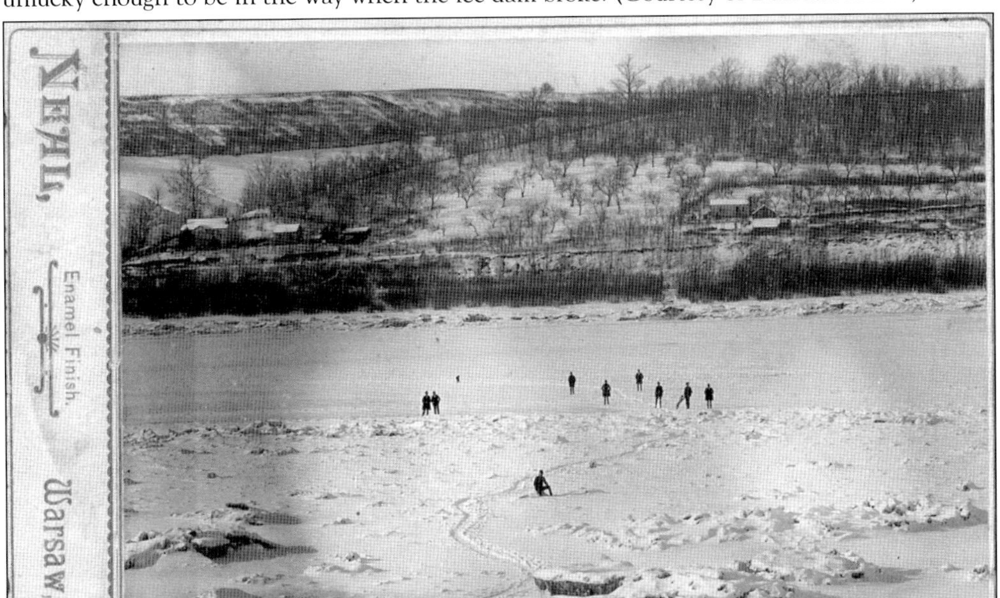

Before the Dam. This photograph, taken around 1900, is believed to have been captured at the site of today's Markland Dam. The narrow path of the river where the men are standing is in stark contrast to the current width due to the dam. The man in the front is kneeling on the Indiana riverbank with the Gallatin hillside in the background. (Courtesy of Darrell Maines.)

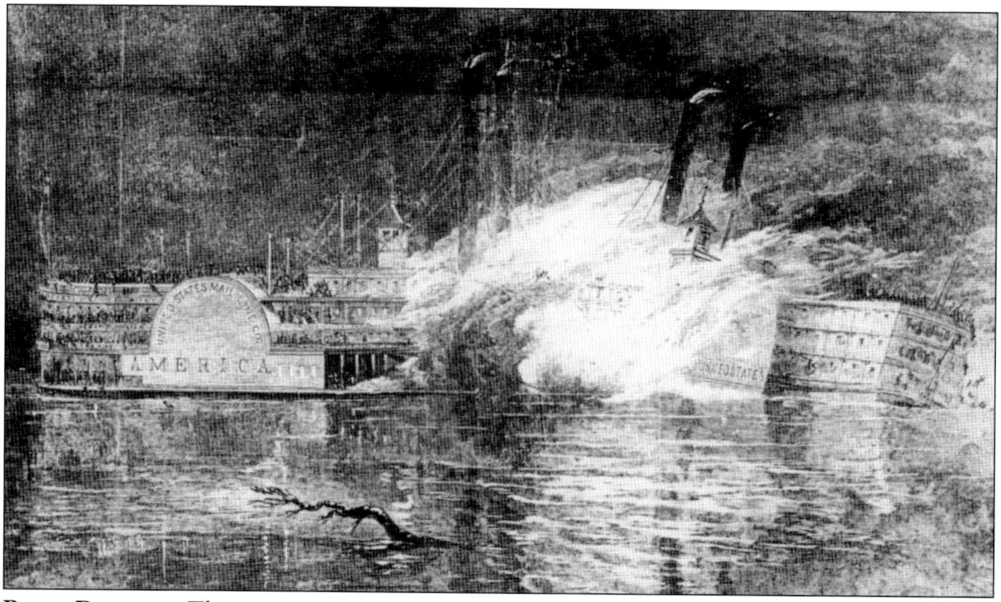

RIVER DISASTER. The worst river tragedy to occur in Gallatin County happened on December 4, 1868, when the *United States* and the *America*, both US Mail Line steamboats, collided just past the Sugar Creek bend in the river, about two miles above Warsaw. The *Harper's Weekly* illustration above depicts the ensuing fire that resulted. Accounts of the disaster state that the captain of the *United States* failed to hear the whistle of the *America* as it was coming around the bend. The *United States* burst into flames, which spread to the *America*, causing passengers to jump overboard as the boats tried to get to the Indiana shore. The Kentucky Historical Marker placed at the Sugar Creek overlook says that 162 people perished in the fire. The map below shows the location of the disaster as well as other riverboat wrecks in the same area of the river. (Both, courtesy of the Gallatin County Free Public Library.)

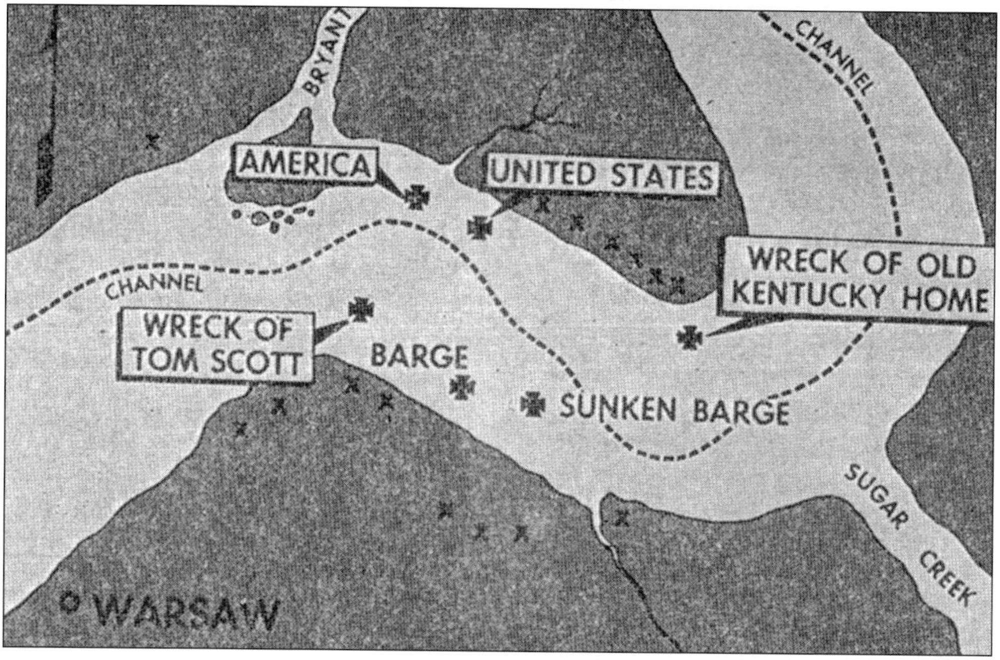

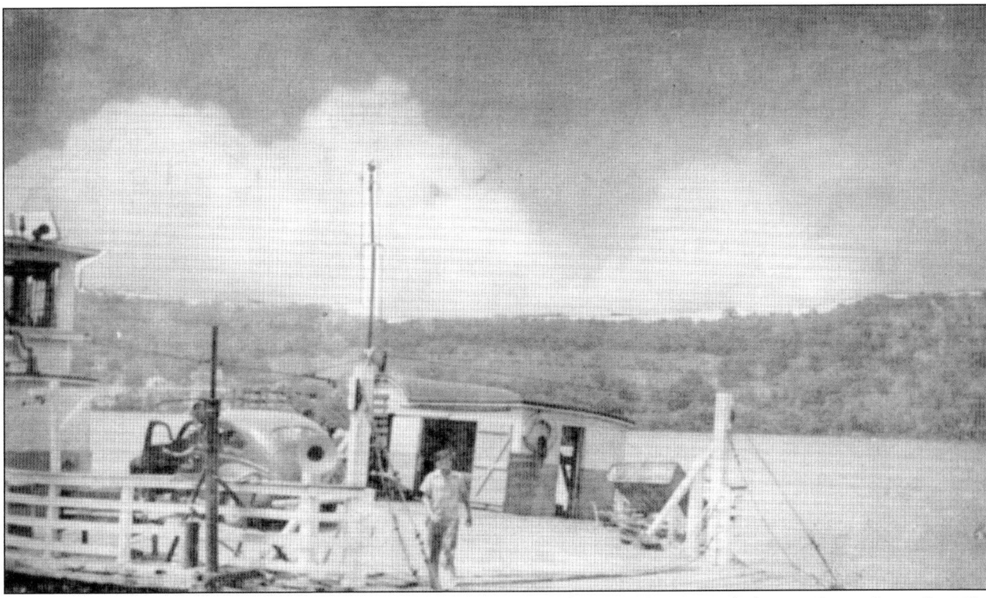

WARSAW FERRY. The ferry stayed busy even after the advent of automobiles and good roads. The 1949 photograph above shows deckhand James Everett Webb at work while the ferry carries a vehicle across the river to Indiana. The ferry was owned by Allan Young (in the pilot house) and Jimmy Hart (sitting in the car) and operated 24 hours a day, seven days a week. The 1950s image of the ferry below shows a newer version of the ferryboat preparing to carry two vehicles to Indiana. (Courtesy of Darrell Maines.)

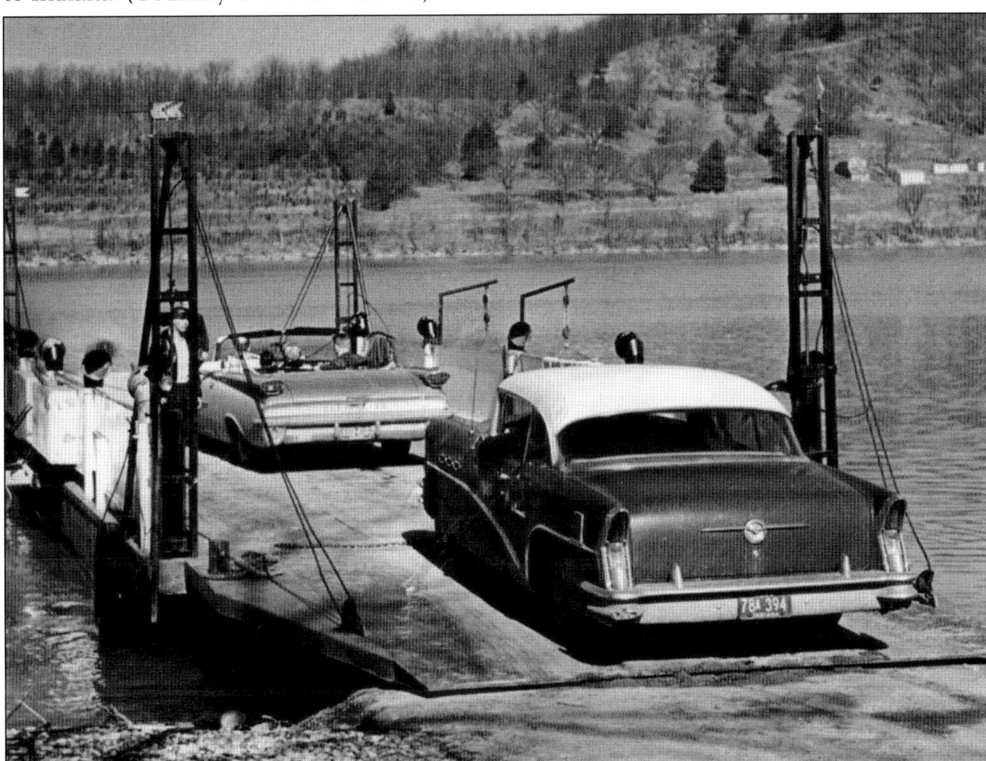

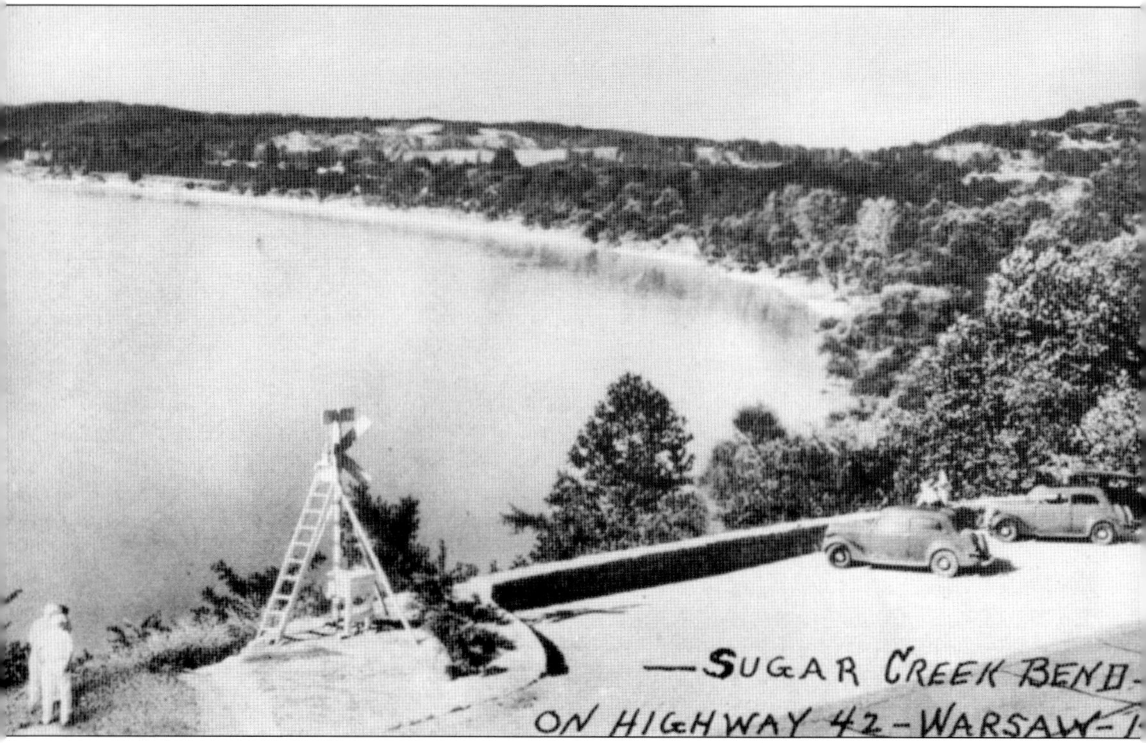

SUGAR CREEK BEND. This 1940s photograph shows the Sugar Creek Bend Overlook. Still in use today, the overlook provides a roadside rest stop for travelers to view the beauty of the Ohio River as it forms a sharp bend passing by the creek. Previously known as Jackson's Landing, the bend was the site of several tragic riverboat accidents due to the lack of visibility while navigating the sharp turn. A historical marker is placed at the site honoring the victims of the *United States* and *America* steamboat accident in 1868. (Courtesy of Darrell Maines.)

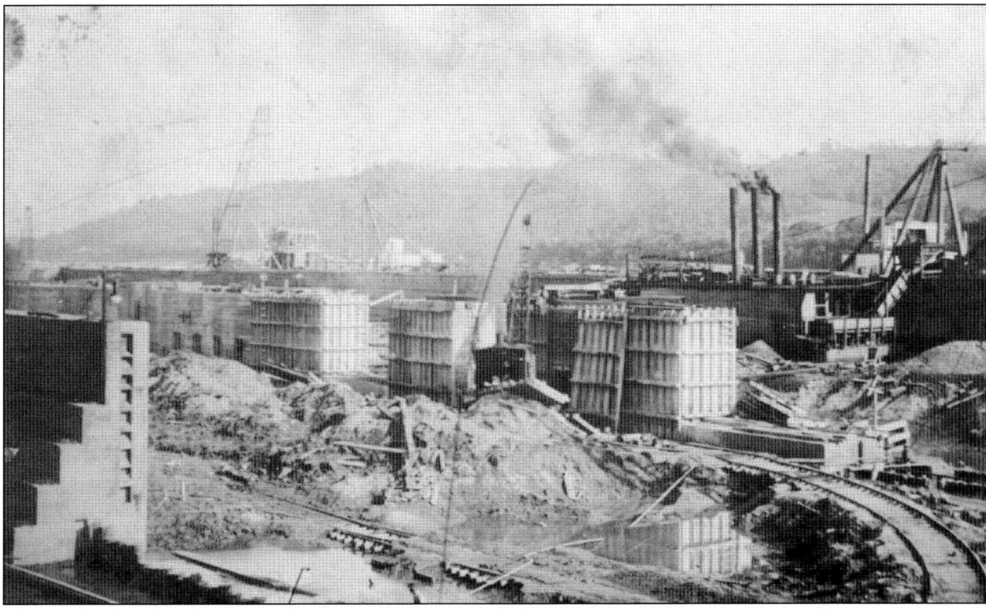

The Dam Era. The Ohio River served as a major trading route during the 19th century, hence a stable water level was vital for the steamboats to navigate the river. At times, the water level would be too low to allow boats to pass, or they would be damaged when stuck in the ice. The Army Corp of Engineers determined that a series of locks and dams from Pittsburgh, Pennsylvania, to Illinois would create a higher and safer water level in the river. The photograph above shows the construction of Lock No. 39 about three miles west of Warsaw. The scene from July 1916 below shows boats clustered near the riverbank during the dam construction. The dam opened in 1921 and raised the pool level six feet. (Both, courtesy of Darrell Maines.)

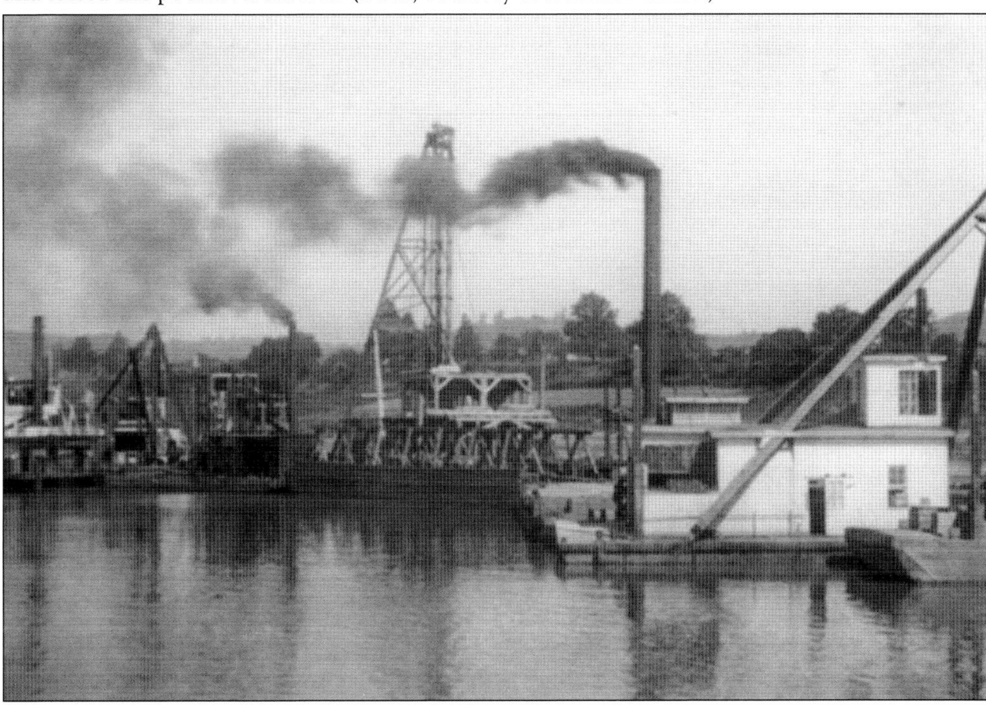

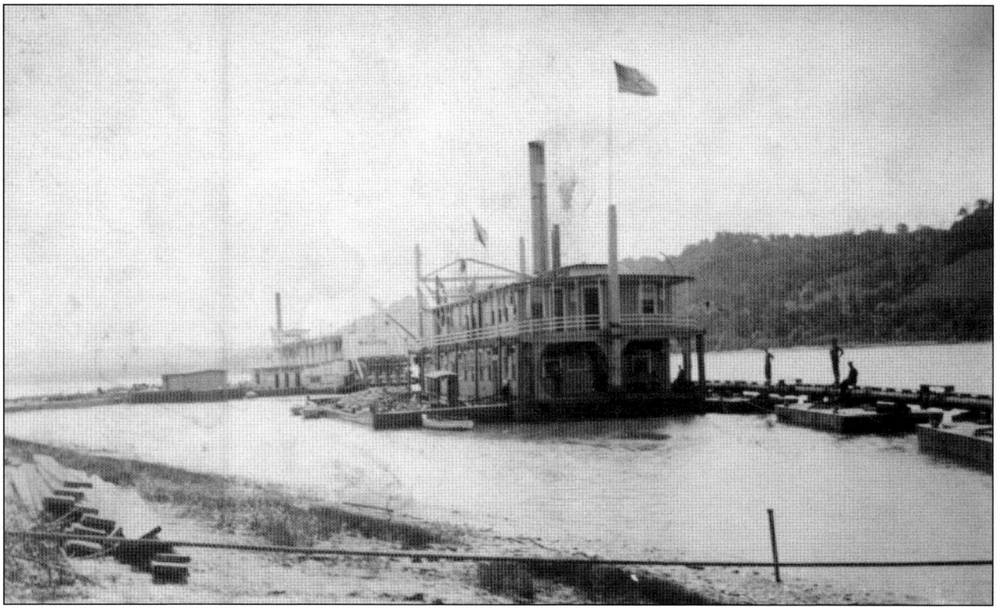

Lock No. 39. These 1920s steamboats are preparing to go through the dam on their trip between Cincinnati and Louisville. Lock No. 39 was built to accommodate larger steamboats, but after World War II, diesel boats came into use, and the old wicket-style dam was difficult for the newer boats to navigate. It was replaced by the Markland Dam in 1964. (Courtesy of Darrell Maines.)

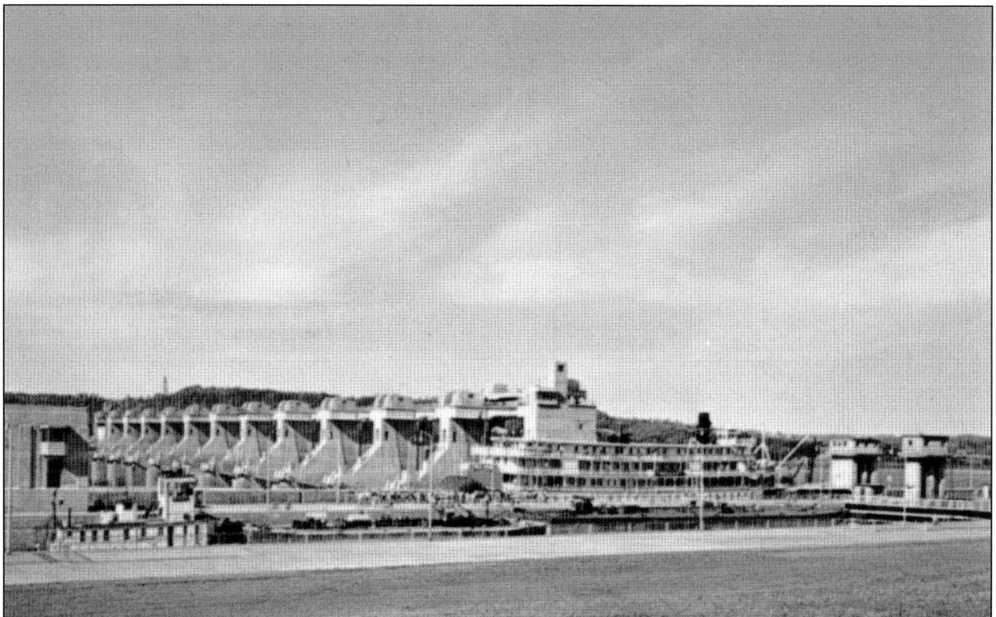

Modern Dam. When it was determined that the Ohio River lock system was antiquated and unsafe for modern diesel boats to use, the Army Corps of Engineers began construction on a new series of dams. Construction of the new dam to replace Lock No 39 began in 1956, and the structure was dedicated as the Markland Dam in October 1963. Pictured here is a boat going through the lock during the construction. (Courtesy of Darrell Maines.)

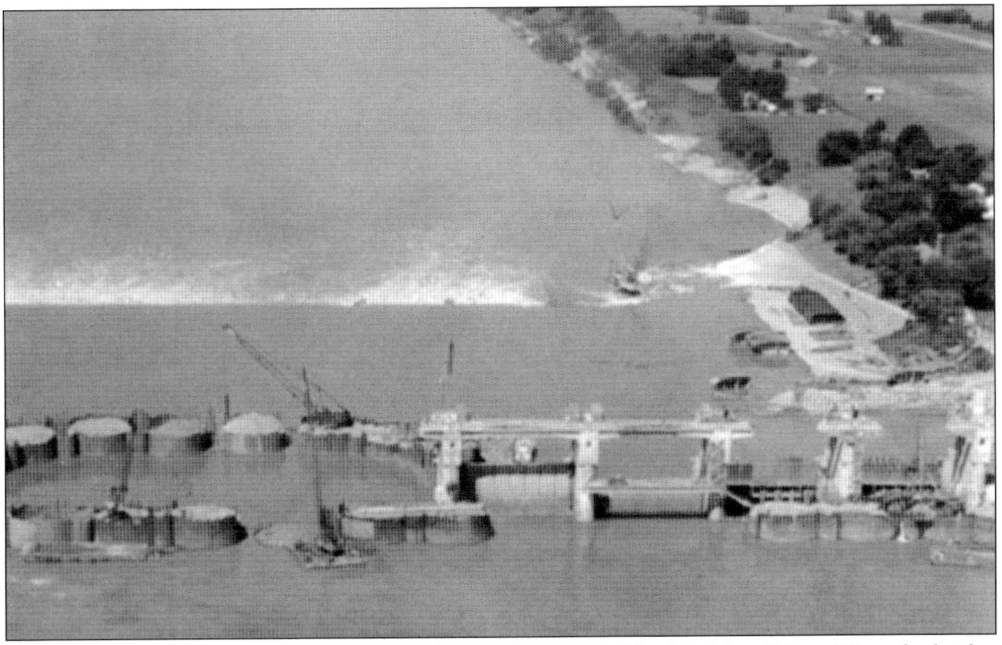

MARKLAND DAM. This aerial view shows the construction of the Markland Dam. Note the bridge is partially completed. The bridge now connects Gallatin County with Switzerland County, Indiana, home of the Belterra Casino. The construction of the dam raised the pool level much higher than the previous dam. The river now maintains a level of 15 to 20 feet, depending on weather conditions. (Courtesy of Darrell Maines.)

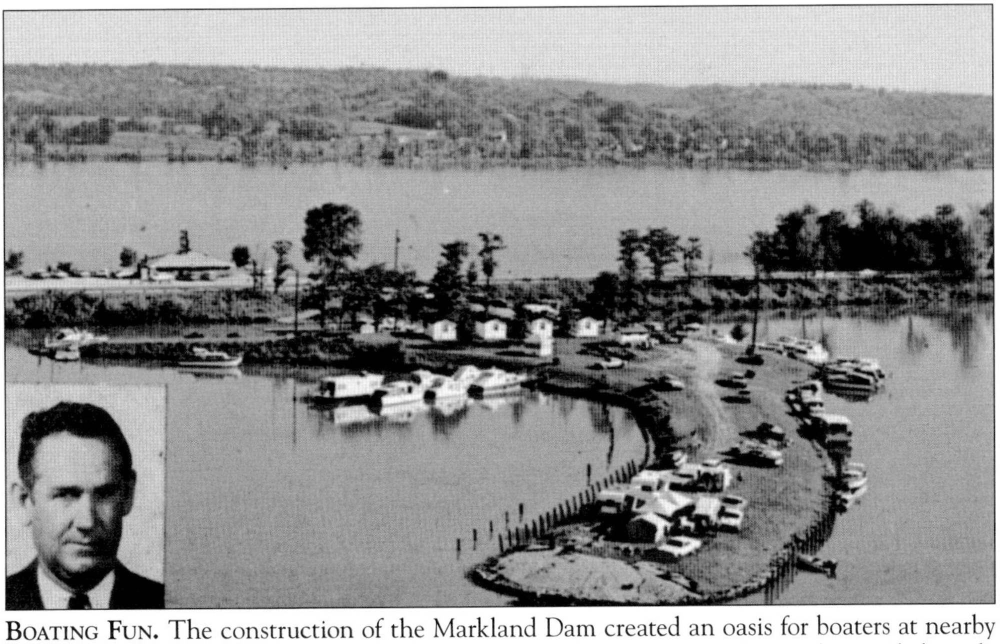

BOATING FUN. The construction of the Markland Dam created an oasis for boaters at nearby Craig's Creek. Located just east of the dam, a cove at the entrance to the creek provided ample space for a marina. This 1960s aerial photograph shows Dan's Marina in the foreground and the restaurant in the background fronting US Highway 42. Owner Dan Webster is pictured at bottom left. Webster was later shot and killed by his son in the 1980s. (Courtesy of Darrell Maines.)

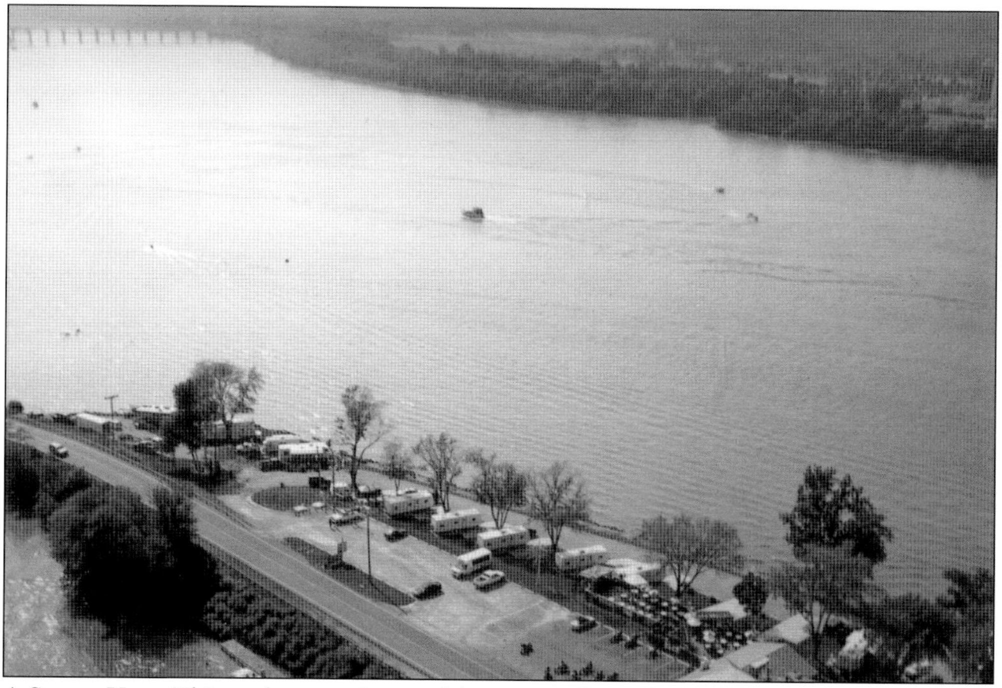

A Scenic View. This modern aerial view of the marina shows the beauty and serenity of the river at Craig's Creek. Boaters enjoy the river while patrons at the Sunset Grille and campground take in the beautiful scenery. The Markland Dam is in the distant background, and the Belterra Casino is partially visible at top right. The restaurant and US Highway 42 are in the foreground. The marina and Sunset Grille restaurant are now owned by Dan Fuehner. (Courtesy of Dan Fuehner.)

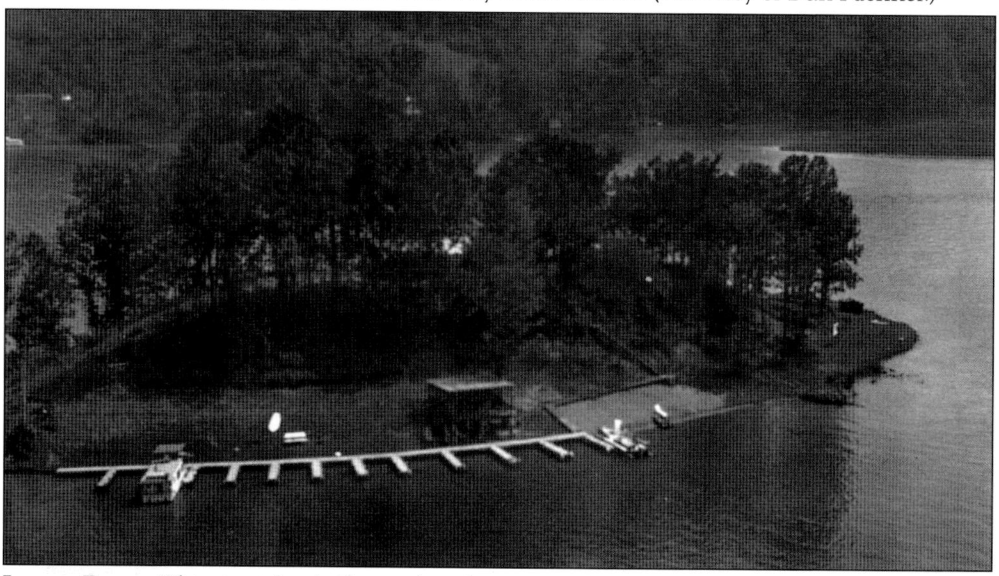

Island Party. This tiny island is located in the cove at Craig's Creek. As this aerial view shows, it was large enough to dock boats and have a shelter for picnics. At one time, it was owned by Russell "Bubby" Hall, owner of the popular Country Kitchen restaurant and the Warsaw Ferry. The peak of the island is all that is currently visible due to the rise in the pool level. (Courtesy of Russell Hall.)

Three

FLOODWATERS

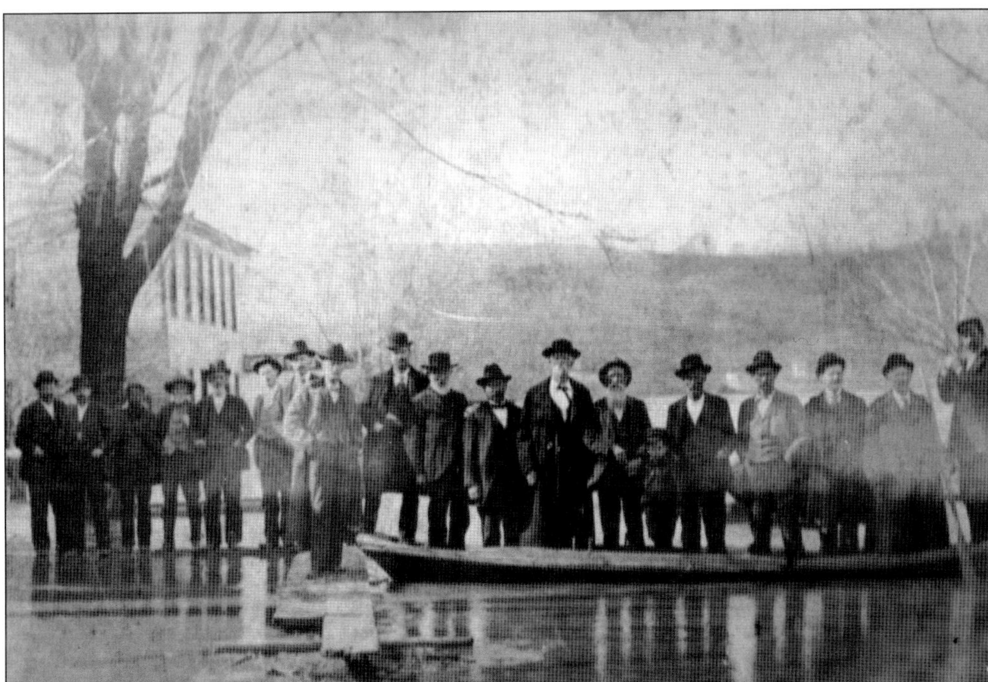

GRIM CIRCUMSTANCES. Warsaw residents show their grim reaction to the flood while standing in water covering the street at the ferry landing. This 1913 photograph is typical of the damage sustained by the under-the-hill area of Warsaw during the many floods it experienced over the years. Major floods occurred in 1883, 1884, 1913, and 1937. Jacob Gardt's saloon is at left. (Courtesy of Darrell Maines.)

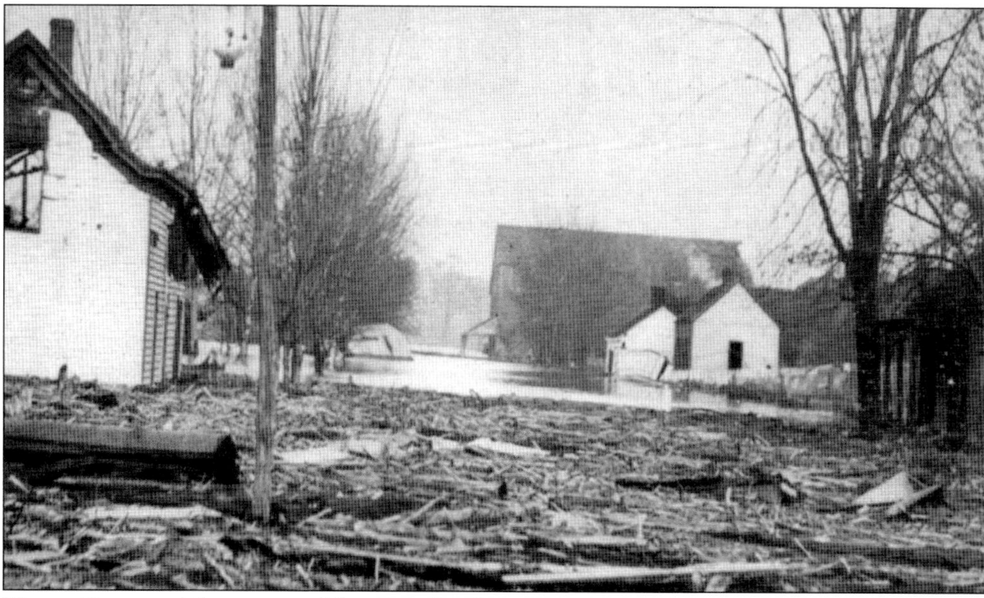

Heavy Damage. This image of the 1907 flood in Warsaw was taken by local photographer F.M. Neal. The view is facing east on Locust Street while Neal stood by the livery stable. The flood caused extensive damage to homes and businesses close to the riverfront. Most houses located there were completely underwater, and all travel was suspended as most of the roads were covered by water. Frequent floods took a toll, with little evidence left of the once-thriving district. (Courtesy of Darrell Maines.)

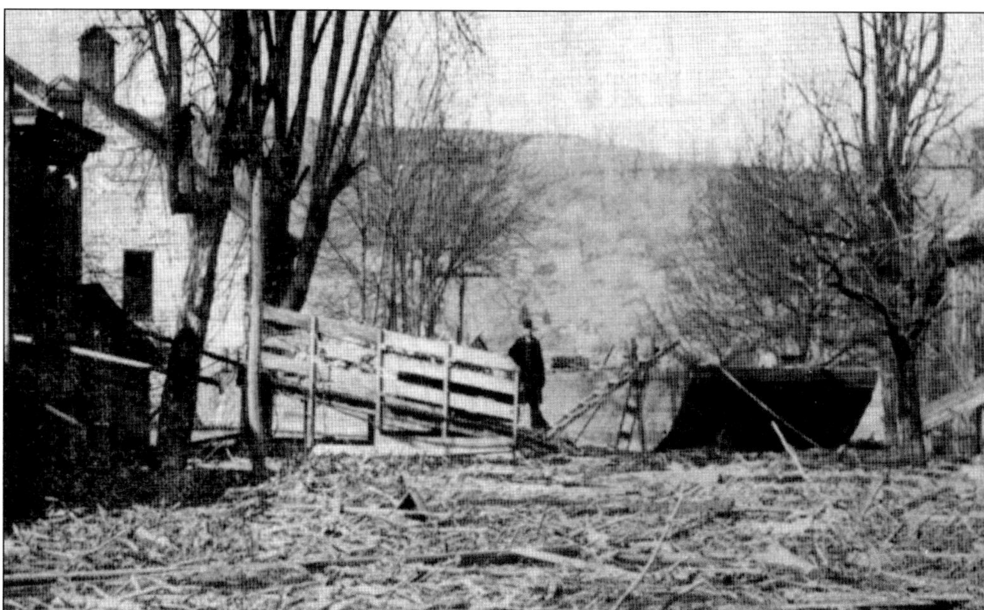

Water Damage. This 1907 photograph also taken by F.M. Neal shows the damage left by the floodwaters. Neal is standing in front of the Lindell Hotel (unseen) looking toward Indiana in the distance. Jacob Gardt's saloon is in the left foreground, with the Eagle Hotel on the left beyond it. The town marshal is standing in front of the Eagle by a barge that was pulled up to the hotel to remove household items. (Courtesy of Darrell Maines.)

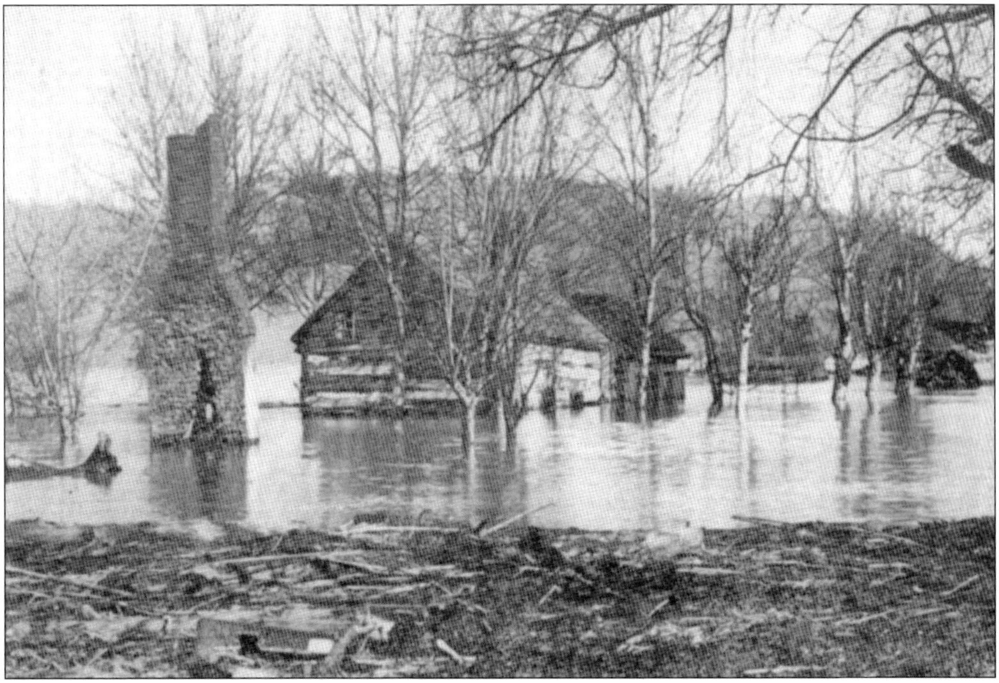

HIGH WATERS. This 1907 image is another view from the Lindell Hotel looking up Locust Street. The water completely inundated the homes and businesses, causing heavy damage. Locust Street is located on the riverfront, between High Street and the river. Today it is mostly gone, replaced by the city park. (Courtesy of Darrell Maines.)

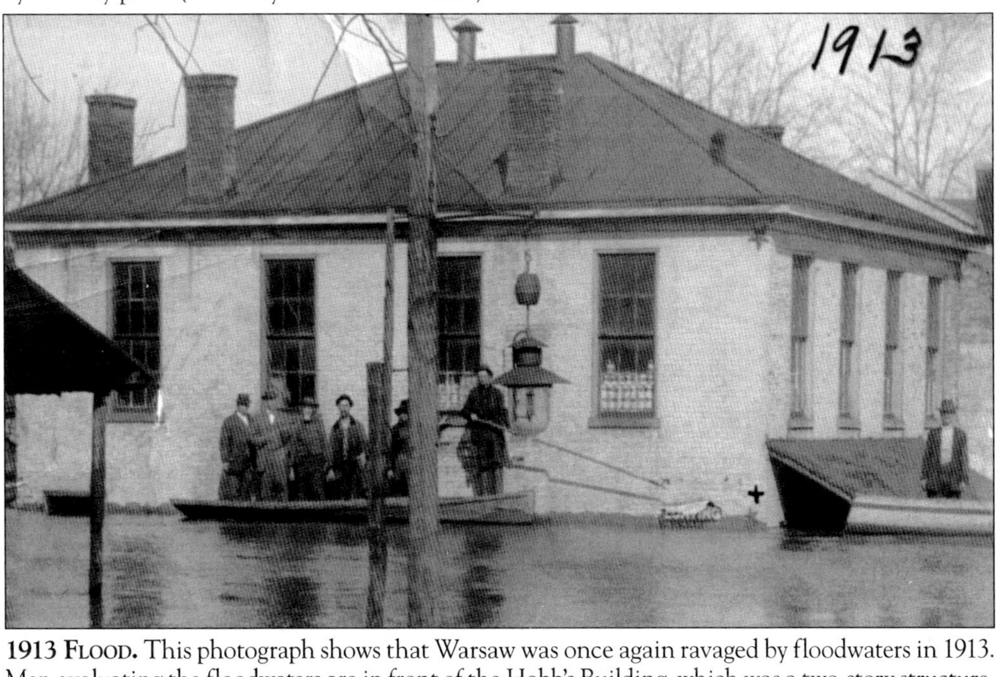

1913 FLOOD. This photograph shows that Warsaw was once again ravaged by floodwaters in 1913. Men evaluating the floodwaters are in front of the Hobb's Building, which was a two-story structure. This view was from the Lindell Hotel, located on the northeast corner of Locust Street and Main Cross. The building was later used as a Coca-Cola warehouse. (Courtesy of Darrell Maines.)

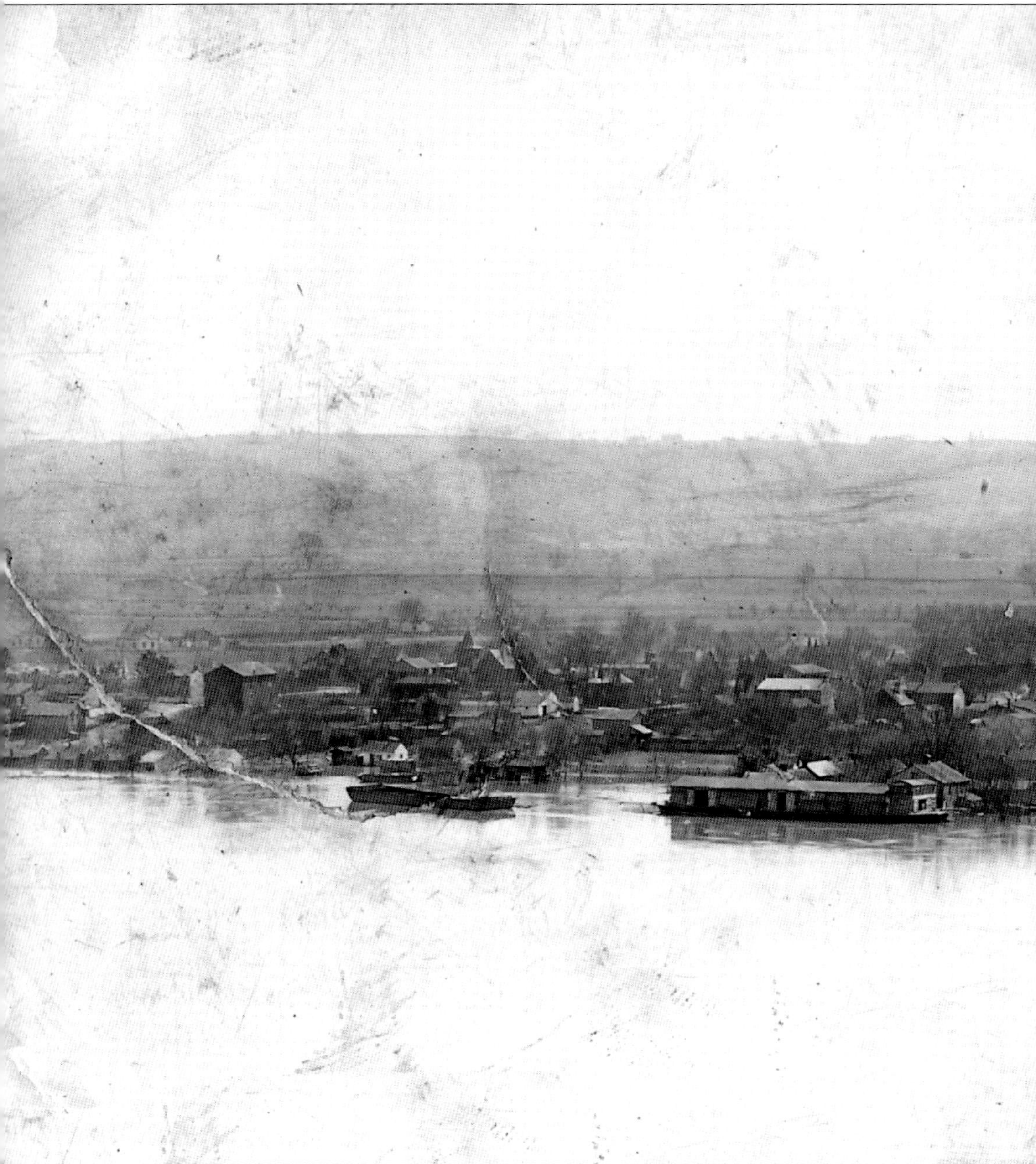

PANORAMIC VIEW. This rare 1913 photograph was taken from Indiana looking south toward Warsaw. The view of the under-the-hill area demonstrates the thriving businesses and residential homes that used to dot the landscape at the riverfront. It is now mostly gone. The courthouse is visible in the distance behind the wharf boat. To the right of the courthouse is the McDanell

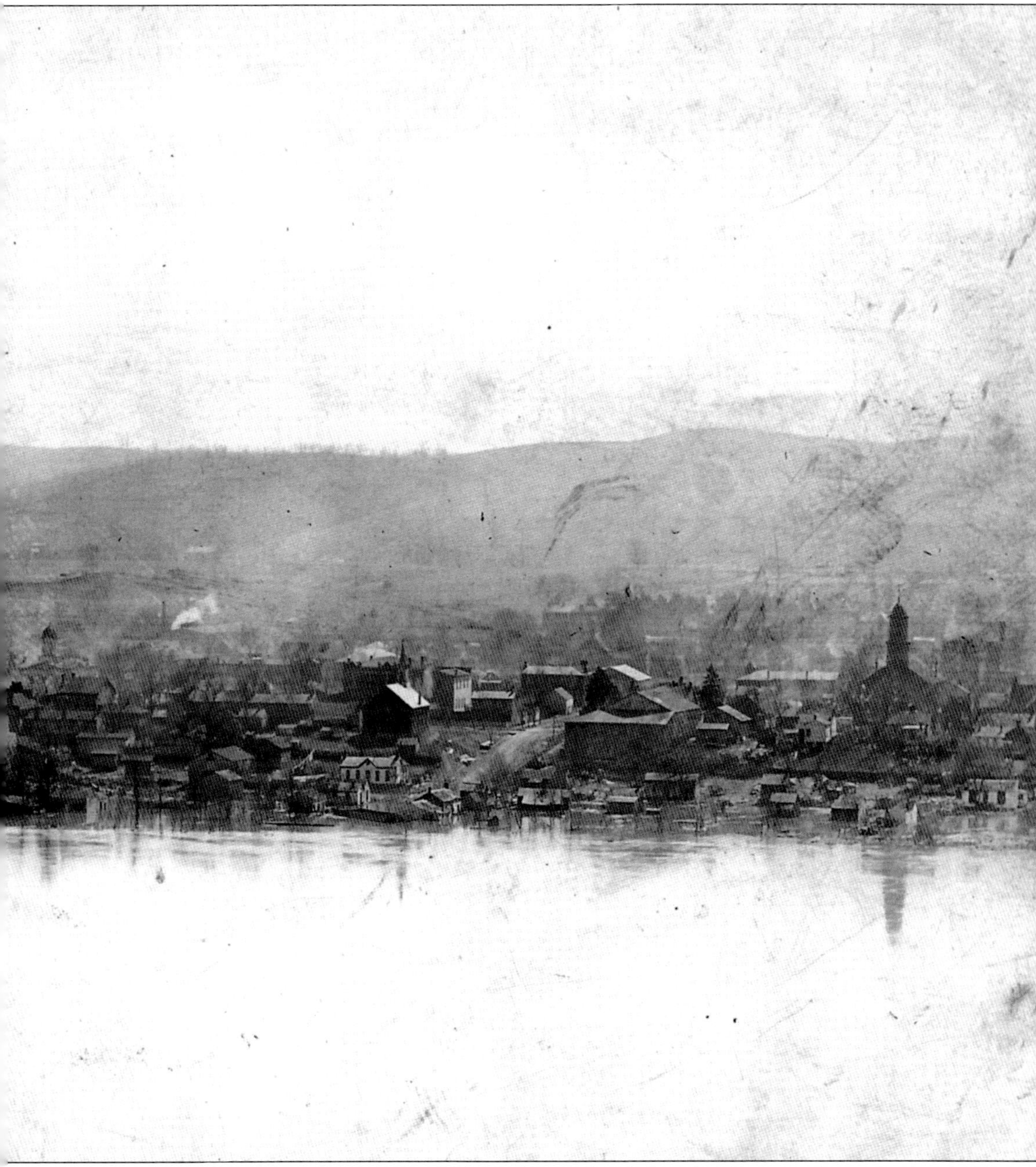

Furniture Factory (unseen, smoke is visible). Hidden behind the wharf boat is the Eagle Hotel; behind it is Gardt's Saloon and the Hobb's Building. The Eagle Hotel was located on Locust Street, which was between High Street and Water Street. Water Street was completely underwater at this point—hence the wharf boat snuggled up to the hotel. (Courtesy of Darrell Maines.)

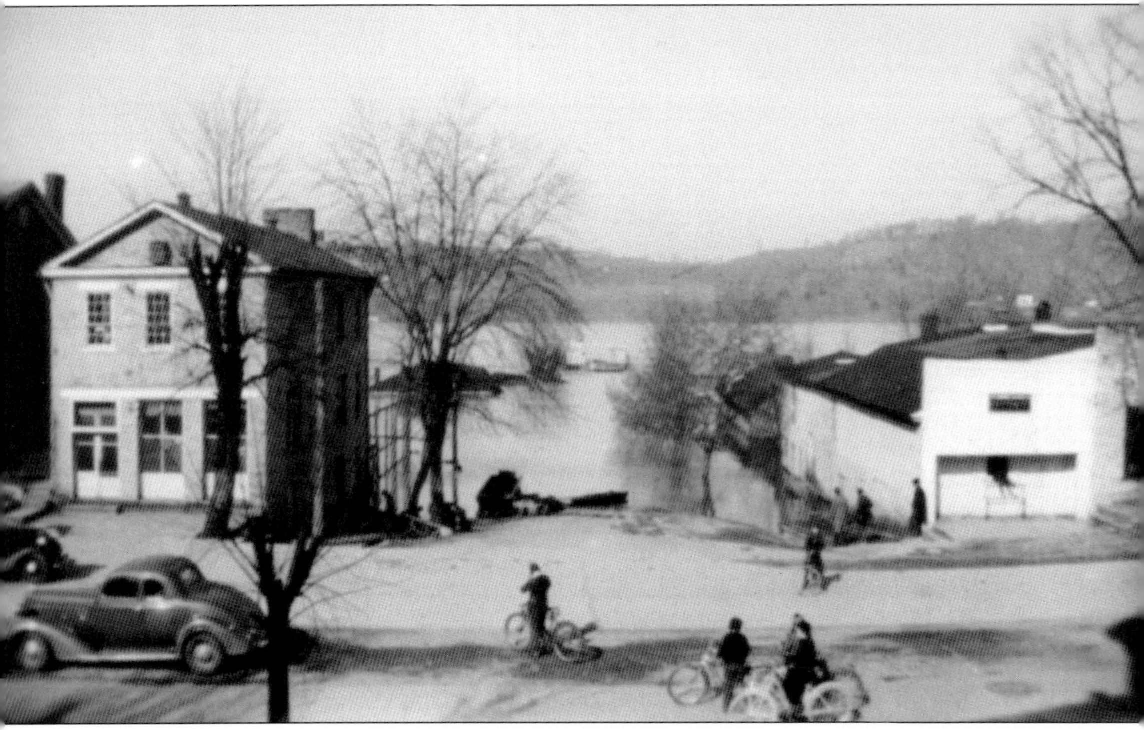

VIEW FROM THE HILL. The 1937 flood was by far the most devastating of all the floods, completely inundating the lower-lying areas along the Ohio River, and the riverfront in Warsaw was no exception. This photograph was taken by local druggist Sam Clore while standing in front of the courthouse, which still faced the river at this point. High Street runs the east-west route where the bicyclists are standing. Main Cross can be seen disappearing into the high waters. On the left is the old Gallatin County Deposit Bank; the building on the right housed the William Craig Furniture and Tin Shop. The submerged building behind the furniture shop is the Webb Hotel, a two-story structure, of which only the second story is visible. The under-the-hill area is invisible under the rising water. (Courtesy of Darrell Maines.)

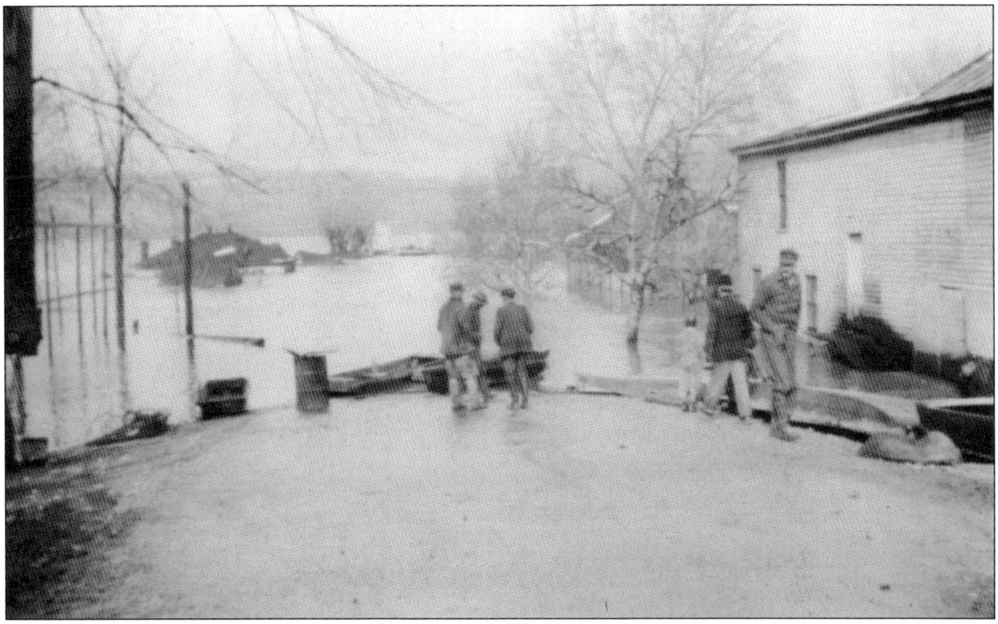

A Closer Look. This photograph was taken while men were standing on Main Cross next to the William Craig Furniture and Tin Shop (on right). Submerged buildings can be seen in the background while looking north toward Indiana. (Courtesy of Robert and Alexandra Weldon.)

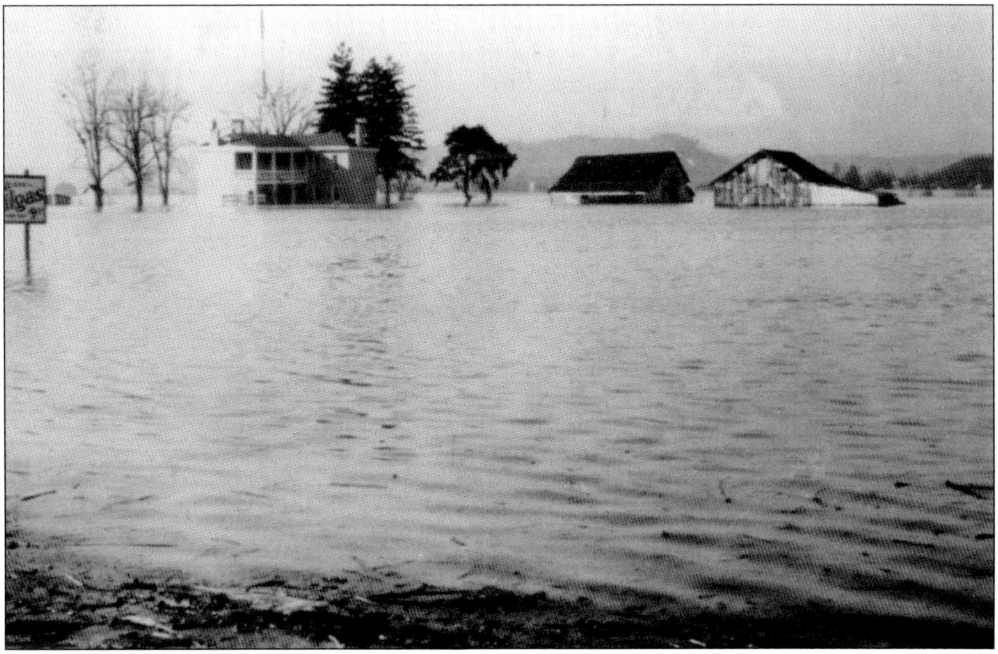

Bledsoe House. This beautiful Federal-style home known as the Melanie Bledsoe house, located between the river and US 42 just west of Warsaw, also suffered major flooding in the 1937 deluge. It was reported that a small boat was able to enter the house and cruise around the rooms, but the house is still standing today. The Philgas sign on the left was next to the highway. (Courtesy of Robert and Alexandra Weldon.)

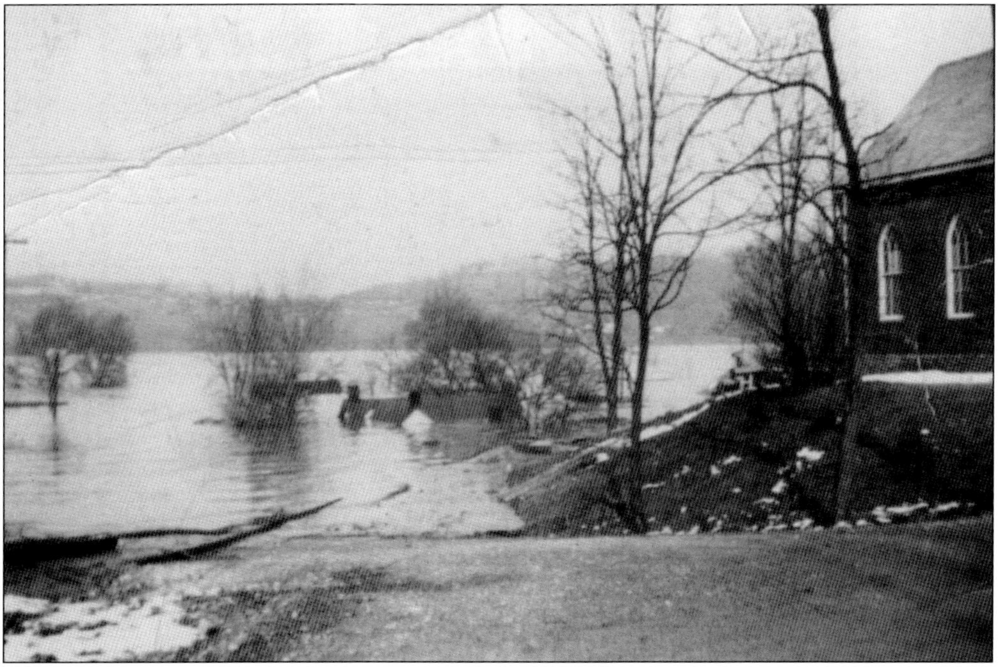

BAPTIST HILL. This 1937 photograph was taken while standing on High Street looking down Third Street toward the river; the roofs of the buildings can barely be seen above the high water. The building on the right is the old Baptist church. (Courtesy of Robert and Alexandra Weldon.)

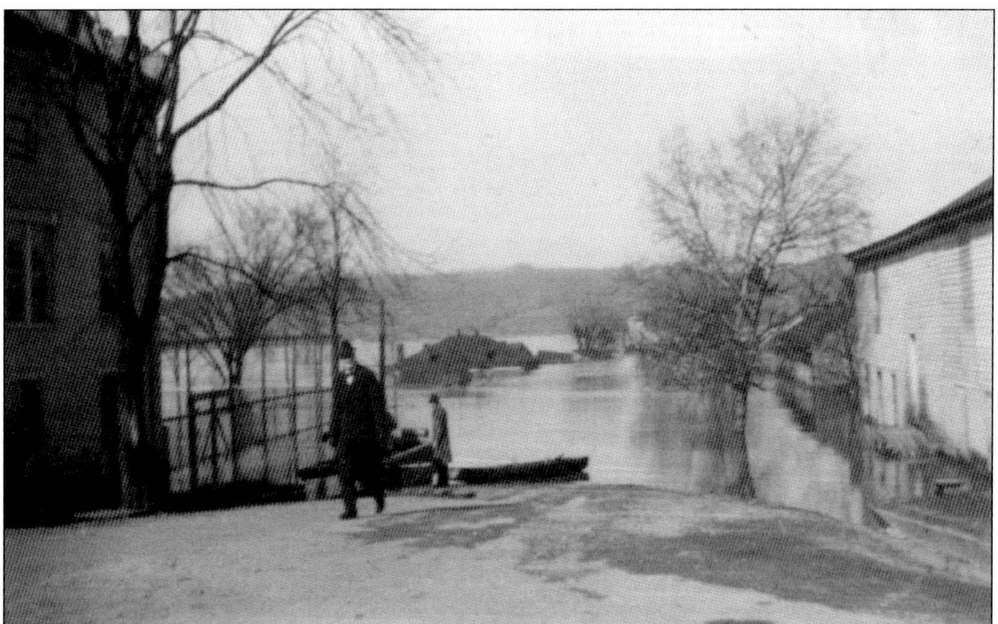

SIGHTSEEING. William R. Payne walks up Main Cross after observing the destruction of under the hill in the 1937 flood. Gallatin County Deposit Bank is on the left; the William Craig Furniture and Tin Shop is on the right. A tennis court was located behind the bank. (Courtesy of Robert and Alexandra Weldon.)

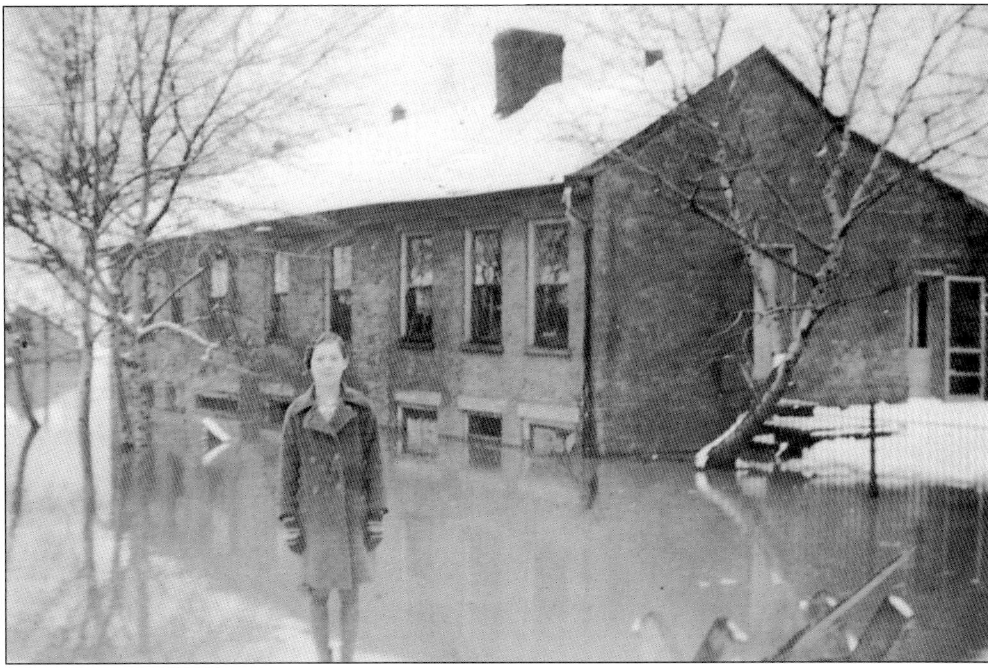

Rising Waters. Rose Dickerson stands in front of the Webb Hotel on Main Cross near High Street. This photograph was taken before the floodwaters rose to the second story of the hotel. The back corner of the Craig furniture shop can be seen on the right. (Courtesy of Dale Samuel.)

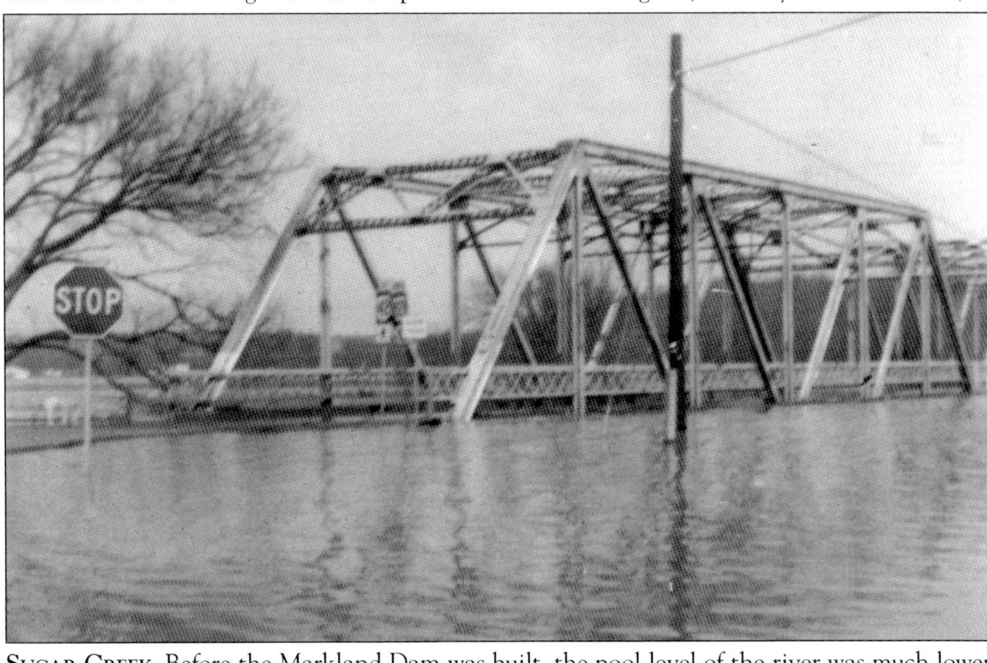

Sugar Creek. Before the Markland Dam was built, the pool level of the river was much lower. At Sugar Creek, the US Highway 42 Bridge crossed mostly dry land when the creek was low. In 1937, the water covered the highway and bridge, essentially shutting down any travel on the east-west corridor between Cincinnati and Louisville. This photograph was taken from State Route 127 looking north. (Courtesy of Dana Benne.)

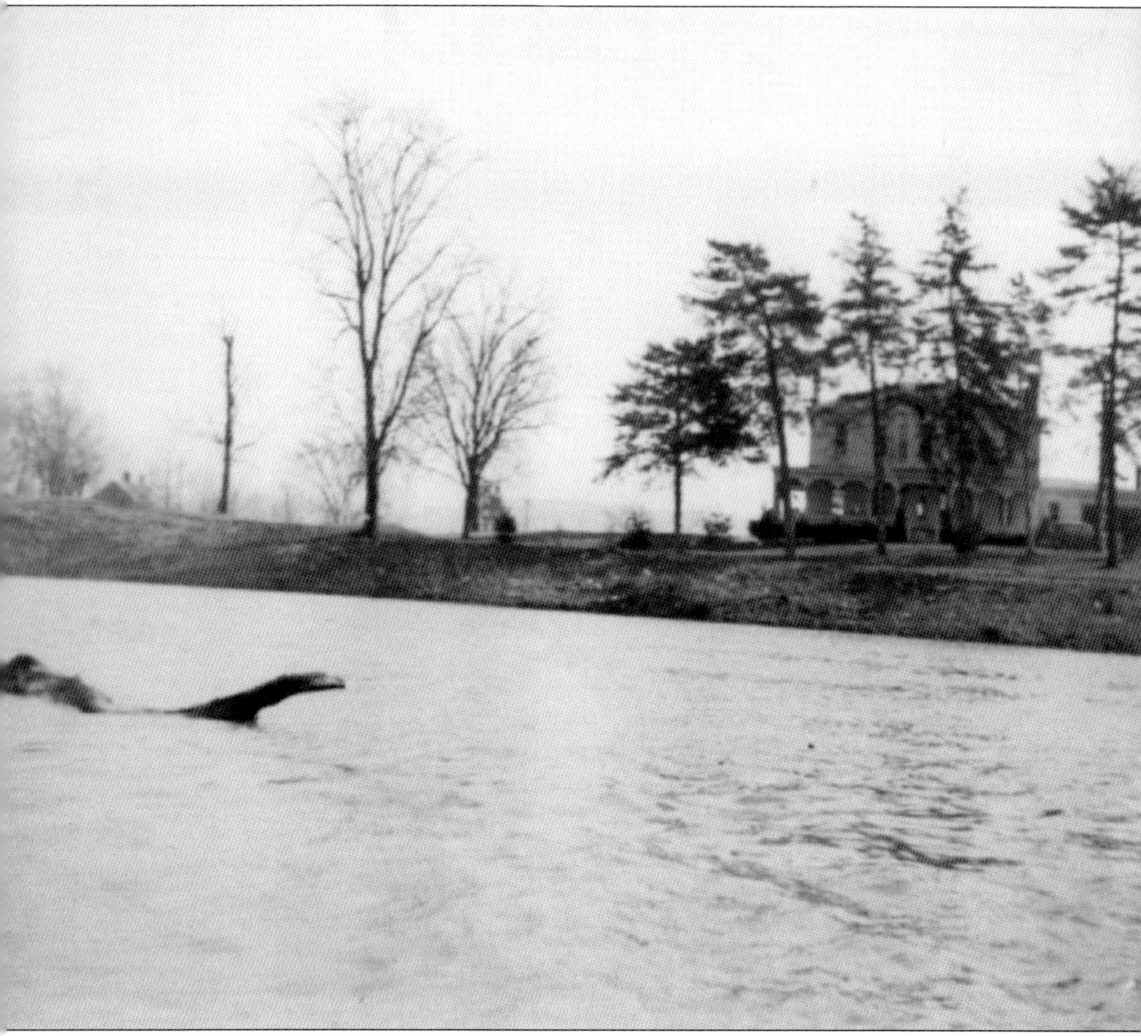

SPARED FROM THE FLOOD. One home lucky enough to be on high ground away from the floodwaters was the stately home known as Seven Pines. Built on a knoll about 1852 by William Payne, this home faces the river where the old River Road ran along the river and US Highway 42 at Fifth Street in Warsaw. (Courtesy of Robert and Alexandra Weldon.)

Four

COMMERCE

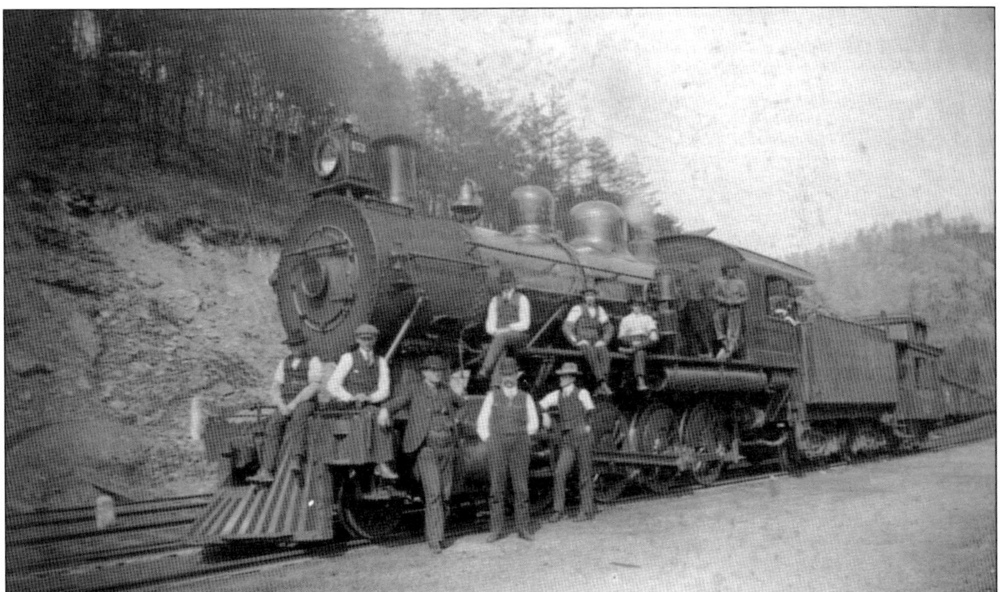

LOUISVILLE & NASHVILLE RAILROAD. The creation of railroads in the mid-19th century changed transportation dramatically, making it much faster and more efficient, and capable of penetrating inland. The first L&N line ran in 1859, but the Civil War caused considerable damage to the line as it cut through both Union and Confederate territory. After the war, the railroad continued to expand and completed the line between Louisville and Cincinnati in 1869. In this undated photograph, unidentified men pose alongside Engine 453 with its freight cars near Sparta. Depots were built in both Sparta and Glencoe, sparking the economy in both towns as freight and passenger trains passed through on their way to the city. (Courtesy of Dana Benne.)

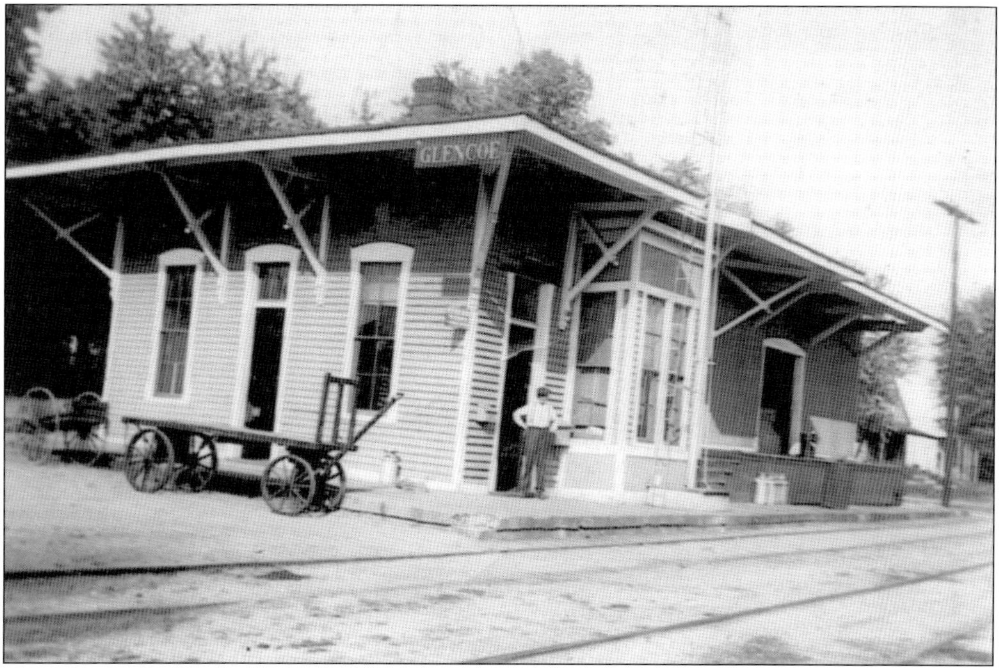

Glencoe Depot. The L&N Railroad line ran alongside the Eagle Creek on the southern border of Gallatin County. Glencoe's depot was small but a busy hub for passenger and freight transportation. Its connection with Warsaw via the Glencoe Turnpike enabled travel between all parts of the county. The depot was located on the north side of the tracks at US 467 and US 127. (Courtesy of Darrell Maines.)

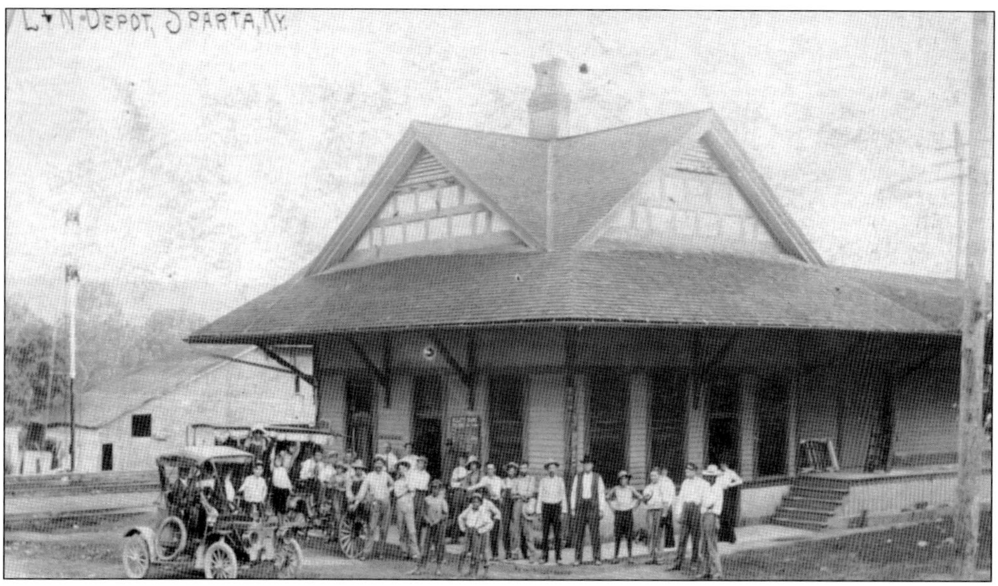

Sparta Depot. Like its neighbor Glencoe, tiny Sparta became a busy hub of activity. Though the population never grew to more than 200 residents, it became an important stop along the L&N line. This depot was located on Main Street, right at the Owen County line. By 1982, the L&N was absorbed into the Seaboard Railroad line. In 1986, it became the CSX Railroad. The depot no longer exists, but the CSX railroad still runs through town. (Courtesy of Darrell Maines.)

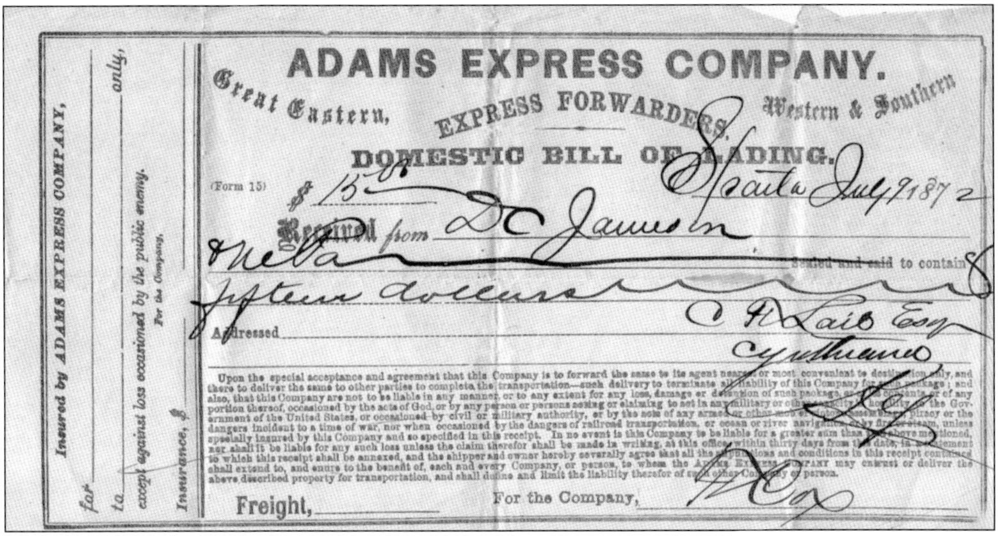

ADAMS EXPRESS COMPANY.

Great Eastern, EXPRESS FORWARDERS, Western & Southern

DOMESTIC BILL OF LADING.

(Form 15) $15 Sparta July 9 1872

Received from D C Jameson

Sealed and said to contain

fifteen dollars

Addressed C R Laib Esq Cynthiana

Upon the special acceptance and agreement that this Company is to forward the same to its agent nearest or most convenient to destination only, and there to deliver the same to other parties to complete the transportation—such delivery to terminate all liability of this Company for such package; and also, that this Company are not to be liable in any manner, or to any extent for any loss, damage or detention of such package, or its contents, or of any portion thereof, occasioned by the acts of God, or by any person or persons acting or claiming to act in any military or other capacity in hostility to the Government of the United States, or occasioned by civil or military authority, or by the acts of any armed or other mob or riotous assemblage, piracy or the dangers incident to a time of war, nor when occasioned by the dangers of railroad transportation, or ocean or river navigation, or by fire or steam, unless specially insured by this Company and so specified in this receipt. In no event is this Company to be liable for a greater sum than that above mentioned, nor shall it be liable for any such loss unless the claim therefor shall be made in writing, at this office, within thirty days from this date, in a statement to which this receipt shall be annexed, and the shipper and owner hereby severally agree that all the stipulations and conditions in this receipt contained shall extend to, and enure to the benefit of, each and every Company, or person, to whom the Adams Express Company may entrust or deliver the above described property for transportation, and shall define and limit the liability thereof of such other Company or person.

Freight, For the Company, W Cox

Insured by ADAMS EXPRESS COMPANY, for to only, except against loss occasioned by the public enemy. For the Company. Insurance, $

Bill of Lading. This 1872 Adams Express bill of lading for $15 is typical of the cargo that passed through Sparta on the L&N Railroad. The railroad enabled businesses to ship cargo to large portions of the country via the connecting railroad. (Courtesy of Dale Samuel.)

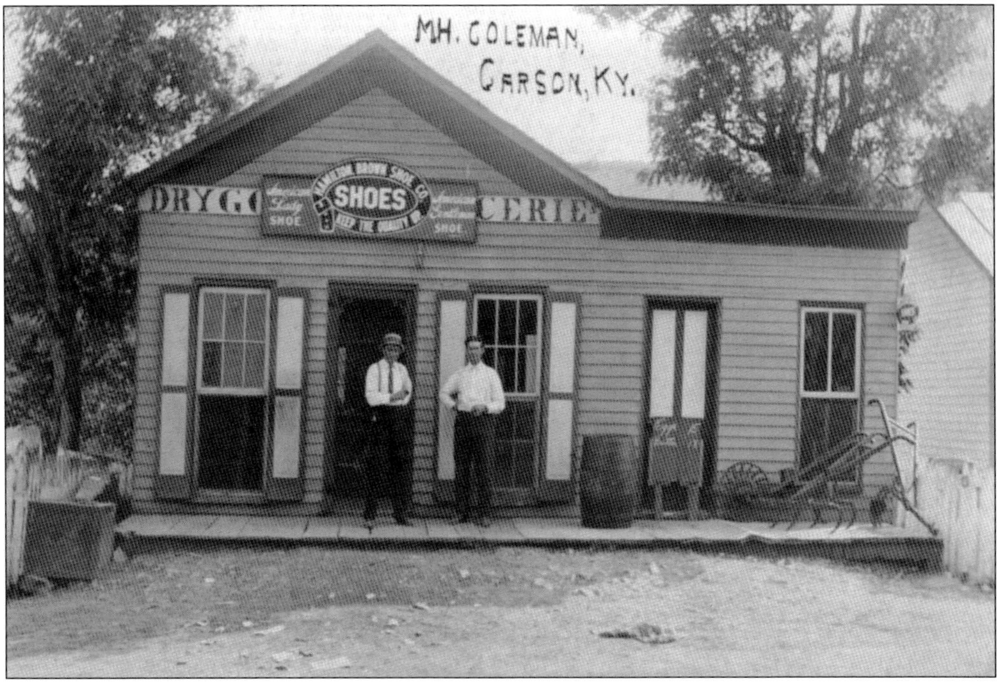

Dry Goods Store. The tiny hamlet of Carson was located near Sparta. Pictured here around 1920 is the small dry goods store and Hamilton Brown Shoe Company. It is unclear which gentleman is M.H. Coleman. This store was located in the area now occupied by the Kentucky Speedway. Carson no longer exists as a community. (Courtesy of Darrell Maines.)

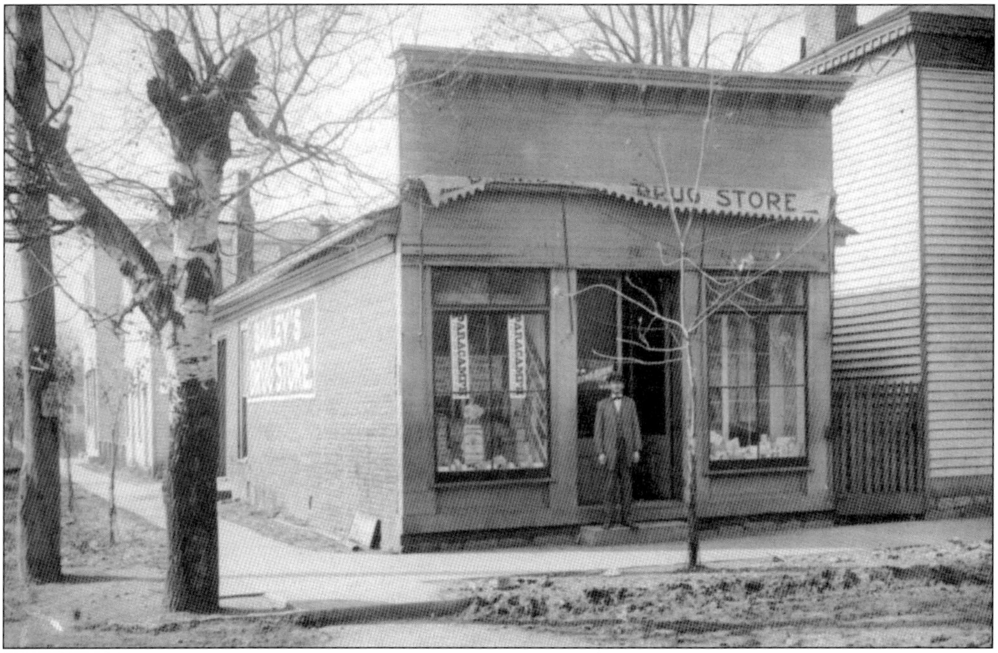

B.K. Bailey's Drugstore. Pictured here around 1900 is the B.K. Bailey Drug Store. It is unknown if the gentleman standing in front is Mr. Bailey. This building stood on the site of the later Warsaw Drugstore on the south side of US 42, going west toward Louisville. (Courtesy of Darrell Maines.)

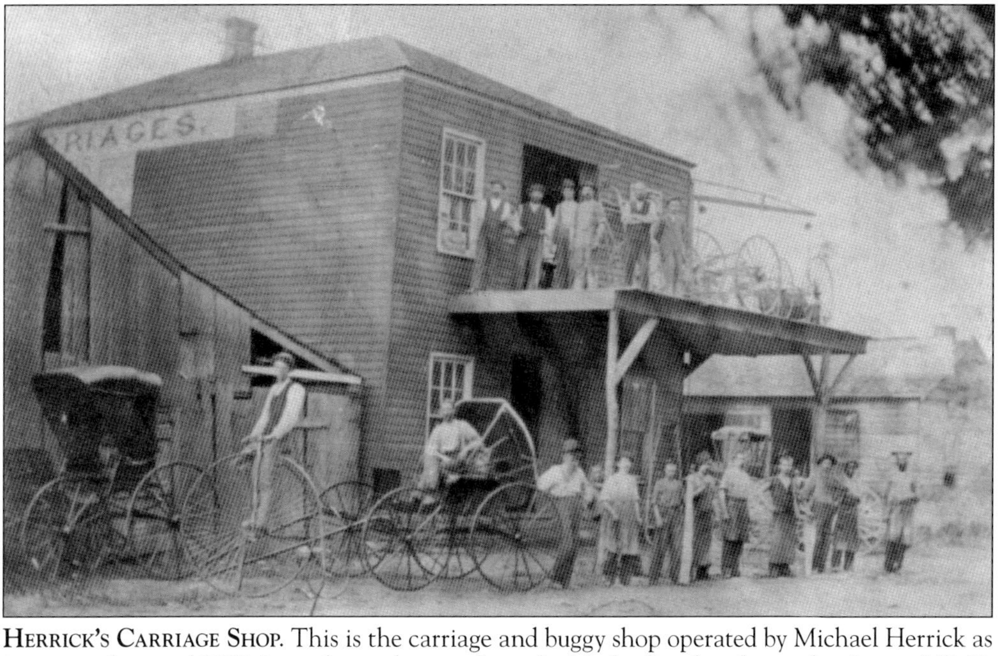

Herrick's Carriage Shop. This is the carriage and buggy shop operated by Michael Herrick as it appeared around 1890. It was located across from the Methodist church on what is now US 42. Herrick was known to make a fine vehicle, with some selling for as much as $600. Likely included in this crowd outside of the carriage shop are Michael Herrick and his son, but their positions are unknown. (Courtesy of Darrell Maines.)

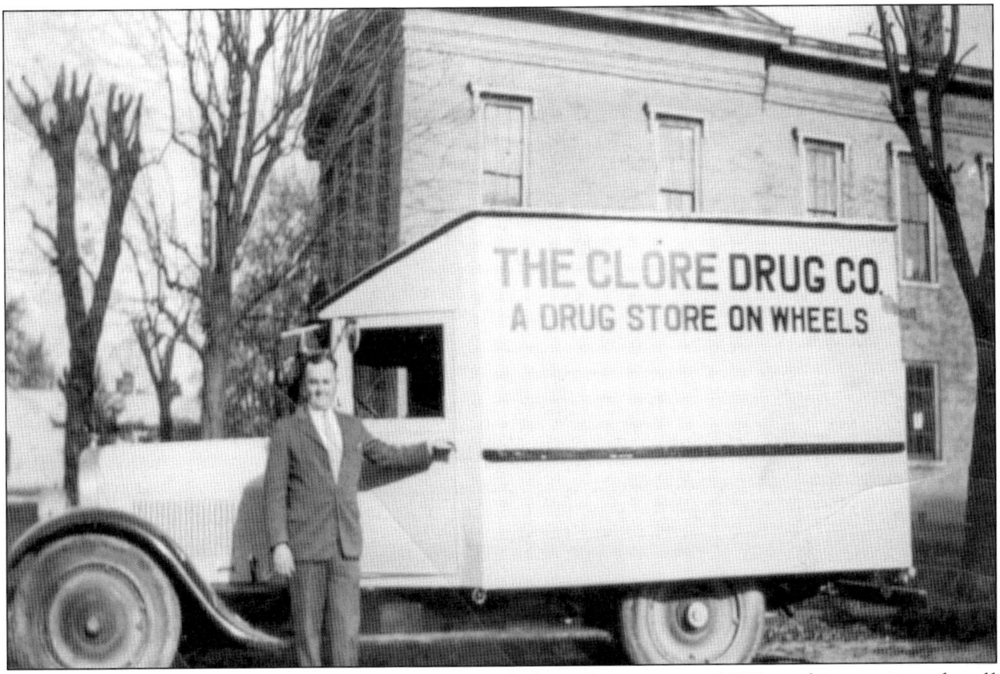

CLORE DRUGSTORE. H.D. and Sam Clore started their drugstore in 1877, and it continued well into the 20th century. This is a 1940s photograph of Mack Furnish beside the company delivery truck, which is parked in front of the courthouse. (Courtesy of Dana Benne.)

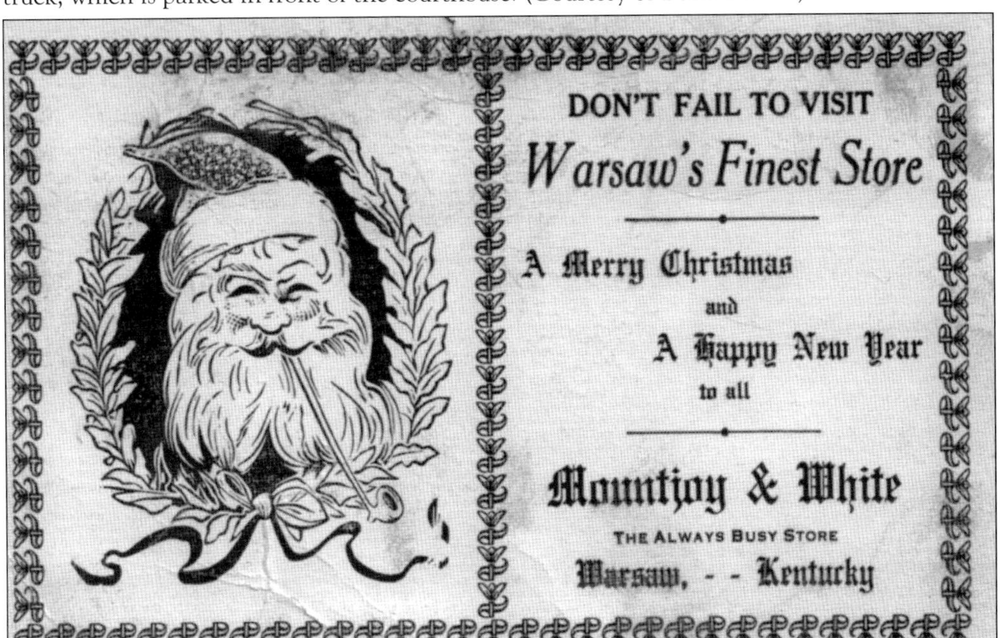

SEASONS GREETING. Mountjoy & White Dry Goods was established in 1877 by J.E. Mountjoy, who was well known in his trade to carry the best and sell for the cheapest. One location was the building on the courthouse square that once served as Maines Hardware. (Courtesy of Darrell Maines.)

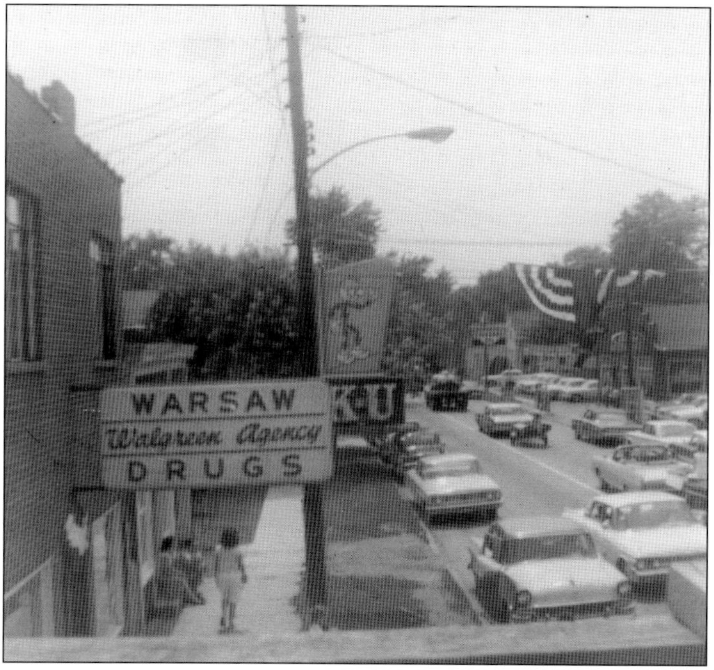

WARSAW DRUGSTORE. This 1960s image of Main Street (US 42) in Warsaw shows a busy thoroughfare. The Warsaw Drugstore, a division of the Walgreen Company, is in the left foreground. B.K. Bailey's drugstore was previously located here, and Kentucky Utilities is next door. (Courtesy of Dana Benne.)

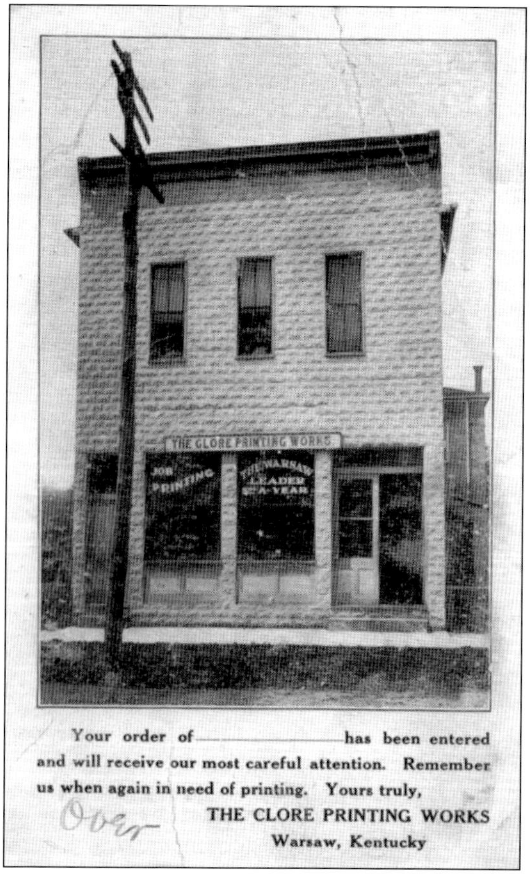

PRINTING COMPANY. The Clore family also owned a printing company in addition to their drugstore business. This building was located on High Street near the courthouse. It was later home to the *Warsaw Leader* around 1910. (Courtesy of Darrell Maines.)

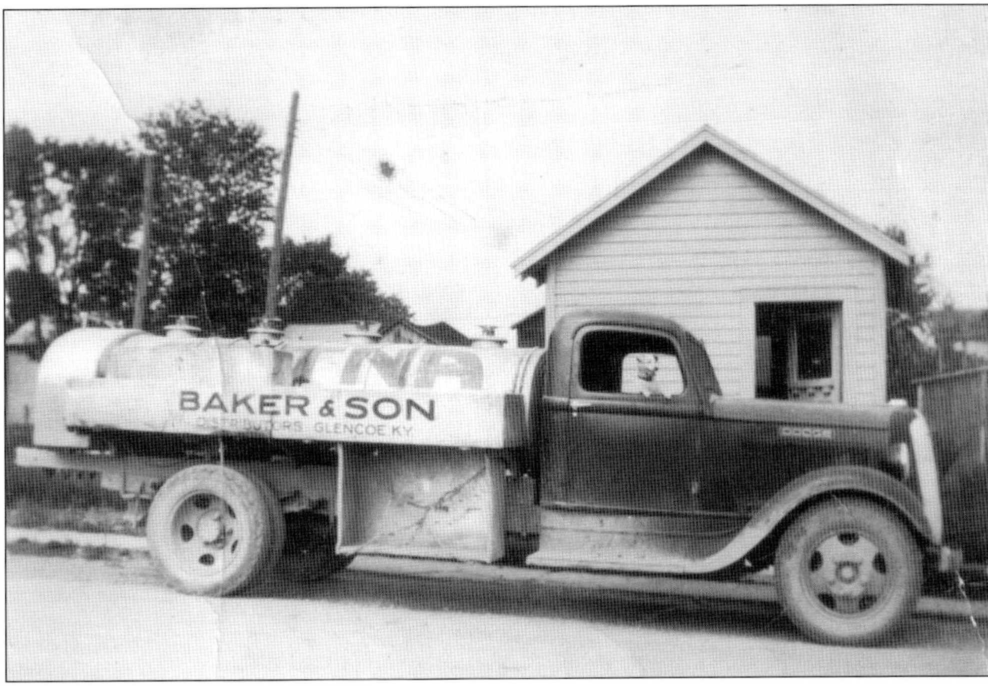

The Dog Rules. Baker & Son was an Aetna Gas distributor based in Glencoe. Apparently, the dog is in charge in this 1940s photograph. (Courtesy of Dana Benne.)

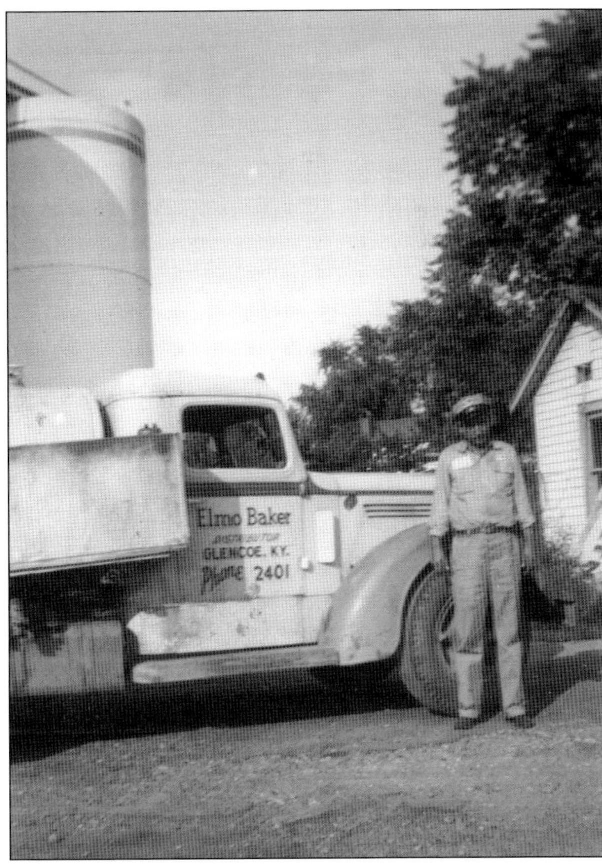

Businessman. This is a 1940s photograph of Elmo Baker, who operated the Baker & Son Aetna Gas distributing company in Glencoe. He lived on Second Street in Warsaw. (Courtesy of Dana Benne.)

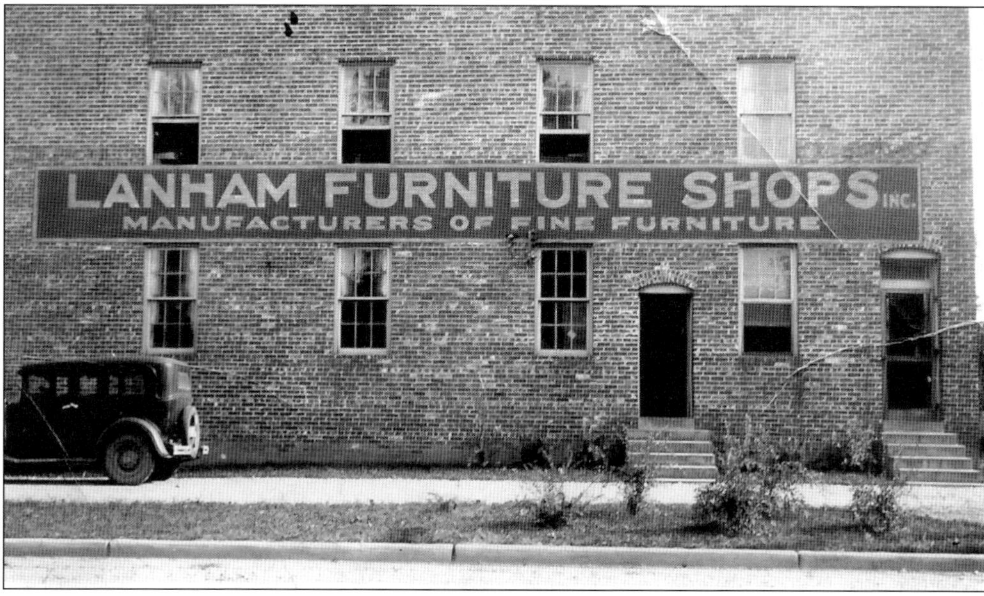

LANHAM FURNITURE SHOPS. This 1930s photograph shows the Lanham Furniture Shop, located on Main Street behind where Kentucky Motors is today. It was one of three furniture shops in Warsaw, but it burned down on June 27, 1940. (Courtesy of Darrell Maines.)

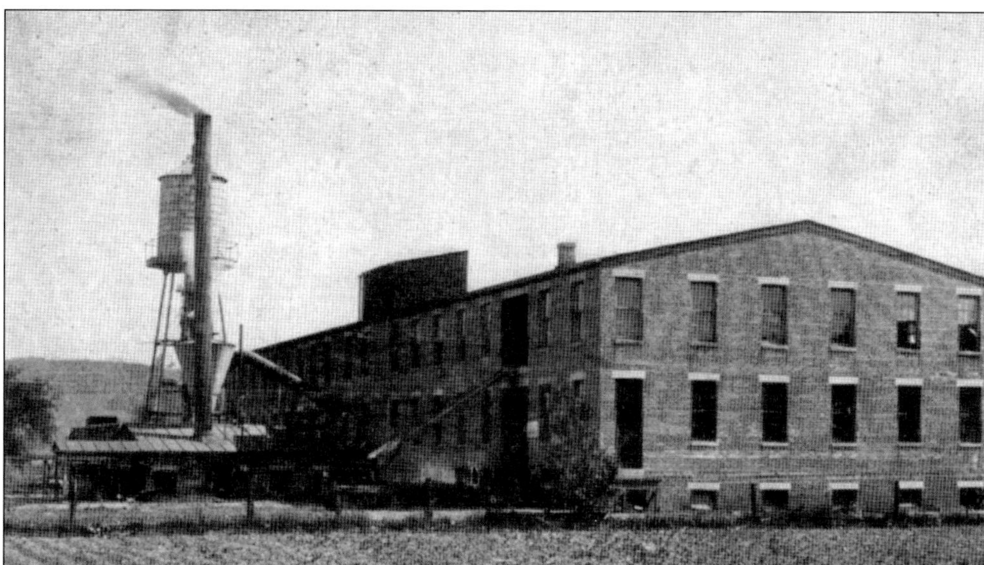

MAJOR BUSINESS. In the early 1900s, Warsaw had three furniture shops. McDannell was by far the largest, with its plant between Second Street and Sparta Pike. It burned in 1905, striking a major blow to the local economy, as it employed a large number of residents in its factory. It was quickly rebuilt and operated for 40 more years. (Courtesy of Darrell Maines.)

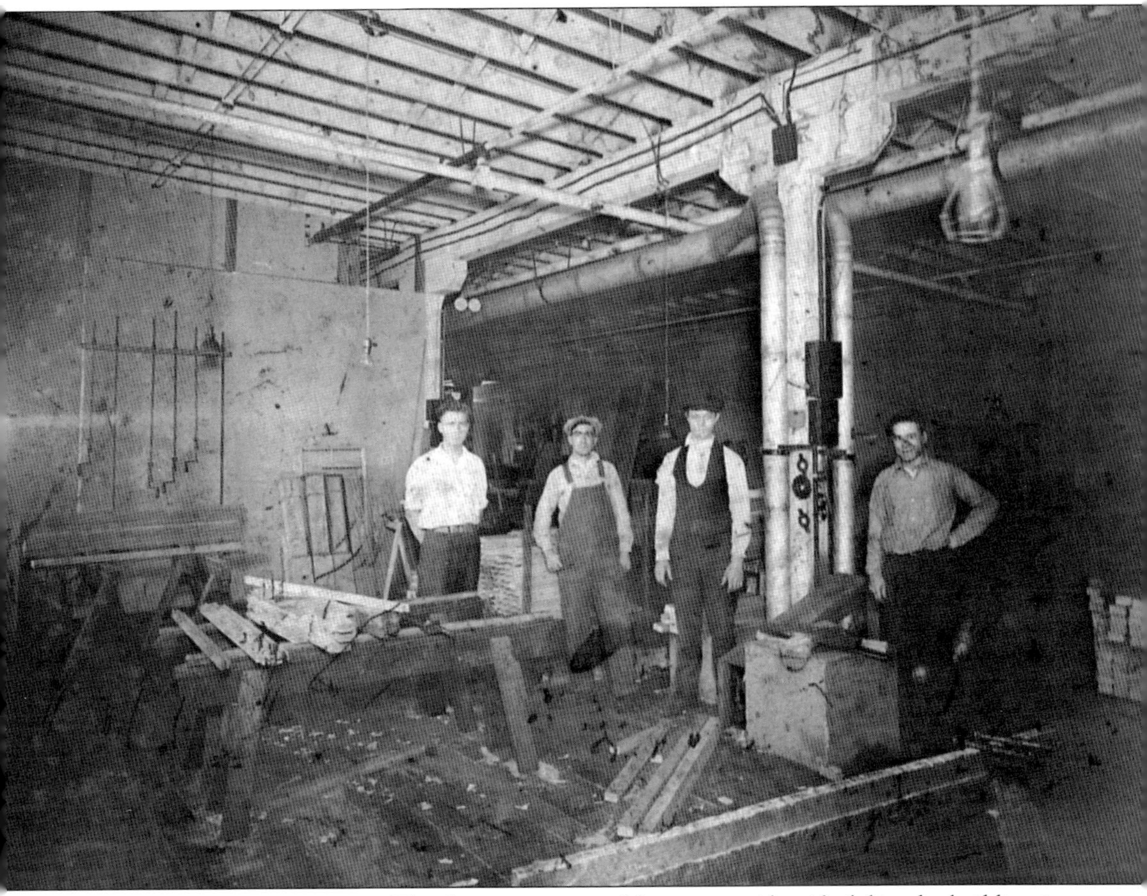

Warsaw Furniture Factory. The four men pictured here are unidentified, but the building is the Warsaw Furniture Factory. Also known as the Bogardus Factory, later owned by Barry Brown, the operation began in 1902. Originally, it manufactured dining room and hall furniture, which was shipped to all 50 states, Canada, Mexico, and South America. The factory was across US 42 from the cemetery, and it was torn down about 2004. (Courtesy of Dale Samuel.)

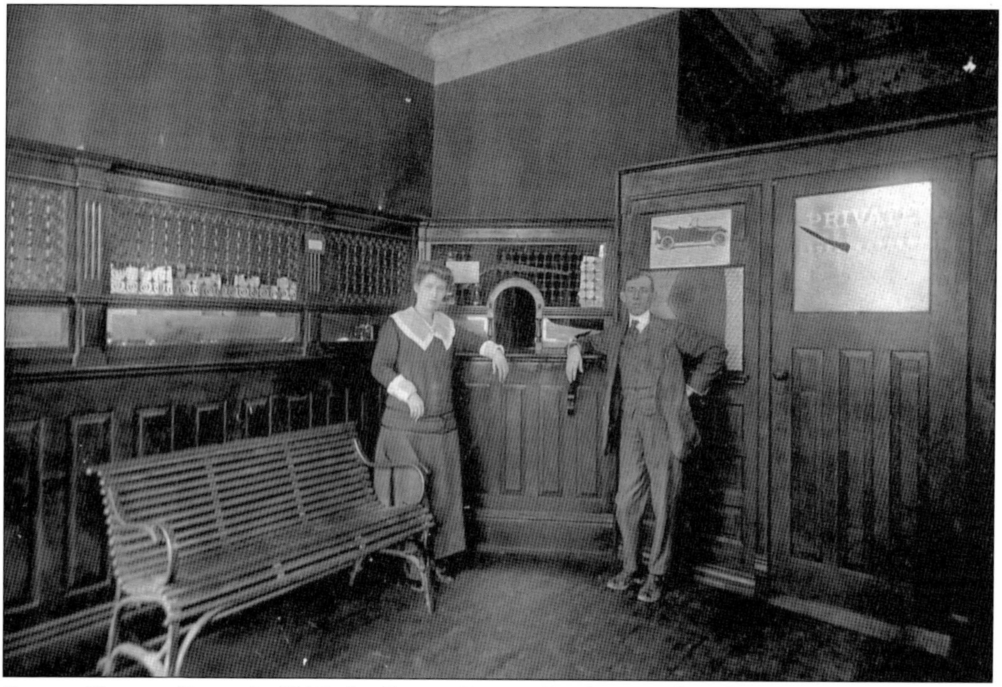

SPARTA DEPOSIT BANK. In 1900, the Sparta Deposit Bank opened its doors. The institution was a great boon to the farmers and businesses in the town. Pictured here are Virgie and Walter Records, whose family helped establish the bank. (Courtesy of Dale Samuel.)

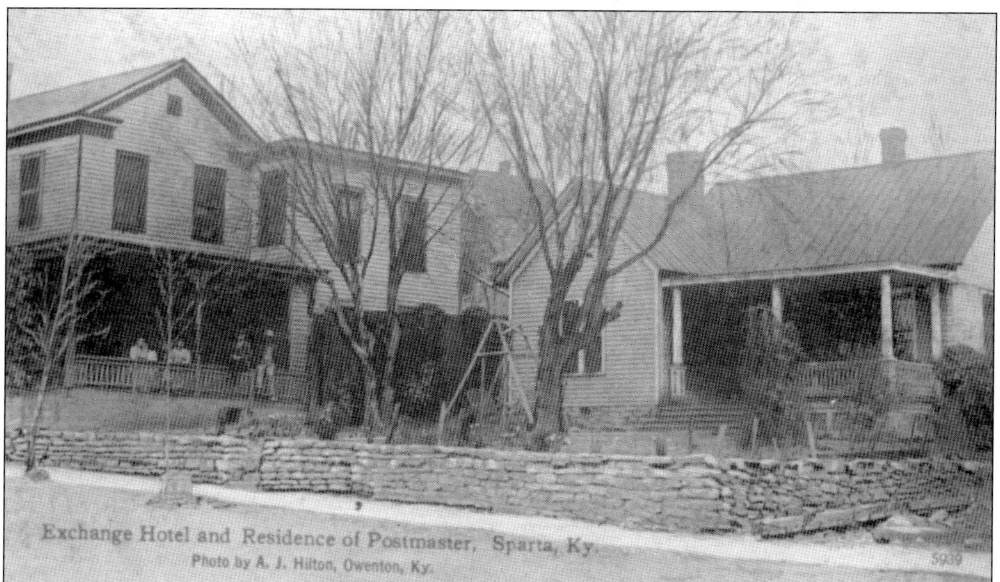

EXCHANGE HOTEL. Hotels were common in most towns during the 19th and early 20th centuries. The small hamlet of Sparta had the need for a more commodious hotel with the advent of the railroad, and Scott Moore opened the Exchange Hotel there in the late 19th century. The large hotel next to the postmaster's house on the right is pictured here around 1910. Both were located on Main Street about a block east of the depot. The stone wall still exists. (Courtesy of Darrell Maines.)

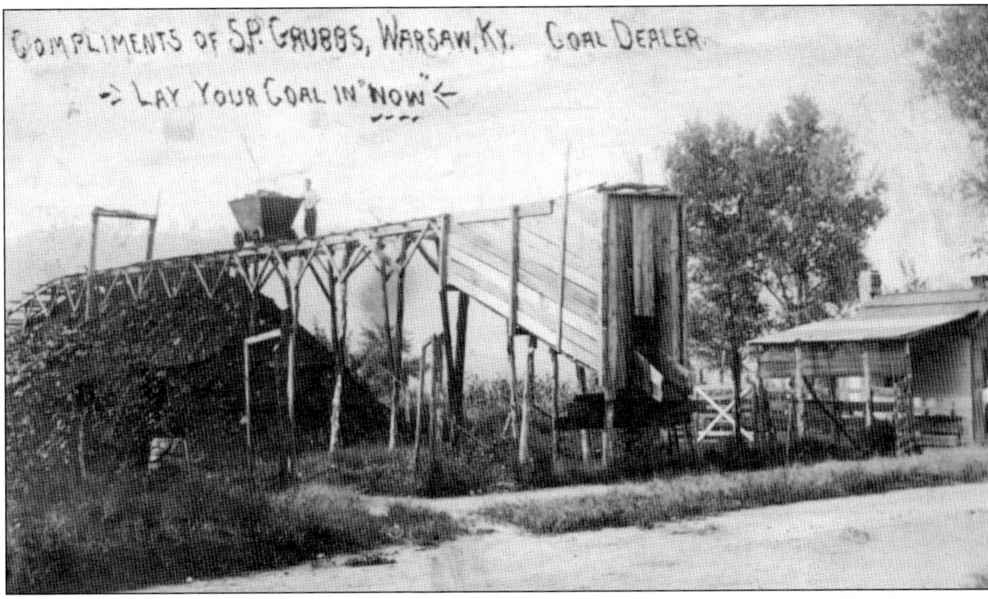

LAY COAL IN NOW. Coal was vital to both businesses and homes for heating. The fuel source was typically loaded and unloaded from barges by hand, which was a long, difficult process. Improvements came with the invention of the coal elevator. Samuel P Grubbs built this coal elevator in 1910 near the riverfront on Locust Street, between Main Cross and Second Street. Coal was scooped by machinery on and off the barges, greatly reducing the labor needed. Grubbs operated the yard until his death in 1931. (Courtesy of Darrell Maines.)

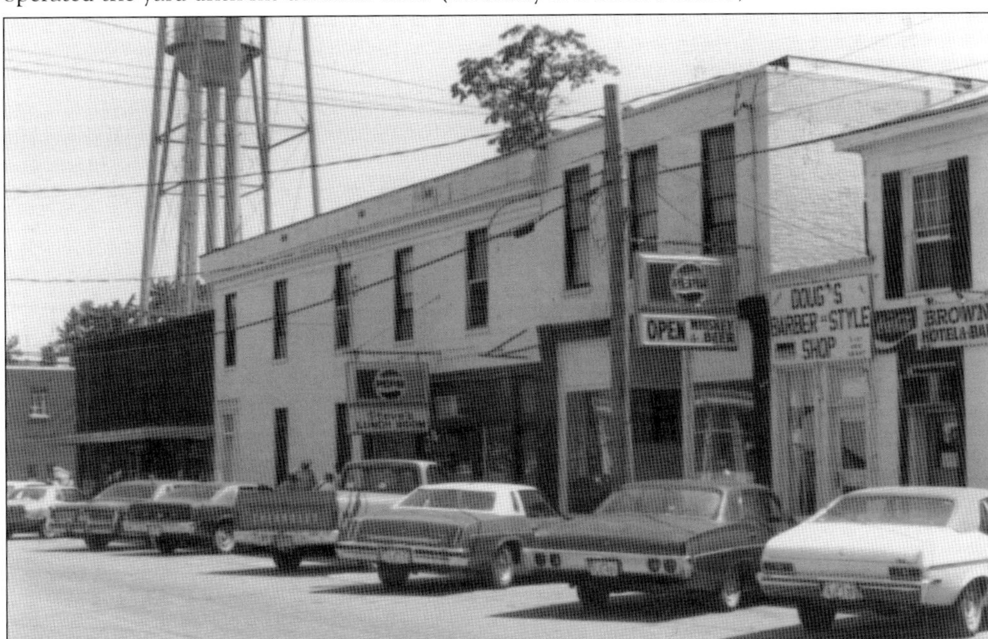

WEST SIDE OF MAIN CROSS. This 1960s photograph captures the businesses that lined the street on Main Cross. The Brown Hotel (front, right) was on the corner, facing Main Street (US 42). Next to it was Doug's Barber Shop and Steve's Lunch Room. Though the businesses are gone, the buildings still remain. (Courtesy of Darrell Maines.)

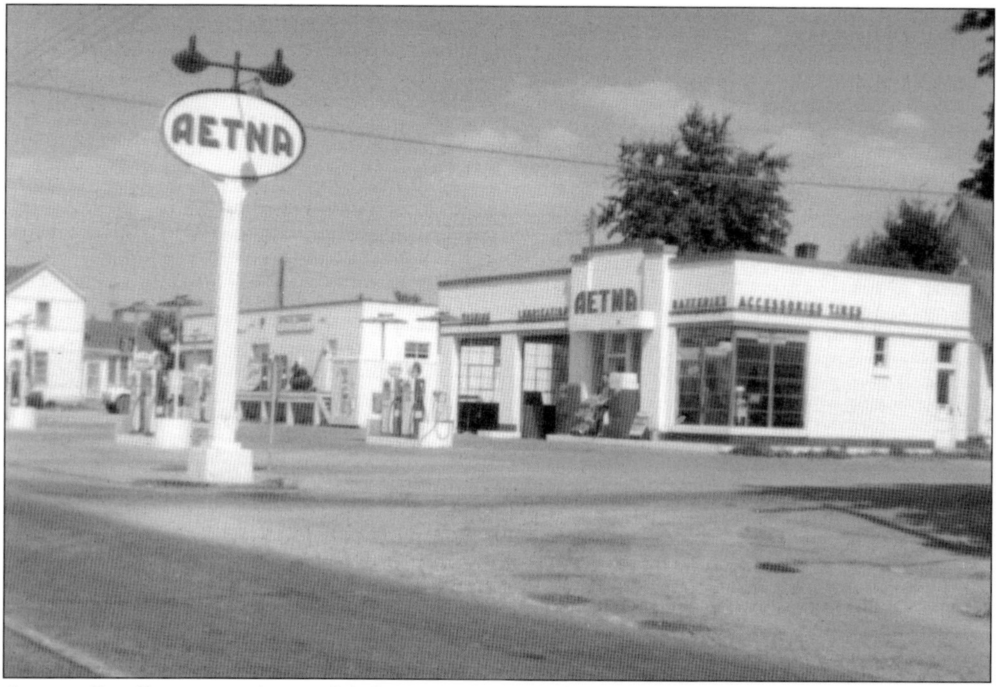

AETNA OIL COMPANY. Aetna Oil Company operated three locations: Warsaw, Glencoe, and nearby Carrollton. This 1957 photograph is of the Warsaw location on US 42 (site of the current Family Dollar, across from the Methodist church). (Courtesy of Dana Benne.)

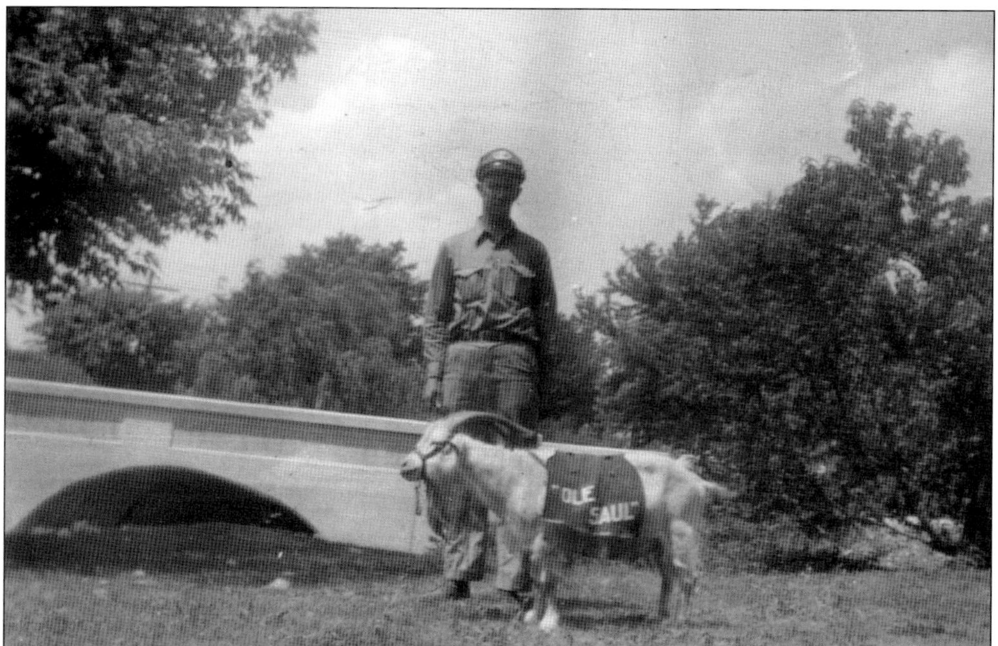

OLE SAUL. An unidentified Aetna Oil employee poses with the company mascot Ole Saul in the 1950s. It is unclear why the goat was chosen as the mascot and where this photograph was taken. (Courtesy of Dana Benne.)

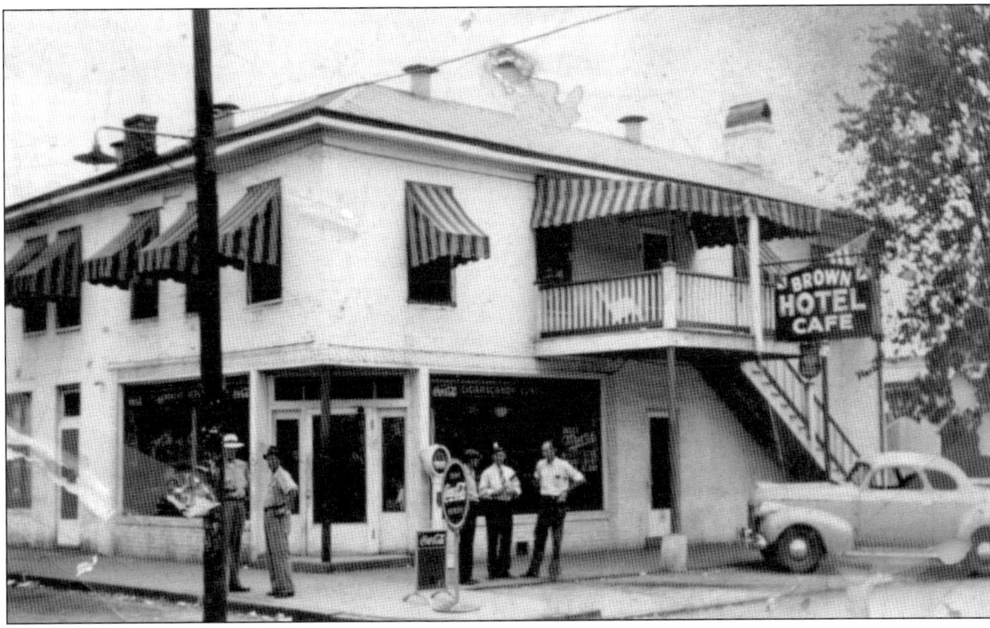

The Brown Hotel. Pictured above in the 1950s, the Brown Hotel occupied the southwest corner of Main Cross in Warsaw from when it was built to the day in burned down on November 21, 1985. The structure did not always serve as a hotel. It was originally built in 1835 as a grocery and residence by John. R. Brown but was later purchased by Bruce Meyers, who established it as the Brown Hotel in 1929, shortly after the opening of US 42. The photograph of the interior of the hotel below shows the small lunch counter. It was also used as a grocery, photography studio, and ice-cream parlor. (Both, courtesy of Darrell Maines.)

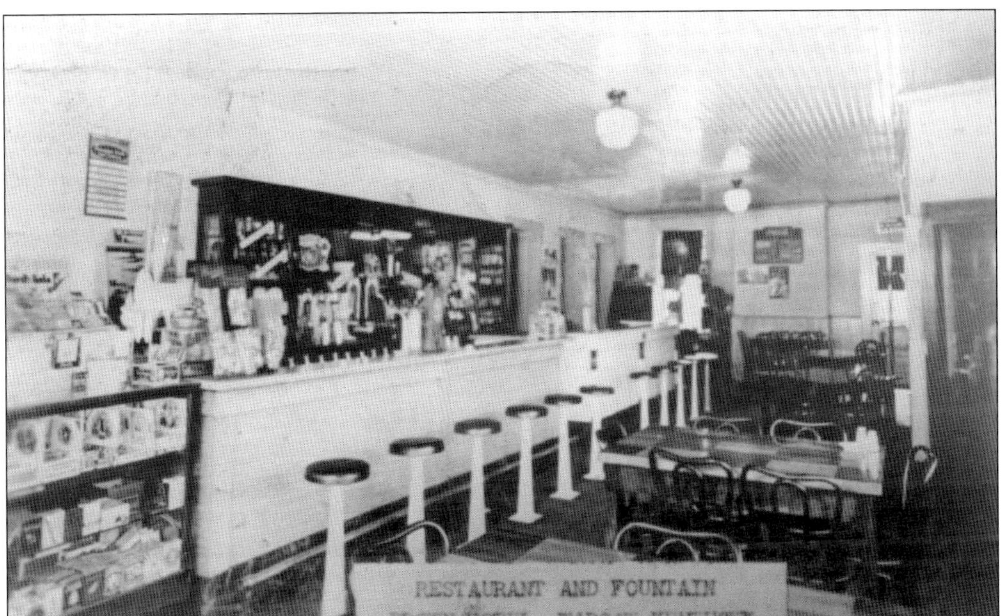

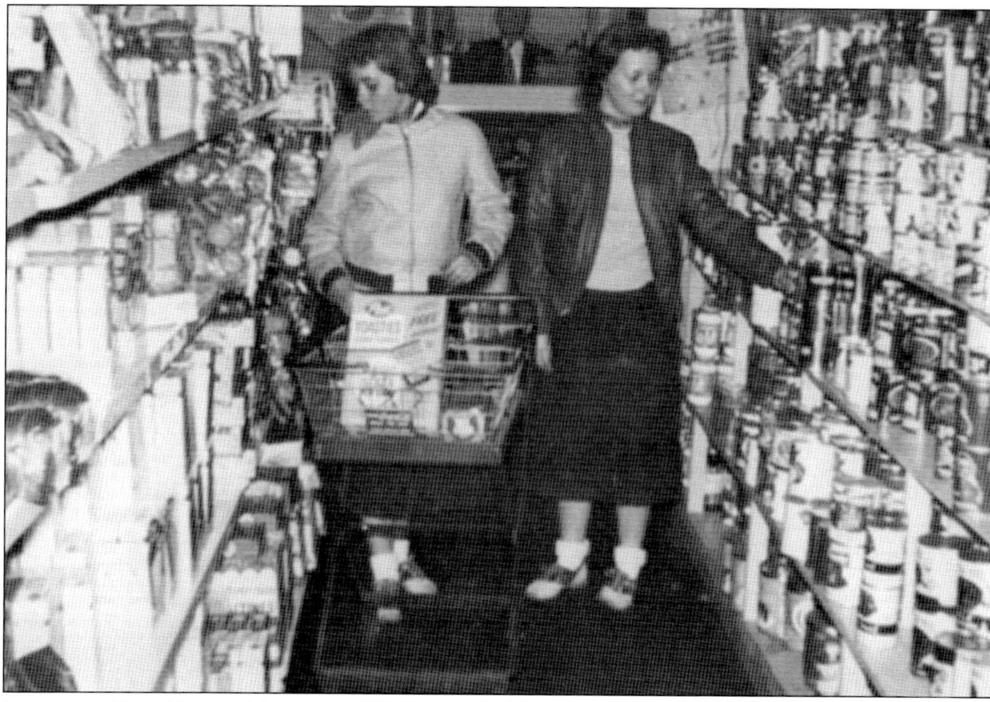

Shopping Day. Pictured here in 1957, Janice (left) and Judy VanHorn shop for groceries at the G.H. Poland Grocery in Glencoe. In the background is the owner, George Henry Poland. The store was located on Route 16 across from the Glencoe Bank. (Courtesy of the Gallatin County Free Public Library.)

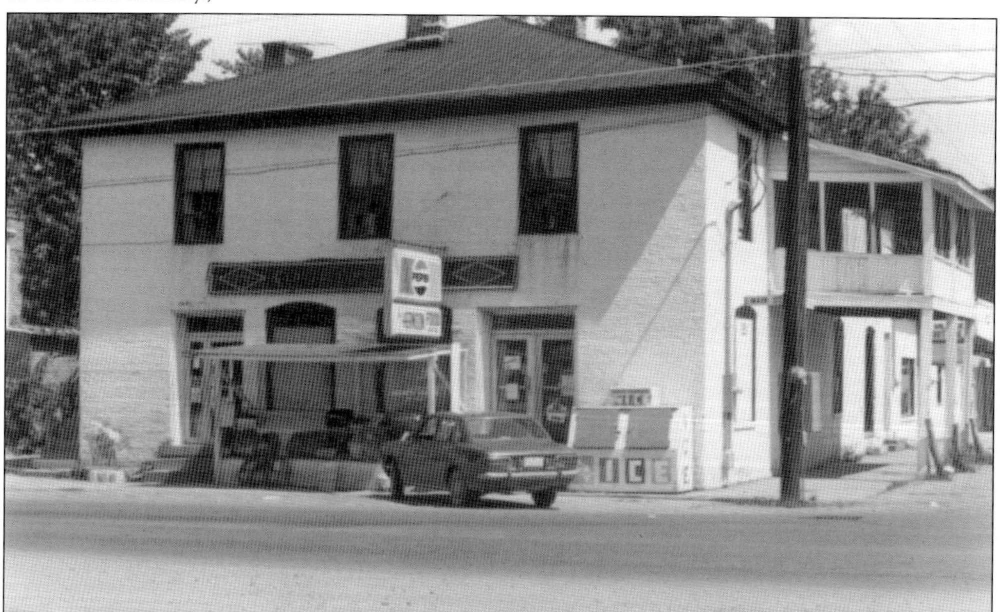

Ken Herndon's Food Store. Ken Herndon's grocery, on the southeast corner of US 42 and Main Cross, is known today as the immensely popular restaurant owned by Justin and Rena Mylor, Jewell's on Main. (Courtesy of Darrell Maines.)

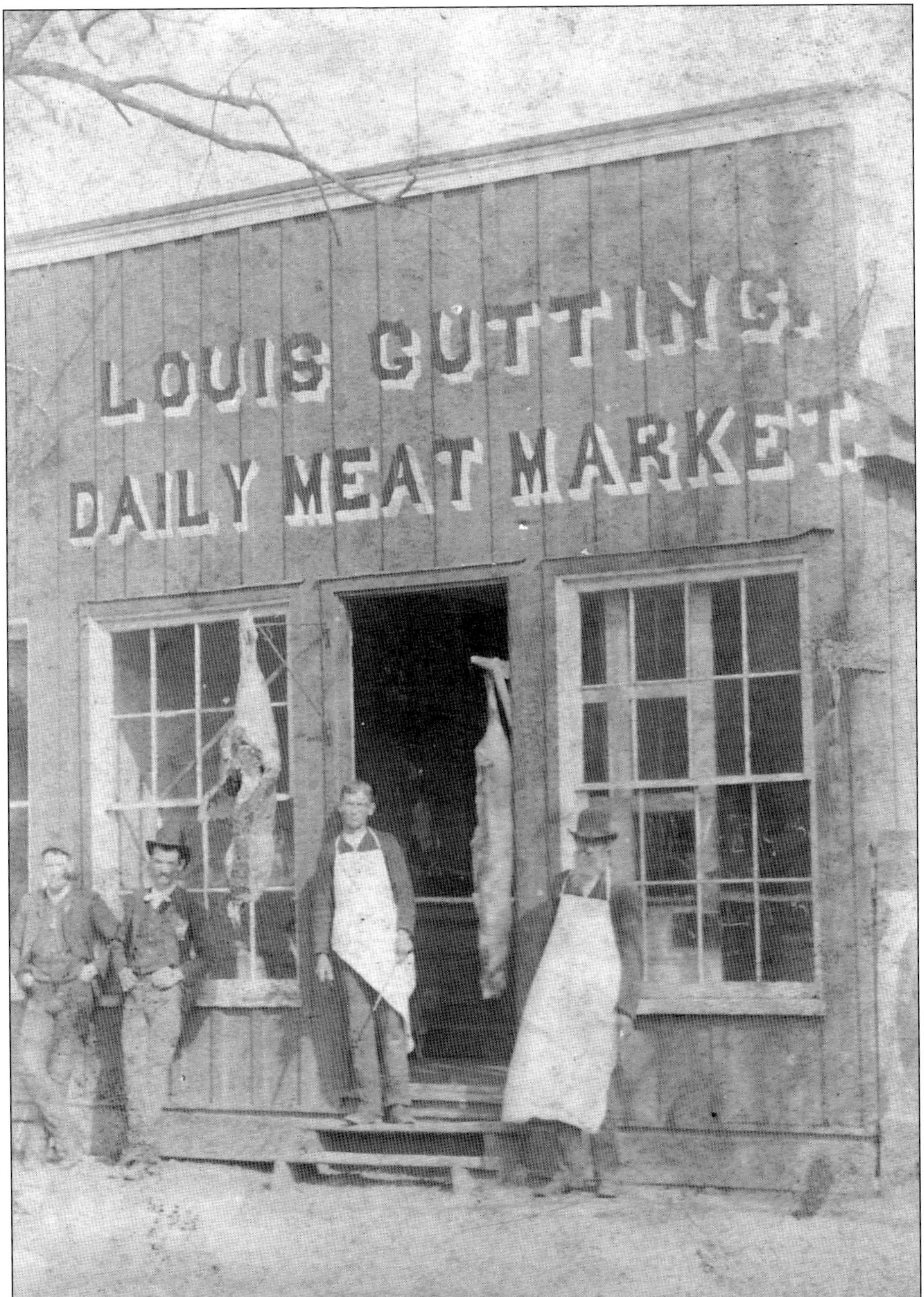

Louis Gutting's Meat Market. Located on the east side of Main Cross in Warsaw, Louis Gutting was in the meat market business for 51 years. His shop sustained substantial damage in the 1937 flood. Standing in front of the shop around 1900 are, from left to right, Clarence Abbott, Hugh Griffin, Mr. Brown, and Gutting. Brown was Gutting's store clerk. Notice the little dog in the shop behind Brown. Gutting was taken ill later in 1937 and died of uremic poisoning. The *Warsaw Independent* printed a tribute to the popular businessman, stating, "No citizen in Warsaw had more friends and was more popular than this man." (Courtesy of Darrell Maines.)

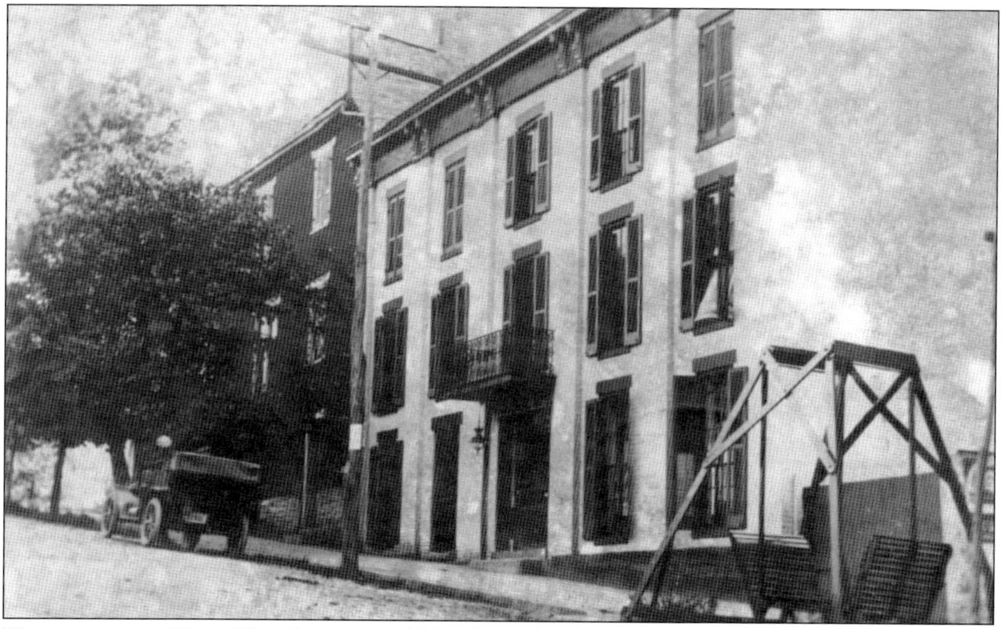

HOTEL ON THE HILL. The Commercial Hotel was located on Main Cross behind the Gallatin Deposit Bank, just beyond the courthouse square, conveniently placed in the heart of the town's business center. It was built and operated by Walter Brown, who came here from Owen County. From the *Warsaw Independent*, in an entry marked January 22, 1898, Commercial Hotel landlord Mr. R. Weldon is praised for his thriving business, which was an "ably-managed, well-kept hostelry, clean, light and inviting, with rates of only $3.50 per day." (Courtesy of Robert and Alexandra Weldon.)

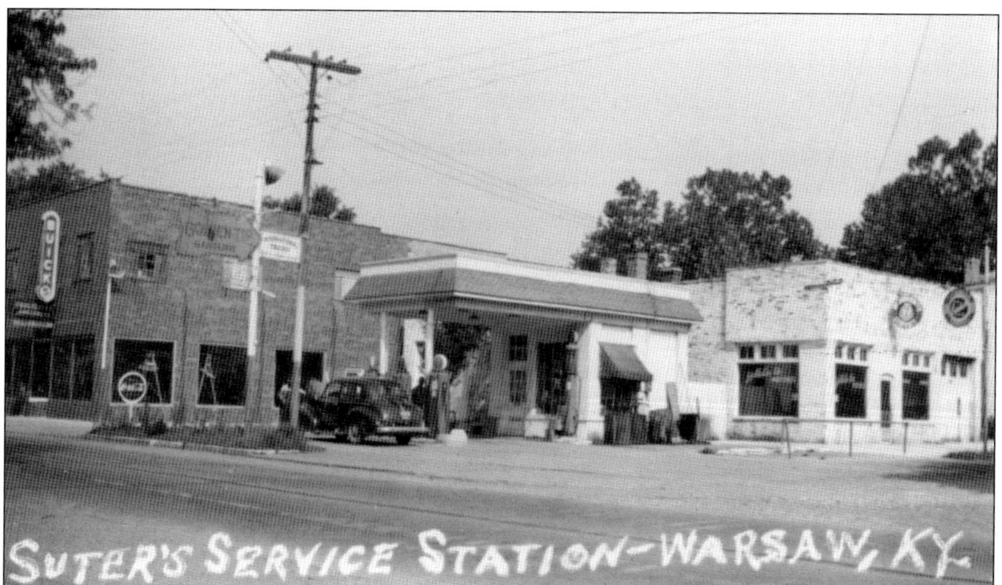

SUTER'S SERVICE STATION. This 1940s photograph shows Suter's Service Station in Warsaw. It was located on the corner of Third Street and US 42. Note the Golden Tip gasoline sign in front. The building next door sold Frigidaire appliances and is now home to the popular Deaton's Market. (Courtesy of Darrell Maines.)

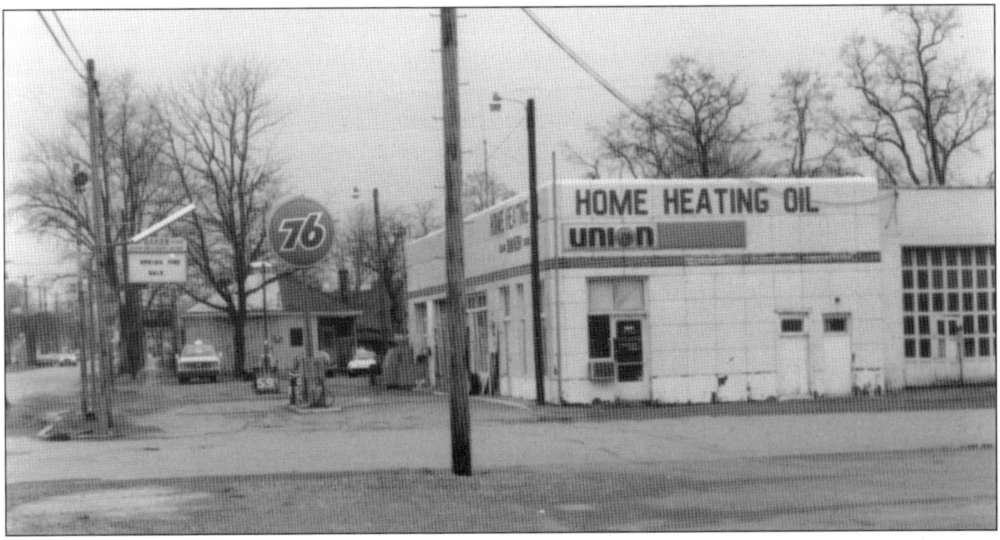

Glencoe Business. Homes were often heated with oil, and most towns had their own heating oil companies. This 76 Oil distributor was located in Glencoe on State Route 127 near the L&N depot. (Courtesy of Dana Benne.)

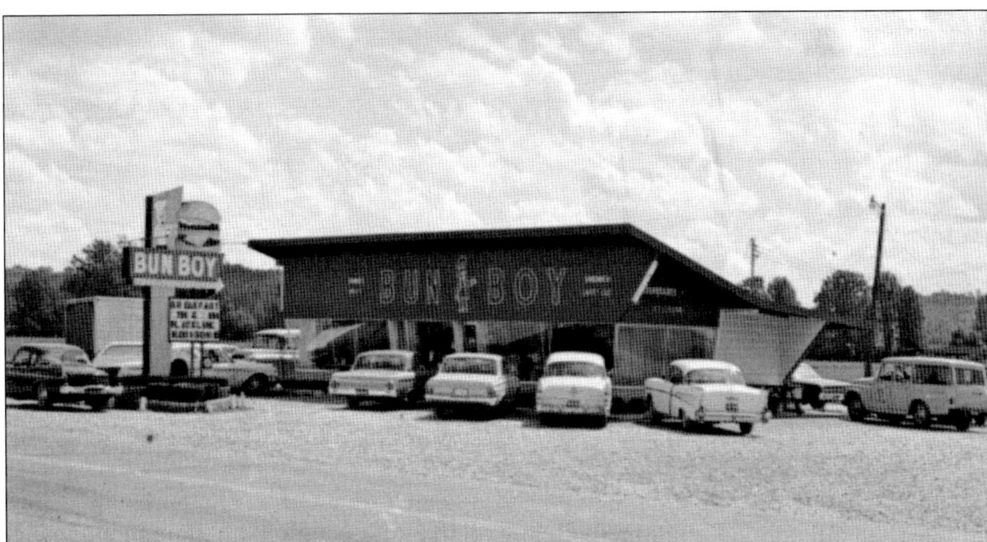

Popular Restaurant. The Bun Boy was a popular restaurant in Warsaw for over 40 years. Pictured here around 1967, the restaurant on east US 42 near the Gallatin County High School was a regular stop for many families after church every week. It is now the location of a Subway restaurant. (Courtesy of Darrell Maines.)

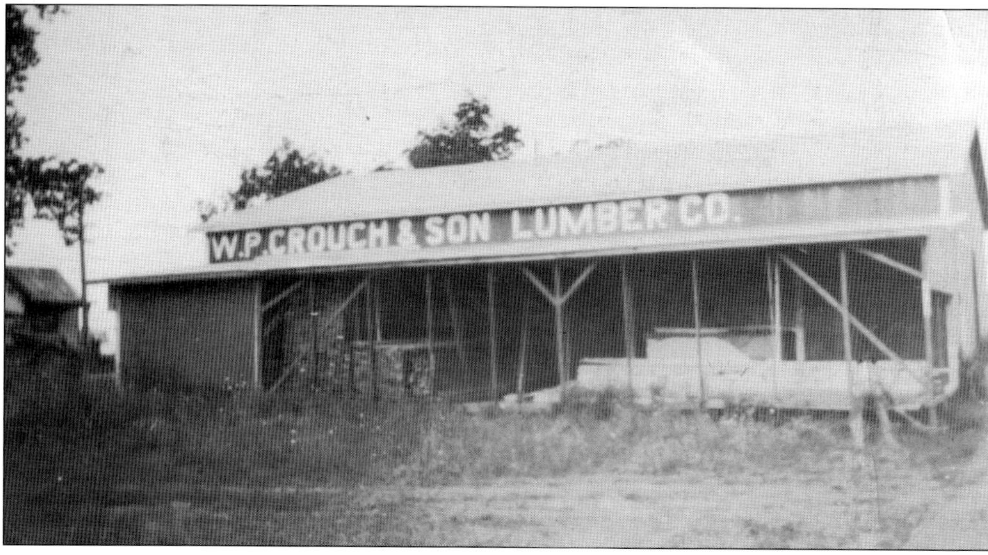

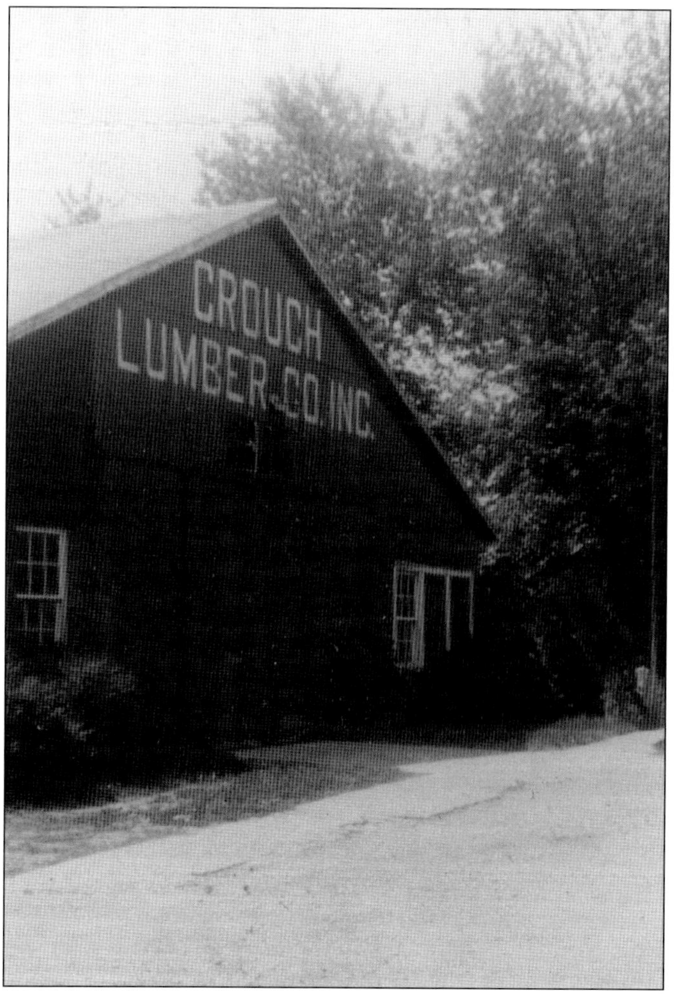

Crouch Family Lumber Company. The Crouch family has lived in the Glencoe area for several generations, and this lumberyard was originally run by O.P. Morton before the Crouches bought the business. They ran it successfully for many years, supplying building materials to customers all over the tri-county area. A son, Clifford Crouch, later founded the Crouch Gas Service. (Courtesy of Dana Benne.)

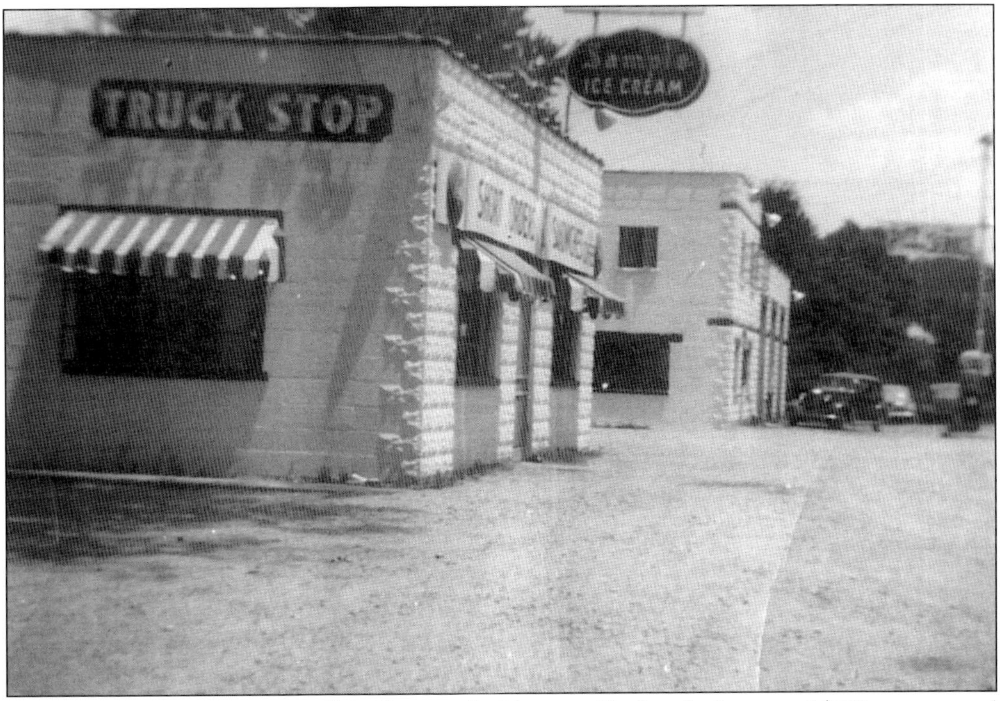

THE COUNTRY KITCHEN. Russell Hall was only 24 years old when he borrowed $750 to open and run what he later referred to as his pride and joy, the County Kitchen Truck Stop/Restaurant. Established in 1946, this well-known restaurant still sits on US 42 midway between Warsaw and Ghent. The building is known to locals today as a once-popular bar called the Green Door, but it is currently vacant with no plans to reopen. (Courtesy of Russell Hall.)

AMONG THE BEST. The Country Kitchen may not have been very big, with just four booths and eight stools, but it was such a favorite with truckers and worldwide travelers that a national magazine (*Argosy*), named it among the best truck stops in America. As seen here, restaurants that were repeatedly recommended were distinguished with an asterisk. (Courtesy of Russell Hall.)

KENTUCKY

25	*Huff's Dinner Bell, 25 mi. south of Cincinnati.
42	*Country Kitchen, near Warsaw, 30 mi. south of Cincinnati.
42	Gipsy Grill, near Caroline, 60 mi. south of Cincinnati.
Jct. 25E, 25W	*Pike's Coffee Shop, at Corbin.
25, 42	Dixie Dew, 7 mi. south of Covington.

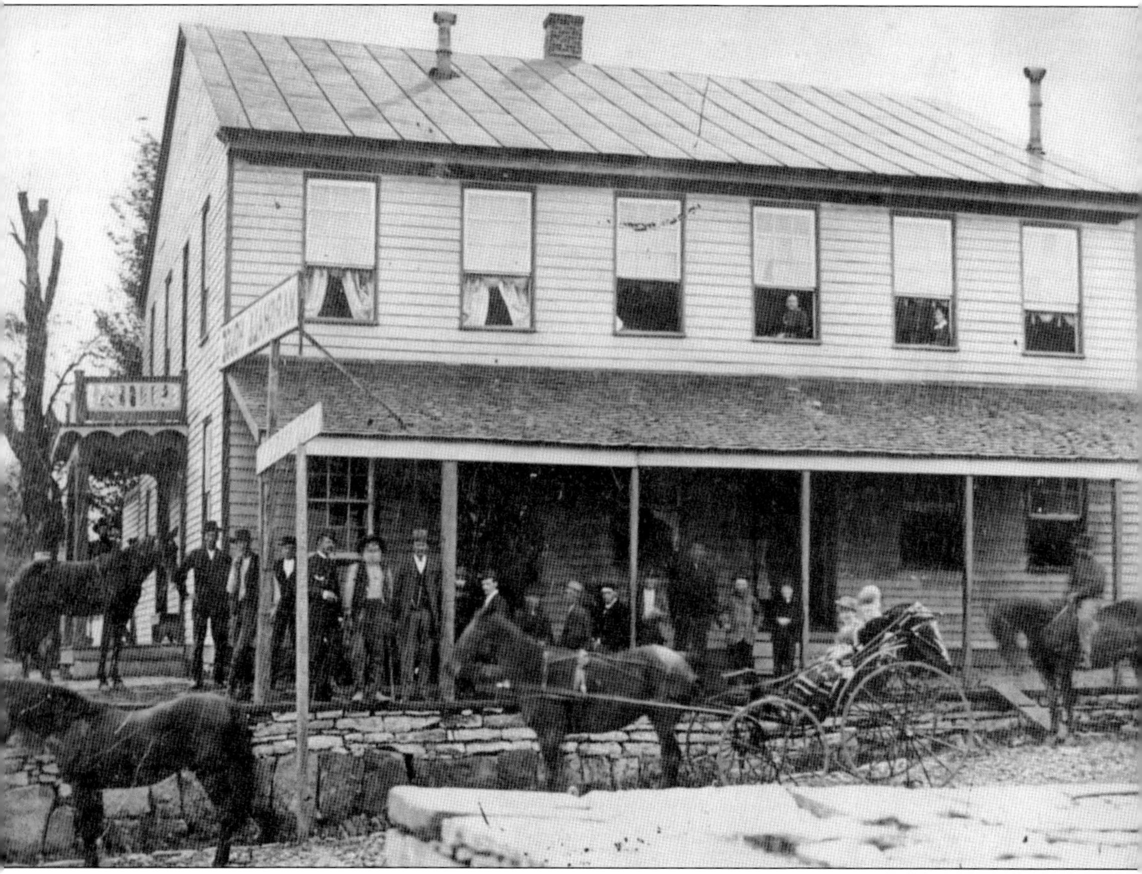

Marshall House. Pictured here around 1880 is the Marshall House hotel, located on the corner of Locust Street and Main Cross, on the riverfront. Operated by Ed Marshall, it was also known as the Eagle Hotel. Note the women in the upstairs windows; their presence suggests the variety of services offered by the hotel. (Courtesy of Darrell Maines.)

Five

EDUCATION

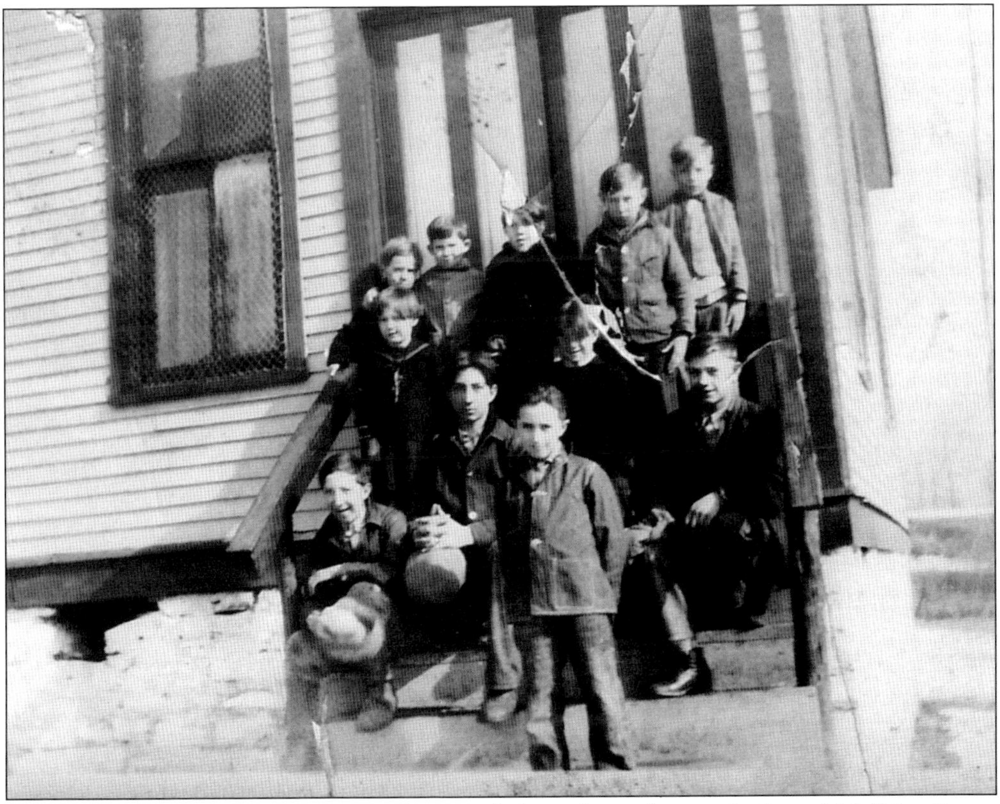

STONE LICK SCHOOLHOUSE. This 1920s photograph shows the students at the Stone Lick Schoolhouse near Craig's Creek, west of Warsaw. The boy at far right in the back is identified as Harold Dickerson. The girl on the third step, behind the two seated boys at left, is identified as Dorothy Dell Dickerson. (Courtesy of Dale Samuel.)

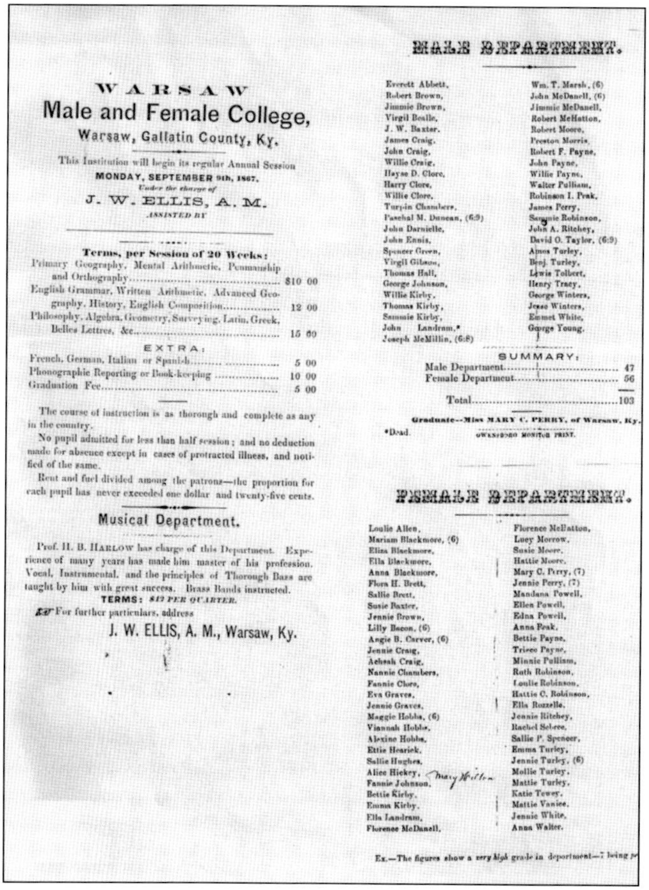

W A R S A W

Male and Female College,

Warsaw, Gallatin County, Ky.

This Institution will begin its regular Annual Session

MONDAY, SEPTEMBER 9th, 1867.

Under the charge of

J. W. ELLIS, A. M.

ASSISTED BY

Terms, per Session of 20 Weeks:

Primary Geography, Mental Arithmetic, Penmanship and Orthography	$10 00
English Grammar, Written Arithmetic, Advanced Geography, History, English Composition	12 00
Philosophy, Algebra, Geometry, Surveying, Latin, Greek, Belles Lettres, &c.	15 00

EXTRA:

French, German, Italian or Spanish	5 00
Phonographic Reporting or Book-keeping	10 00
Graduation Fee	5 00

The course of instruction is as thorough and complete as any in the country.

No pupil admitted for less than half session; and no deduction made for absence except in cases of protracted illness, and notified of the same.

Rent and fuel divided among the patrons—the proportion for each pupil has never exceeded one dollar and twenty-five cents.

Musical Department.

Prof. H. B. HARLOW has charge of this Department. Experience of many years has made him master of his profession. Vocal, Instrumental, and the principles of Thorough Bass are taught by him with great success. Brass Bands instructed.

TERMS: *$12 PER QUARTER.*

☞ For further particulars, address

J. W. ELLIS, A. M., Warsaw, Ky.

MALE DEPARTMENT.

Everett Abbett,
Robert Brown,
Jimmie Brown,
Virgil Bealle,
J. W. Baxter,
James Craig,
John Craig,
Willie Craig,
Hayse D. Clore,
Harry Clore,
Willie Clore,
Turpin Chambers,
Paschal M. Duncan, (6:9)
John Darnielle,
John Ennis,
Spencer Green,
Virgil Gibson,
Thomas Hall,
George Johnson,
Willie Kirby,
Thomas Kirby,
Sammie Kirby,
John Landram,*
Joseph McMillin, (6:8)
Wm. T. Marsh, (6)
John McDanell, (6)
Jimmie McDanell,
Robert McHatton,
Robert Moore,
Preston Morris,
Robert F. Payne,
John Payne,
Willie Payne,
Walter Pulliam,
Robinson I. Peak,
James Perry,
Sammie Robinson,
John A. Ritchey,
David O. Taylor, (6:9)
Amos Turley,
Benj. Turley,
Lewis Tolbert,
Henry Tracy,
George Winters,
Jesse Winters,
Emmet White,
George Young.

SUMMARY:

Male Department	47
Female Department	56
Total	103

Graduate—Miss MARY C. PERRY, of Warsaw, Ky.

*Dead.

OWENSBORO MONITOR PRINT.

FEMALE DEPARTMENT.

Loulie Allen,
Mariam Blackmore, (6)
Eliza Blackmore,
Ella Blackmore,
Anna Blackmore,
Flora H. Brett,
Sallie Brett,
Susie Baxter,
Jennie Brown,
Lilly Bacon, (6)
Angie B. Carver, (6)
Jennie Craig,
Achsah Craig,
Nannie Chambers,
Fannie Clore,
Eva Graves,
Jennie Graves,
Maggie Hobbs, (6)
Viannah Hobbs,
Alexine Hobbs,
Ettie Hearick,
Sallie Hughes,
Alice Hickey,
Fannie Johnson,
Bettie Kirby,
Emma Kirby,
Ella Landram,
Florence McDanell,
Florence McHatton,
Lucy Morrow,
Susie Moore,
Hattie Moore,
Mary C. Perry, (7)
Jennie Perry, (7)
Mandana Powell,
Ellen Powell,
Edna Powell,
Anna Peak,
Bettie Payne,
Trisco Payne,
Minnie Pulliam,
Ruth Robinson,
Loulie Robinson,
Hattie C. Robinson,
Ella Rozzelle,
Jennie Ritchey,
Rachel Sebree,
Sallie P. Spencer,
Emma Turley,
Jennie Turley, (6)
Mollie Turley,
Mattie Turley,
Katie Tewey,
Mattie Vanice,
Jennie White,
Anna Walter.

Ex.—The figures show a *very high* grade in deportment—7 being

THE WARSAW ACADEMY. In 1860, the Warsaw Academy was established by J.W. Ellis. On May 31, 1865, by an act of the General Assembly of Kentucky, the Warsaw Academy was incorporated as the Warsaw Male and Female College. Tuition for this private school was $3 a month. Pictured here is the 1867 school year course descriptions accompanied by both female and male rosters. (Courtesy of Darrell Maines.)

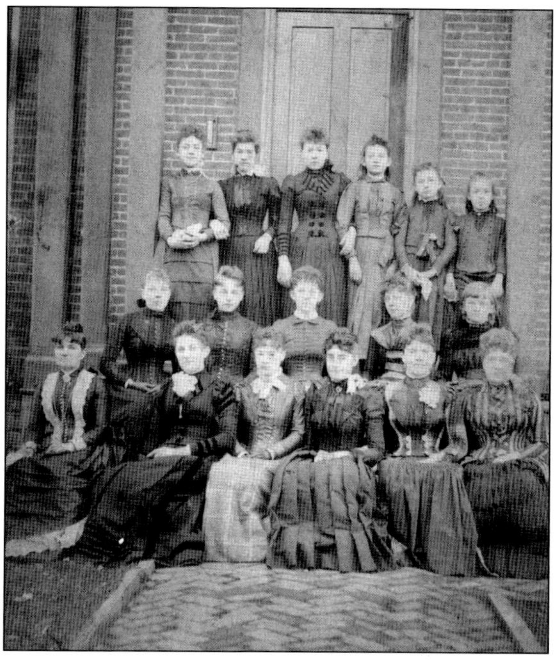

THE FEMALE DEPARTMENT. This is thought to be one of the early female classes to attend the Warsaw Male and Female College. Their location is likely outside of the two-story brick house on Sparta Pike where classes were held. (Courtesy of Darrell Maines)

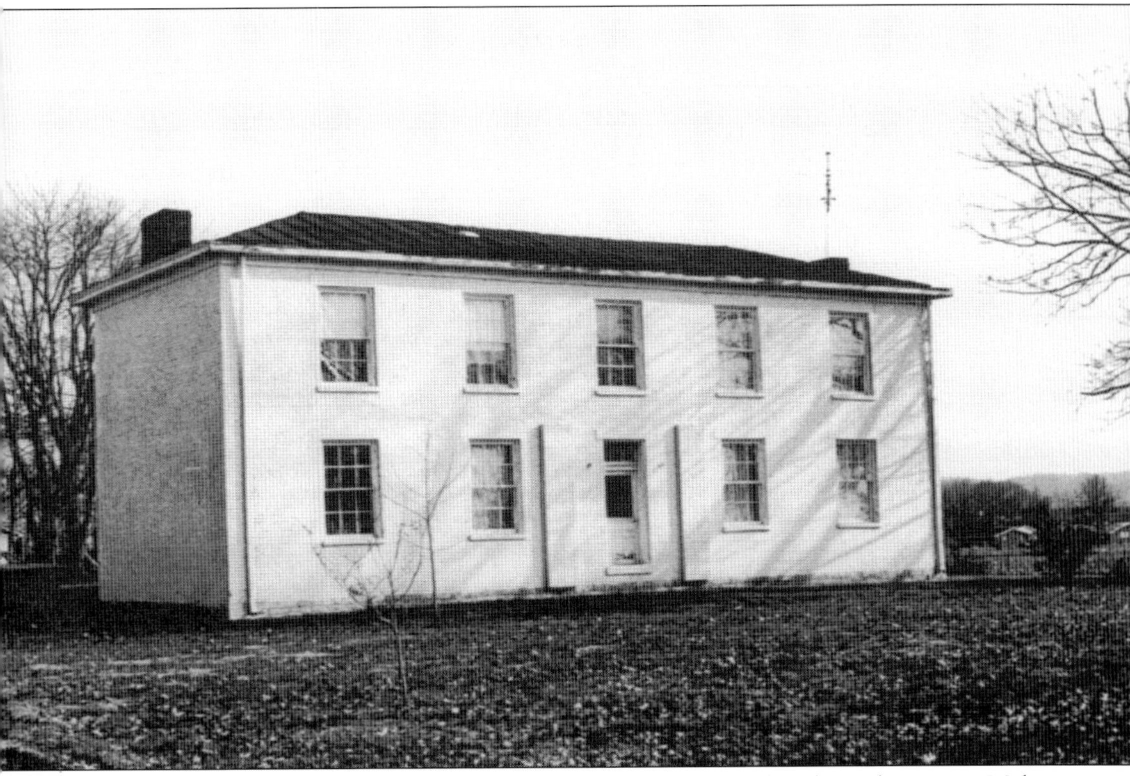

THE CLARA SISSON HOUSE. This two-story brick dwelling once served as the early Warsaw Male and Female College. This building, constructed in 1849 by Whitfield Hawkins, still stands today and is officially referred to as the Clara Sisson House, listed in the National Register of Historic Places. The beautiful military wedding of Ann Graves, the sister of Lorenzo Graves, to Maj. James W. Long, an aide to Pres. Abraham Lincoln, was held here in 1868. The two-story house is located on the edge of Warsaw on Sparta Pike (US Highway 35). (Courtesy of Darrell Maines.)

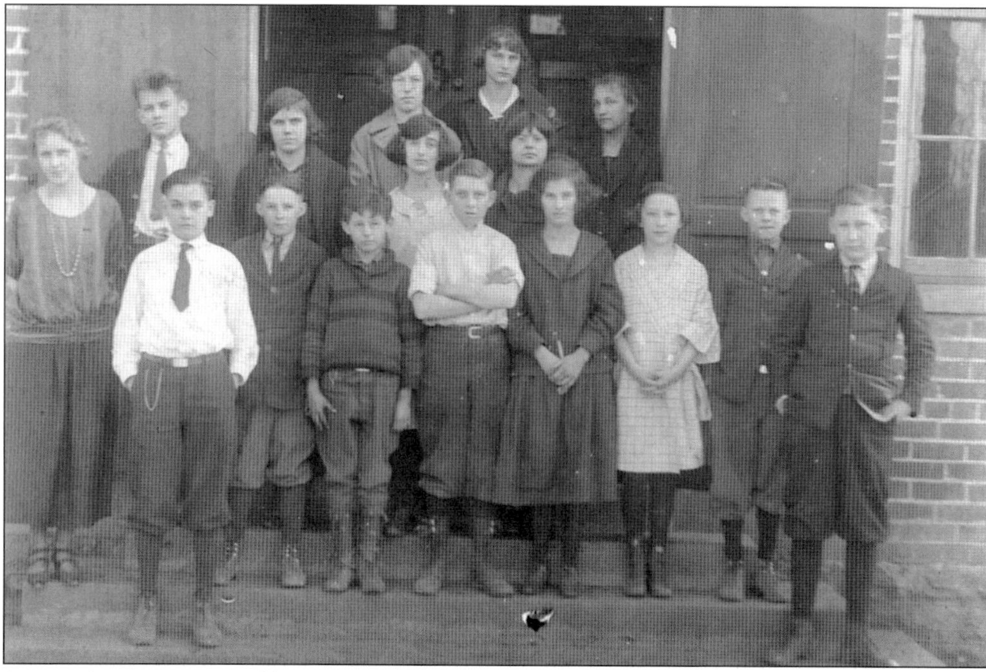

SPARTA SCHOOL. Pictured here are, from left to right, (first row) Robert Wilson, Harry L. Crume, Ernst G. Wilson, Hubert Brock, Geraldine Farrar, Margret Brock, and Lewis Reece Wilson; (second row) Dorthy Smith (teacher), Beulah Jones, and Alma Robinson; (third row) James Gullion, Margaret Harris, Mary Catherine Clark, Leontine Thompson, and Emma D. McCune. (Courtesy of Dale Samuel.)

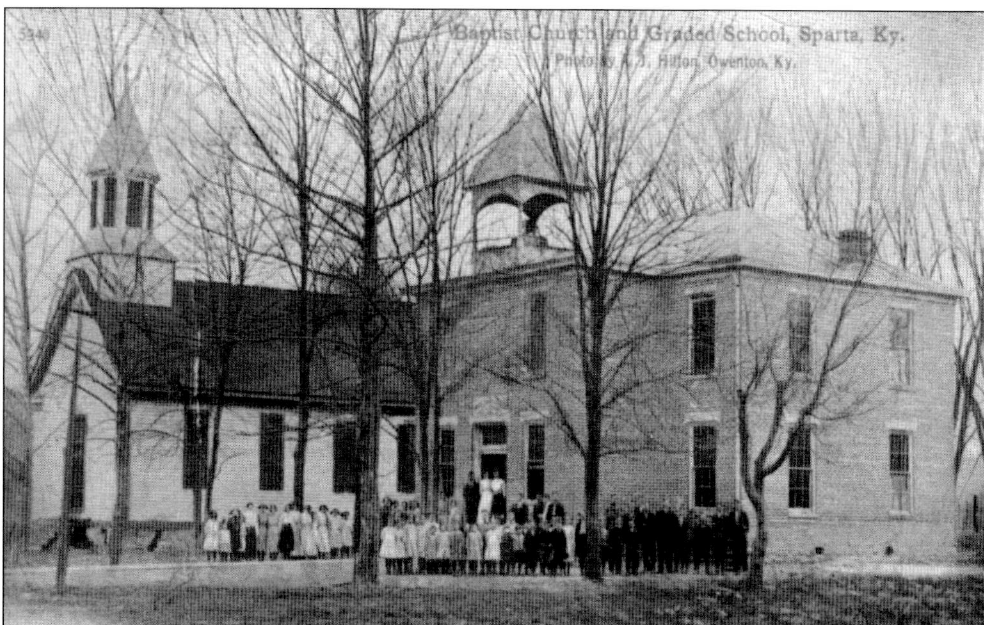

SPARTA SCHOOL AND CHURCH. Students stand outside the Sparta school in this photograph taken around 1900. The old Baptist church is next door. The church building still stands near Eagle Creek on US 35. (Courtesy of Darrell Maines.)

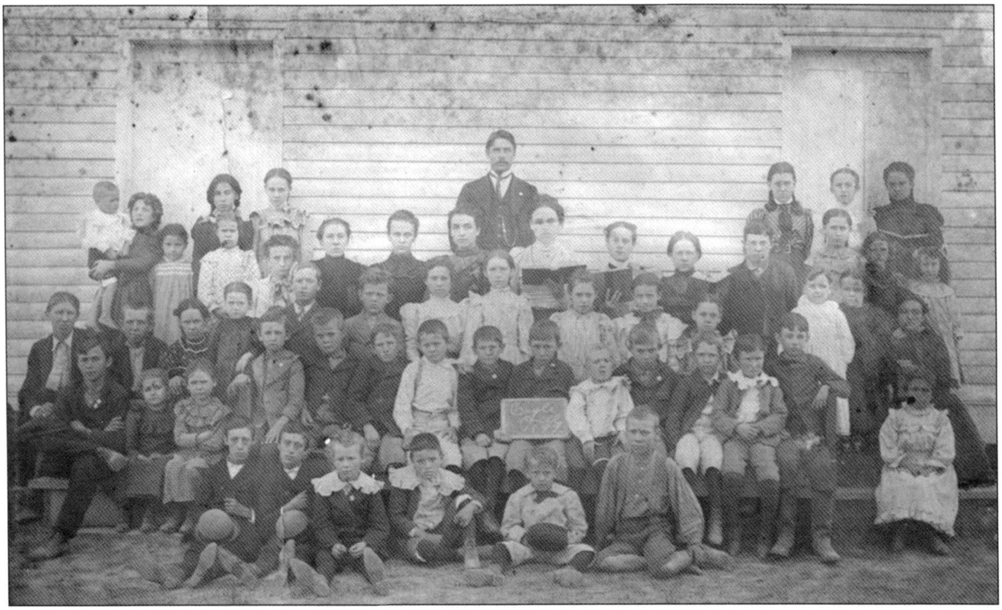

Eagle Hill School Class. The unidentified class members of the one-room schoolhouse at Eagle Hill pose in this 1899 photograph. The school was located near the Eagle Valley at Sparta. (Courtesy of Darrell Maines.)

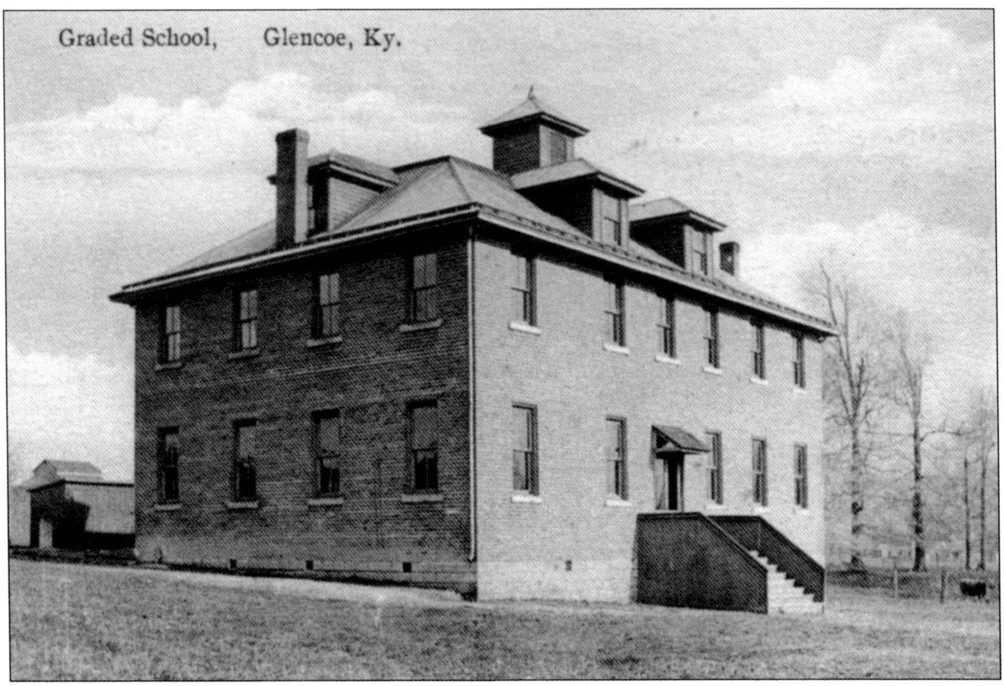

Glencoe School. The Glencoe graded school is pictured here around 1920. Located on US Highway 127 in Glencoe, it burned down in 1955. It was rebuilt on the same site and used until all schools were consolidated into the Gallatin County Public Schools. (Courtesy of Darrell Maines.)

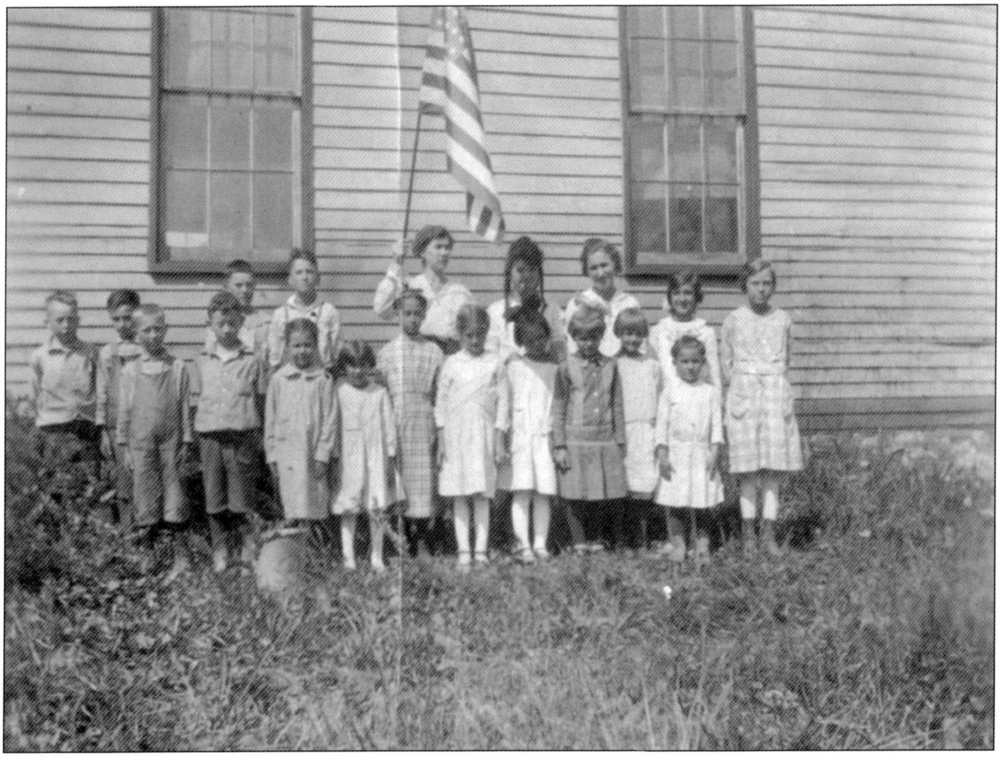

Steeles Creek School. In the 1930s, these students from the Steele's Creek school demonstrate their patriotic spirit by waving the American flag. Steele's Creek is located on the eastern side of the county, near the Boone County line. (Courtesy of Darrell Maines.)

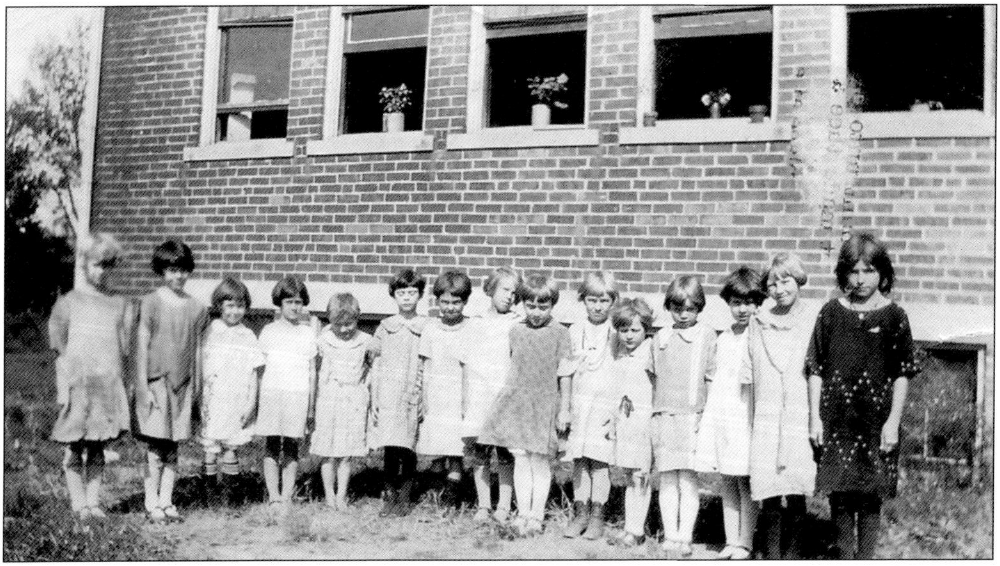

Warsaw School. A group of grade students stand outside the Warsaw School in this 1930s photograph. The fifth girl from the right is identified as Dorothy Dell Dickerson. (Courtesy of Darrell Maines.)

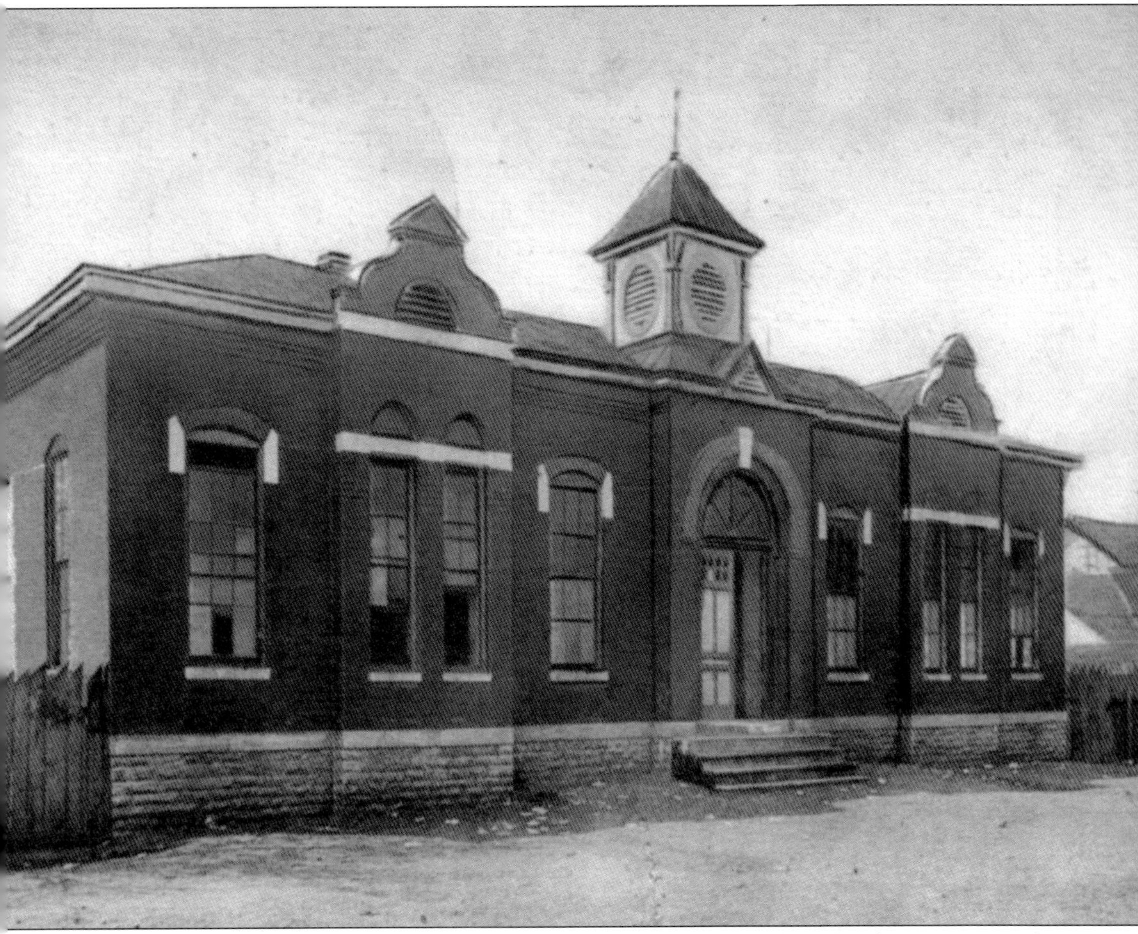

PUBLIC SCHOOLHOUSE. Pictured here around 1900 is the old public school in Warsaw. The official name was the Warsaw Grade School; it was built in 1888 and used as a school until 1913. After the construction of the school building on the east side of town, the old schoolhouse was transformed into a theater. In the 1930s, it housed the *Gallatin County News* office. (Courtesy of Darrell Maines.)

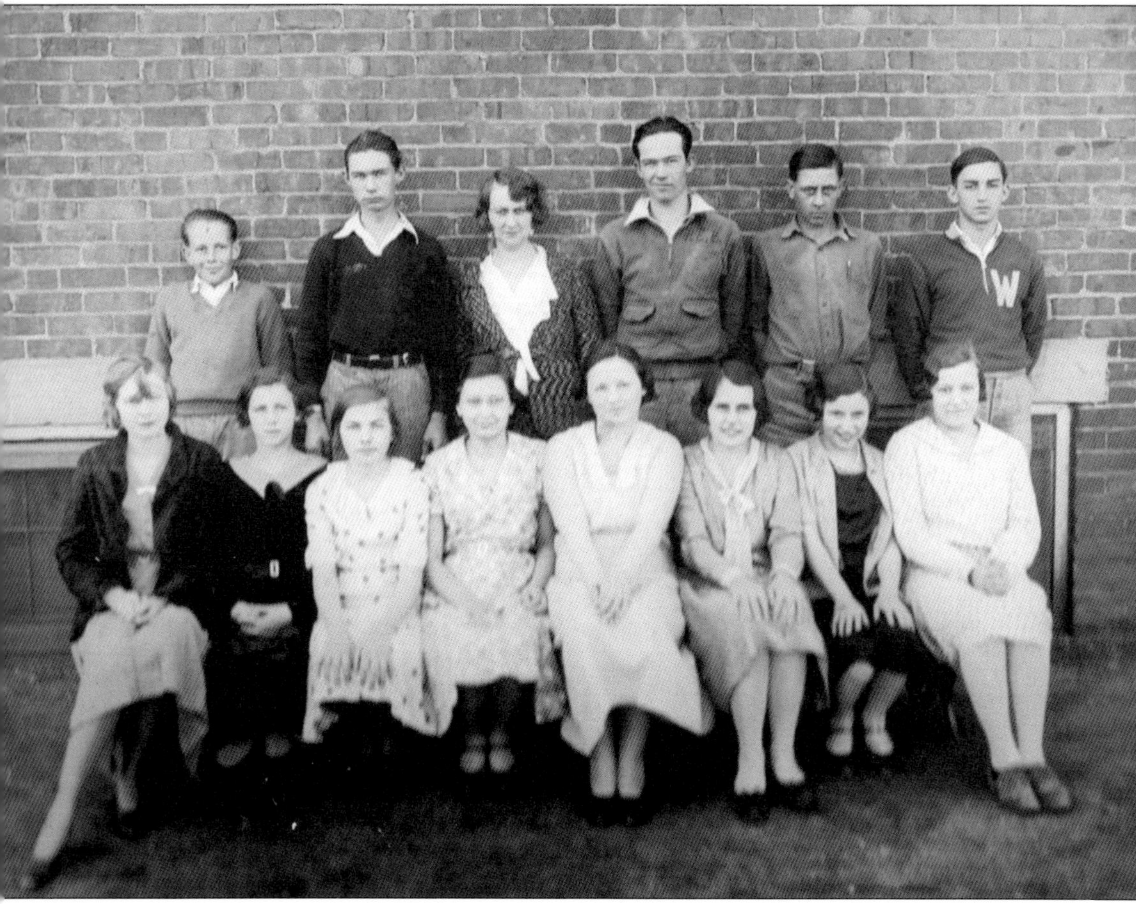

Freshman Class. Pictured here is the Warsaw High School freshman class of 1931. From left to right are (first row) two unidentified, Sarah Lee Whitehead, Harold Brown Conely, Delores Craig, Louvetta Marksberry, unidentified, and Dorothy Hopper; (second row) Robin Milton Hance, unidentified, Willa Beall Spencer Smith (teacher), two unidentified, and Siebert Craig. (Courtesy of Robert and Alexandra Weldon.)

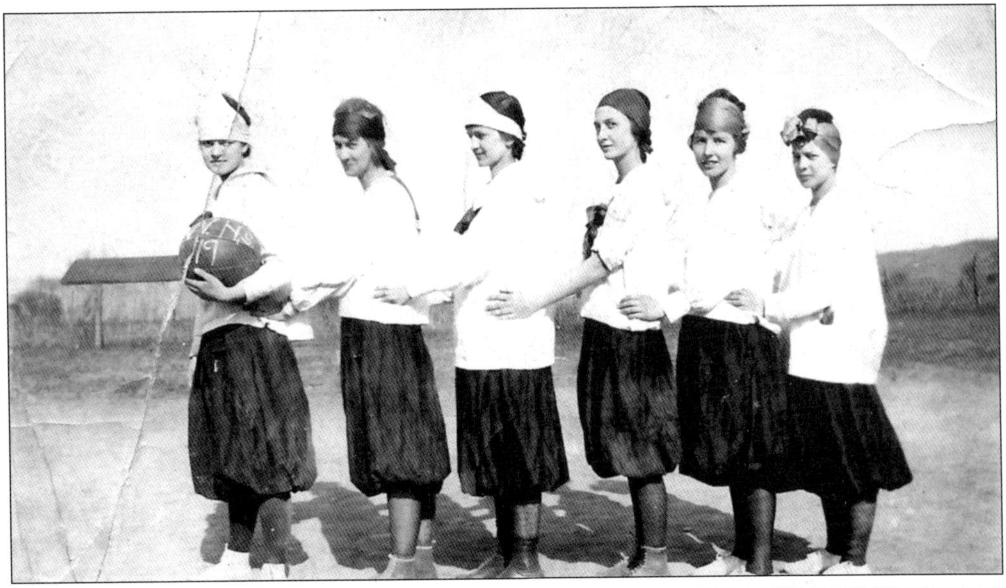

Women's Basketball Team. The 1918–1919 Gallatin County Lady Wildcats pose for a team photograph in their basketball uniforms. (Courtesy of Darrell Maines.)

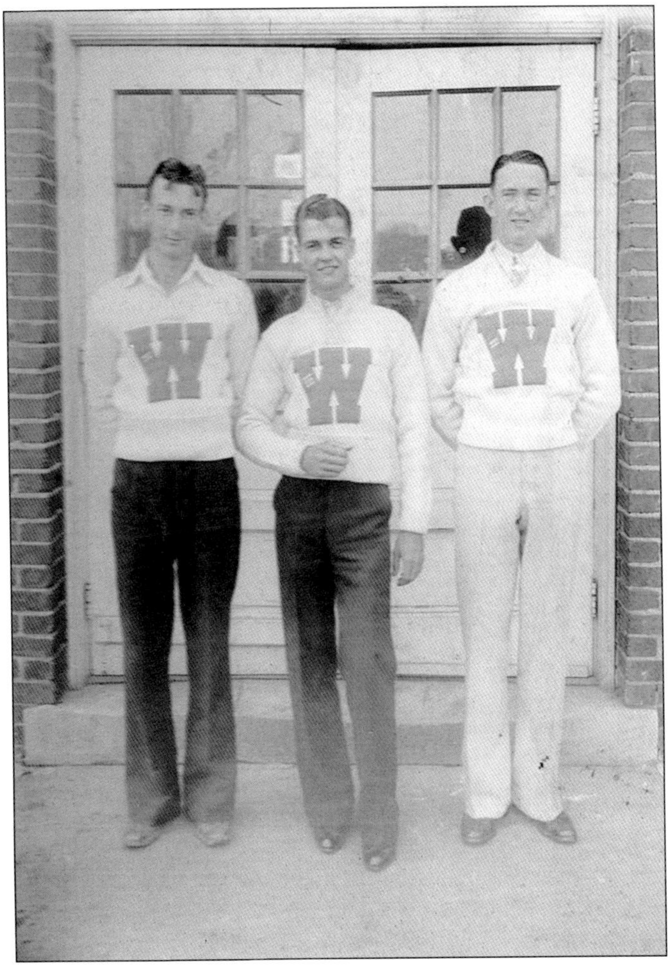

School Spirit. Three young men sport their school spirit by wearing letter sweaters outside of Warsaw's High School. From left to right are Stewart Roberts, Walton Smith, and Rex Wheeler. The school's teams were known as the Warsaw Wildcats. (Courtesy of Darrell Maines.)

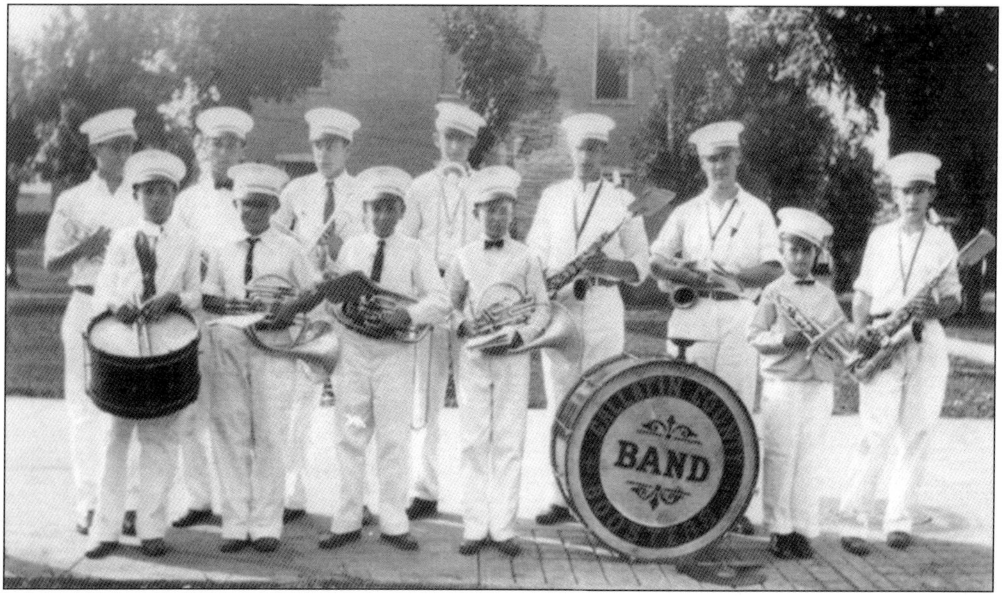

GCHS Band Boosters. This group poses for their yearbook photograph in July 1926. From left to right are (first row) Charlie Lavelle, Hugh John Richards, Charlie Allen, James Warren Ryle, and James William Spencer; (second row) Lem Bledsoe, Russell Ashcraft, Jim Bogardus, Ralph Hart, Wilbur Beyers, Robert Marshall, and Ulous Carlton. (Courtesy of Gallatin County Public Schools.)

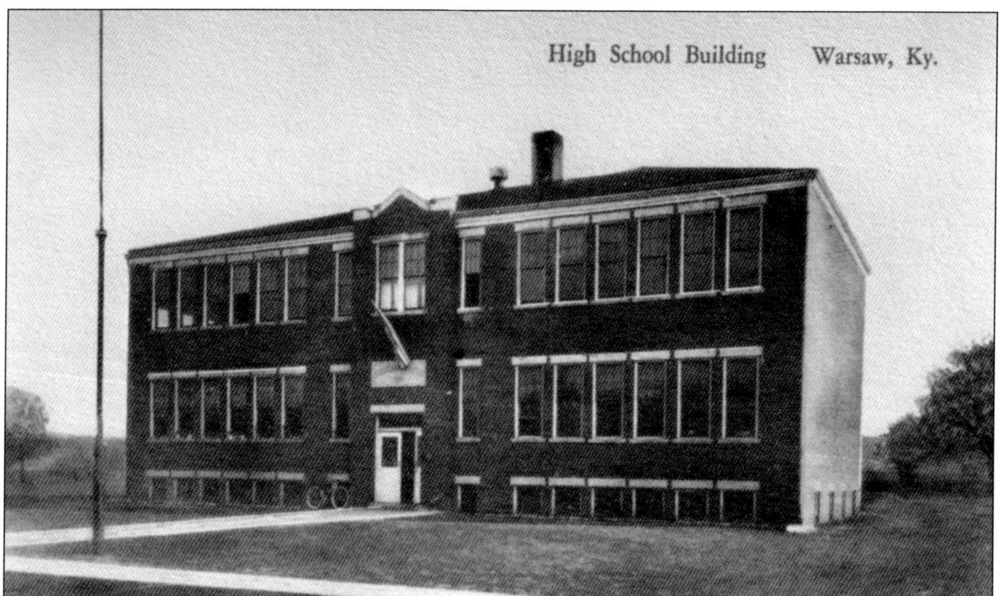

Old GCHS. The Old Warsaw School, (Warsaw's second school) was built in 1913 at a cost of $12,000. This school was used until a new school was constructed in the 1950s. (Courtesy of Darrell Maines.)

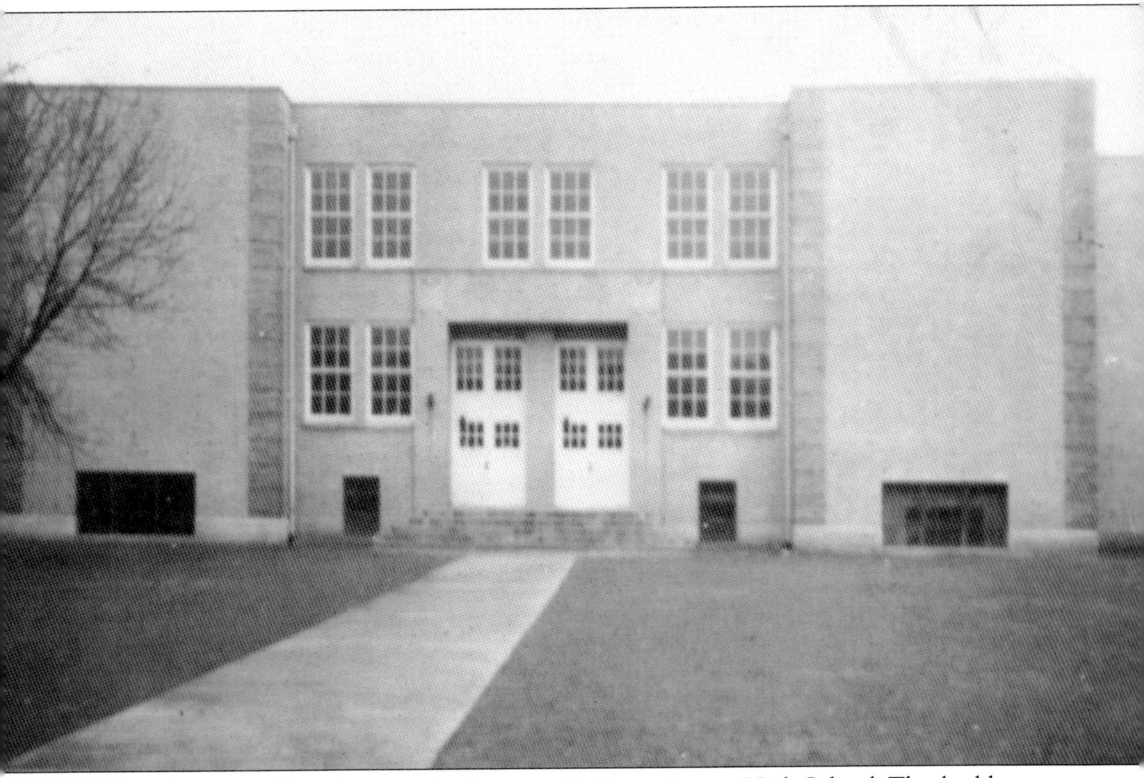

GCHS. This is a 1950s photograph of the new Gallatin County High School. This building was the high school until the construction of the current high school was completed. It was then used as the middle school, a connection to the upper elementary. The building was torn down in 2008 to make room for the new upper elementary and middle school, constructed on the same grounds. (Courtesy of Darrell Maines.)

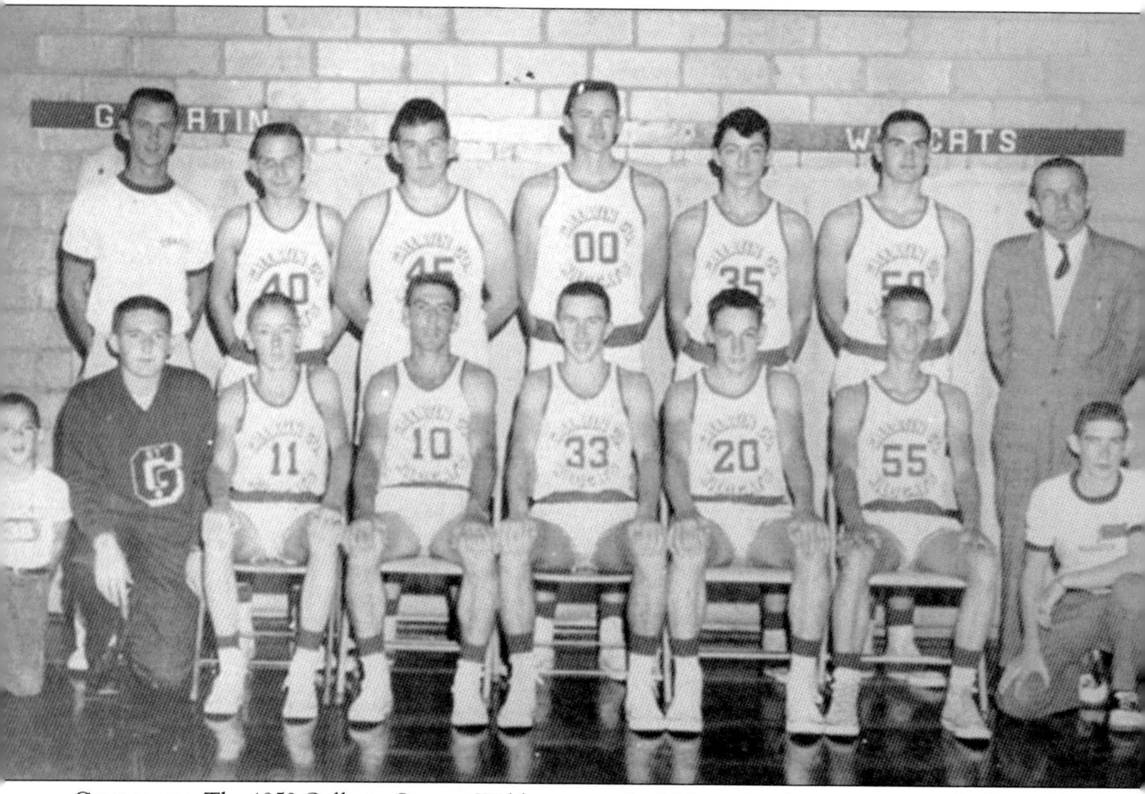

Champions. The 1959 Gallatin County Wildcats won the 10th regional tournament and advanced to the state tournament for the first (and last) time in school history. There they had the unfortunate draw to play the eventual state champions in the first round. Pictured here are, from left to right, (first row) Charlie Sutherland Jr. (mascot), Bill Rea (statistician), Doug Dunavent, Vincent Davis, Rodes Suter, Jim Roberts, Bill McKee, and Dennis O'Connor (manager); (second row) Coach Charles Sutherland, Jerry Hopperton, Mike Roberts, Joe Lowe, Monty Roberts, Barry Baker, and John M. Potter (principal). (Courtesy of Gallatin County Public Schools.)

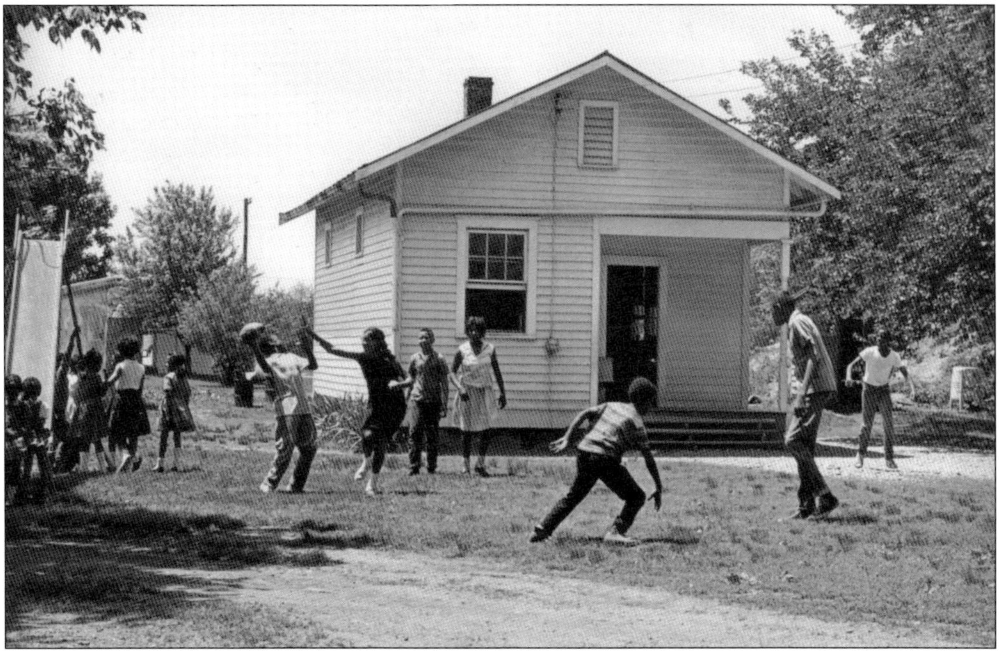

The Rosenwald School. Above is a 1960s photograph of the Rosenwald school in Warsaw, located on the west side of Third Street. This was the second school for African Americans in Warsaw. The first was built under the hill and then relocated to the one-room schoolhouse pictured here. The image below was taken during class. From left to right are (first row) Mike Nevels, Connely Green, Mitchell Sanders, and teacher Naomi Johnson; (second row) unidentified and Emmy Green; (third row) Karen Yates and Delores Nevels. (Courtesy of Robert and Alexandra Weldon.)

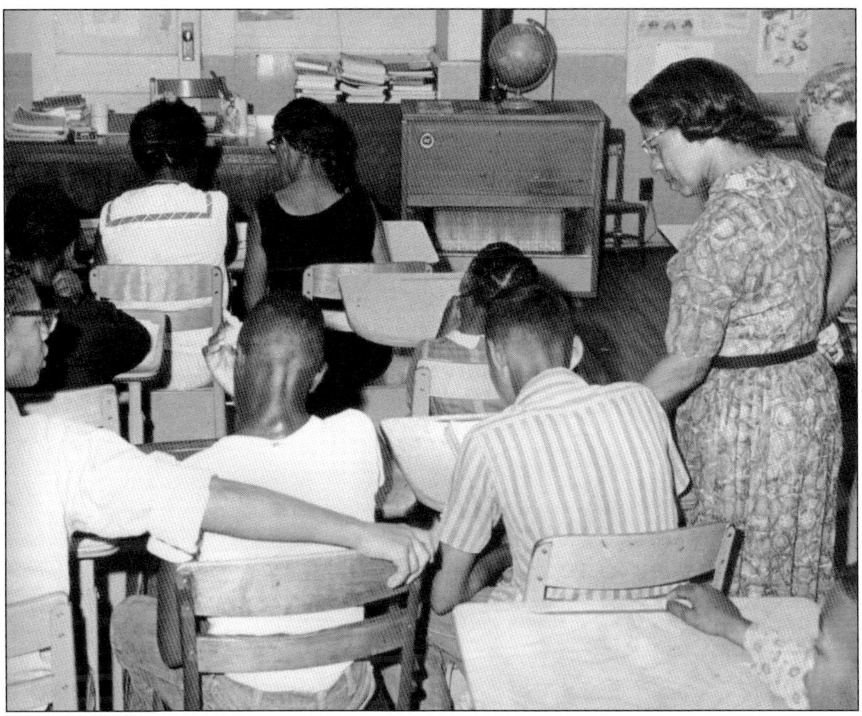

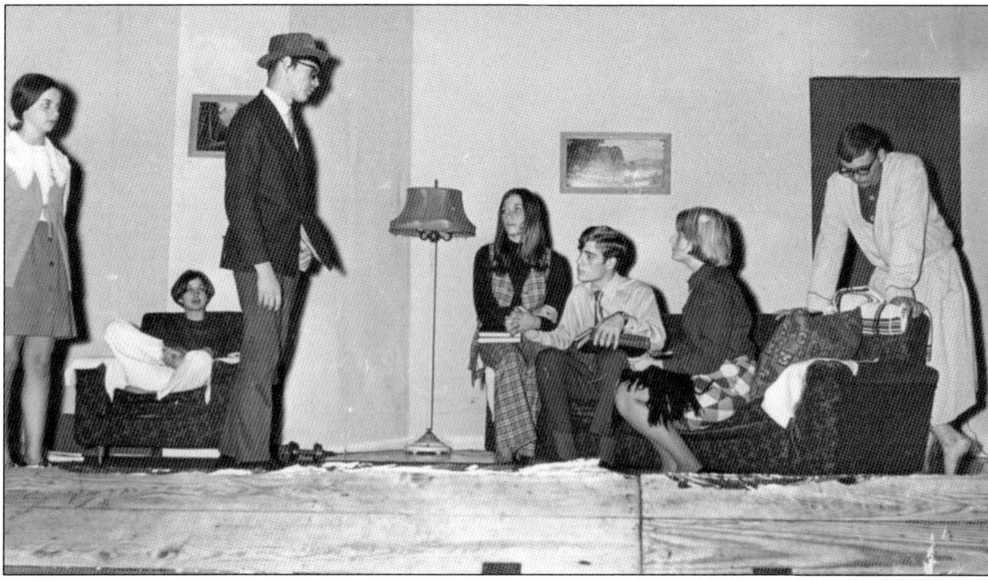

Rest Assured. The 1970–1971 Gallatin County High School senior drama club presents the comedy *Rest Assured* as their senior play. Actors are, from left to right, Debbie Perkins, Gary Hughes, Barby Haymond, Gregory Dickerson, Sharon Morris, and Monty Shinkle. (Courtesy of Gregory Dickerson)

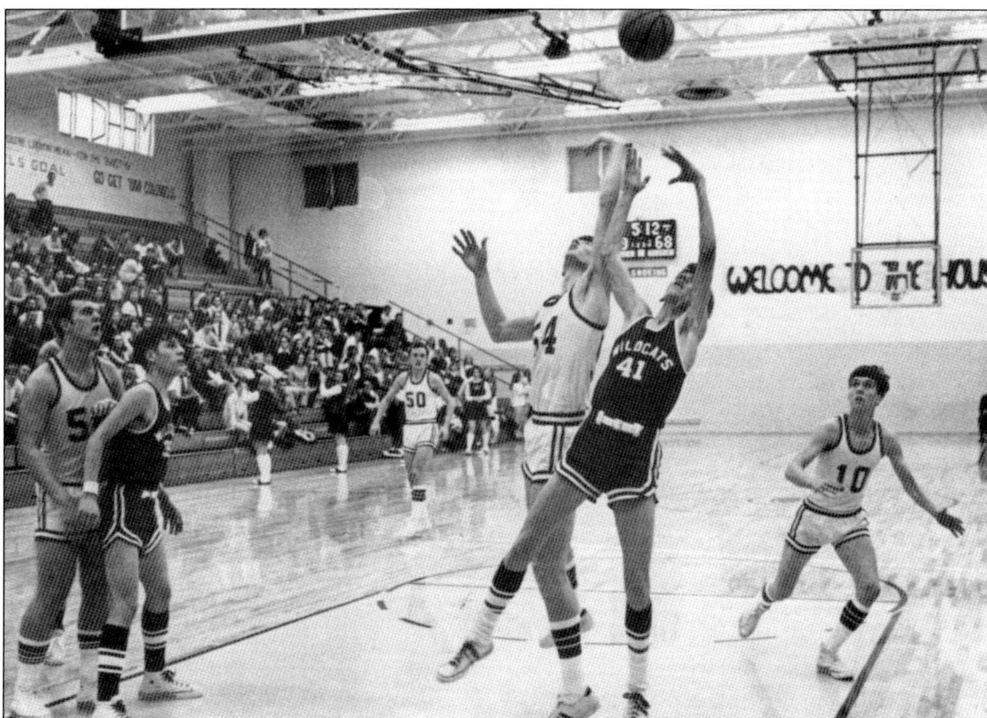

Welcome to the House. The 1970–1971 GCHS men's basketball team takes on Oldham Co. at home. Going for the ball (41) is Wildcat senior Harold Shupie Brown, and boxing out on left is senior Gary Marsh. (Courtesy of Gregory Dickerson.)

Six

RELIGIOUS FOUNDATIONS

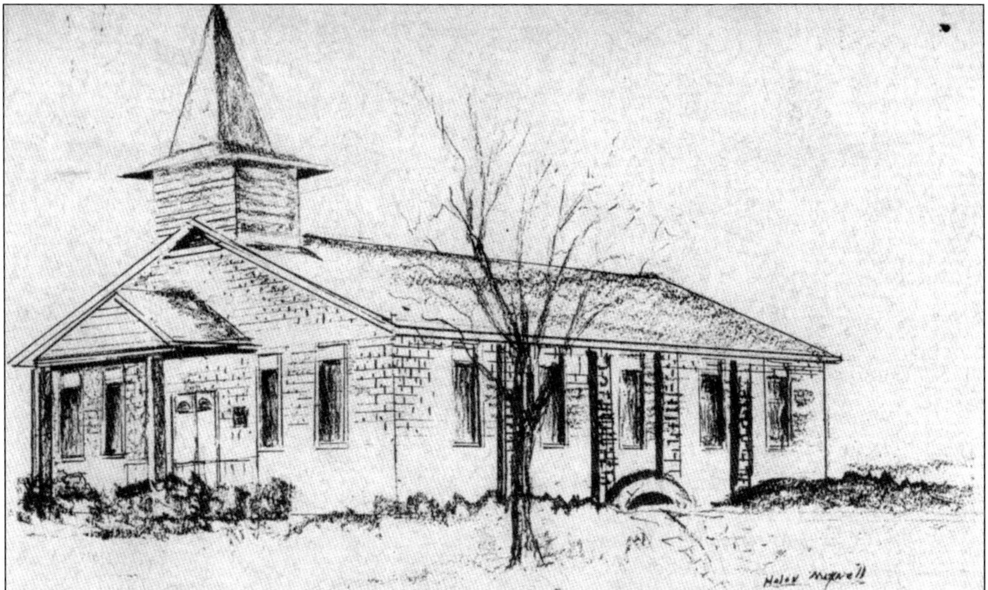

TEN MILE BAPTIST. The history of churches in Gallatin County begins with Ten Mile Baptist Church, which dates back to 1804. Elder David Lillard (1782–1861) organized the Ten Mile Baptist Association in 1831. It is the fifth-oldest Baptist church in Kentucky. (Courtesy of Gallatin County Free Public Library.)

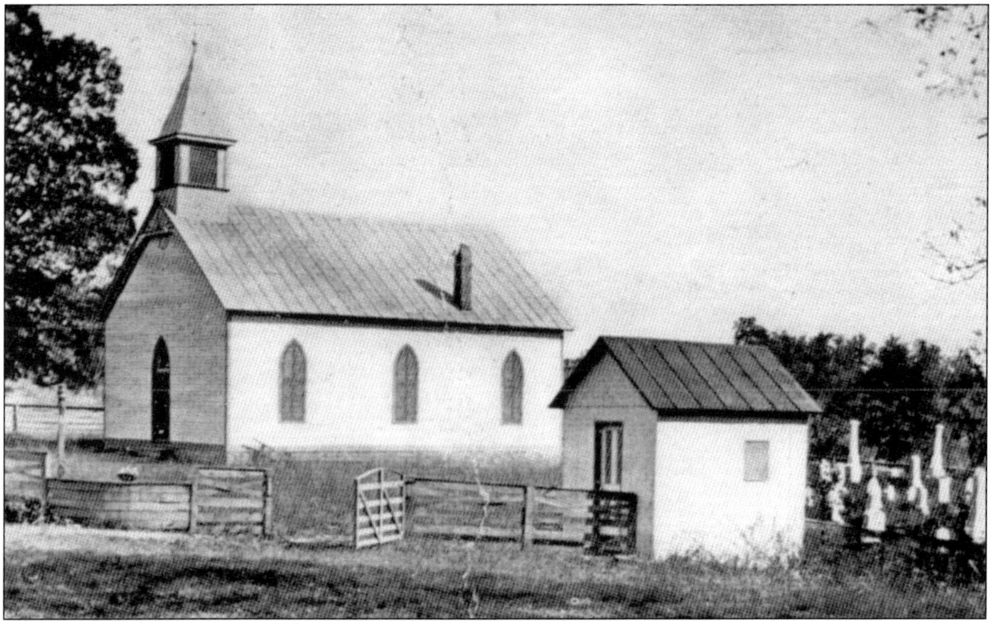

Concord Baptist Church. The need for churches to serve the largely rural areas of the county was realized in the early days. This church officially formed in 1856 and was located in the Concord neighborhood along Route 16 near Verona at the Boone County border. This building was dedicated in 1906 and remains standing today. (Courtesy of Darrell Maines.)

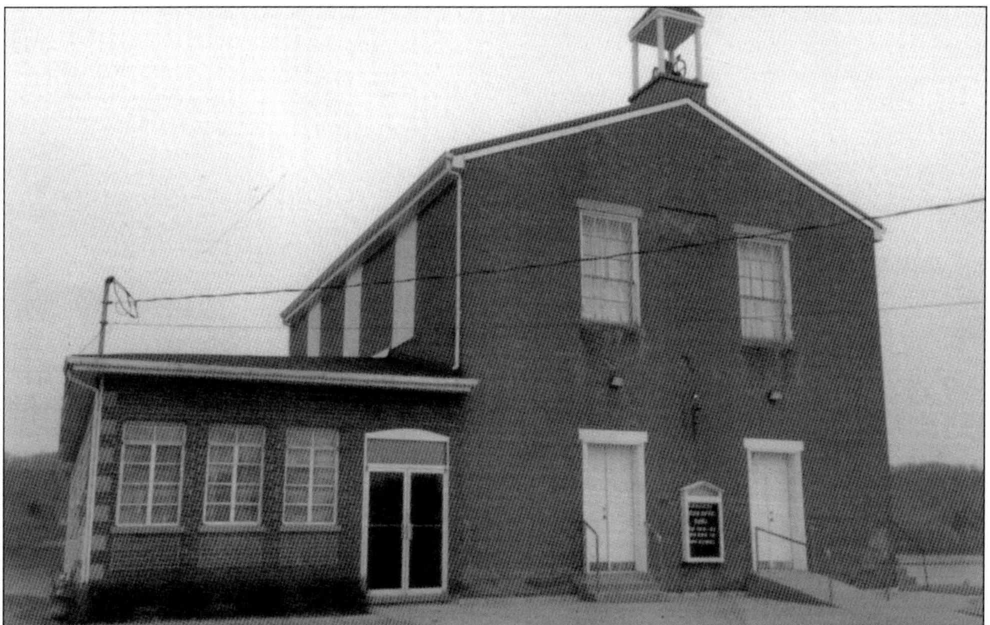

Second Consolidated Baptist Church. This African American Baptist church is located on High Street in Warsaw near the river. It is the oldest church building in Warsaw. The church was originally built in 1851 as the home of the Warsaw Presbyterian Church but has been a black congregation since the late 1800s. "Consolidated" was added to the name as there were two black Baptist churches in Warsaw that merged in 1944. (Photograph by Rebecca Riesenberg.)

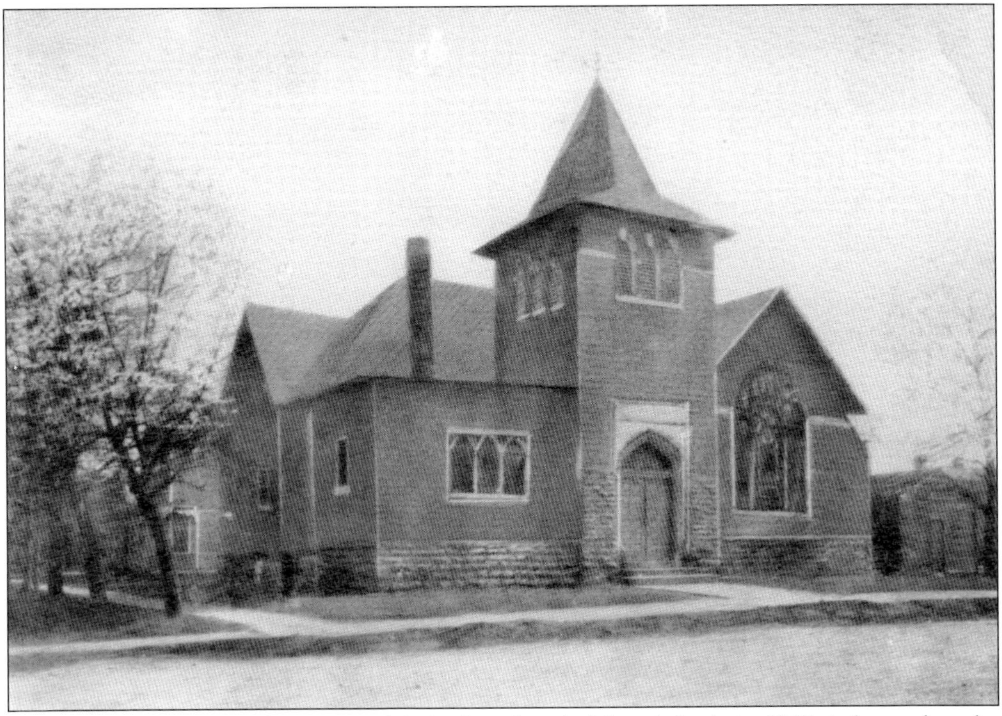

Methodist Church. The current Methodist church (above), built in 1901, is located at the corner of First Street and US 42 in Warsaw. The previous building was constructed in 1830 on the same site. The church was officially formed in 1844, although meetings were held as early as 1824. The Methodist men's group (below) formed during the 1960s. Here they stand outside the church. The man standing in the background at left is Alva Dickerson, on the far right is John Heier, and 11th from the left is Jess Wheeler. (Above, courtesy of Darrell Maines; below, courtesy of Dale Samuel.)

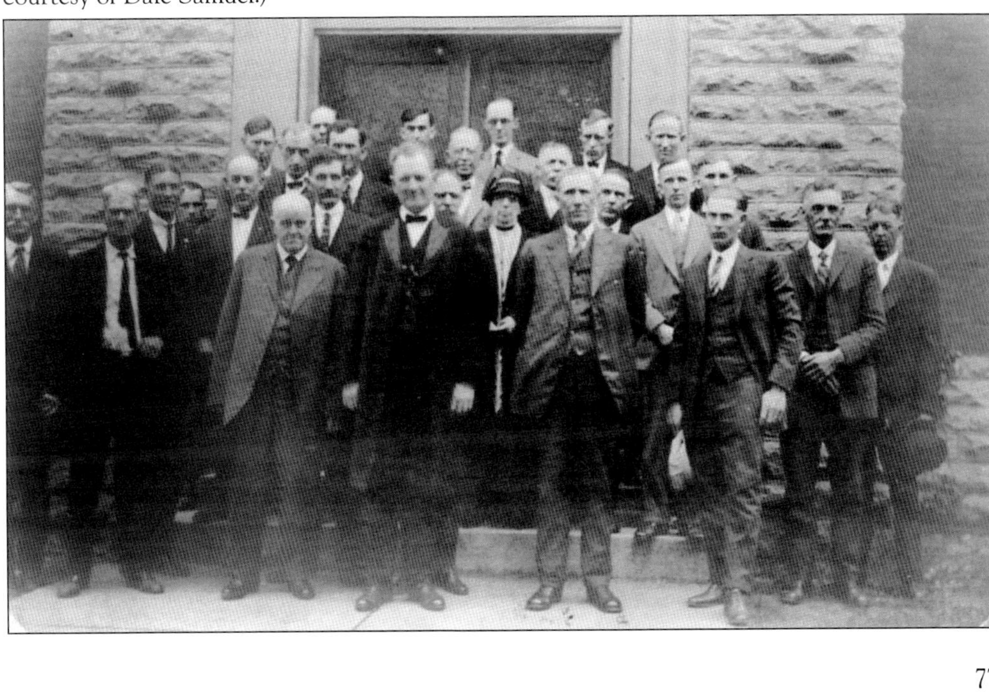

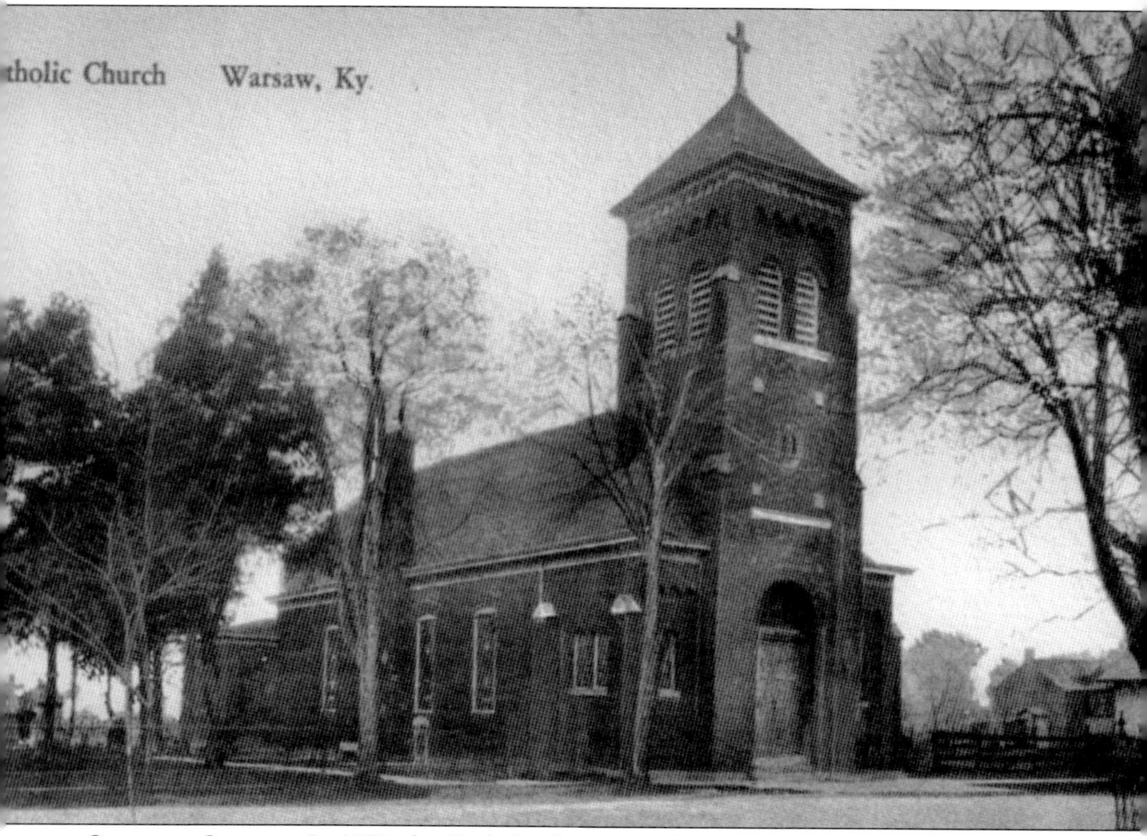

Catholic Church. In 1857, the Catholic diocese in Covington, Kentucky, sent a priest to Carrollton to perform masses. Warsaw Catholics attended services there until 1858, when they were attached to the diocese as a station and received their own mass once a month. In 1868, the parishioners purchased some land on Sparta Pike on the corner of modern-day Kirby Street. This church and cemetery were completed the same year. In 1920, the church was remodeled, and the bell tower was added in 1921. The church and cemetery are still in use today. (Courtesy of Darrell Maines.)

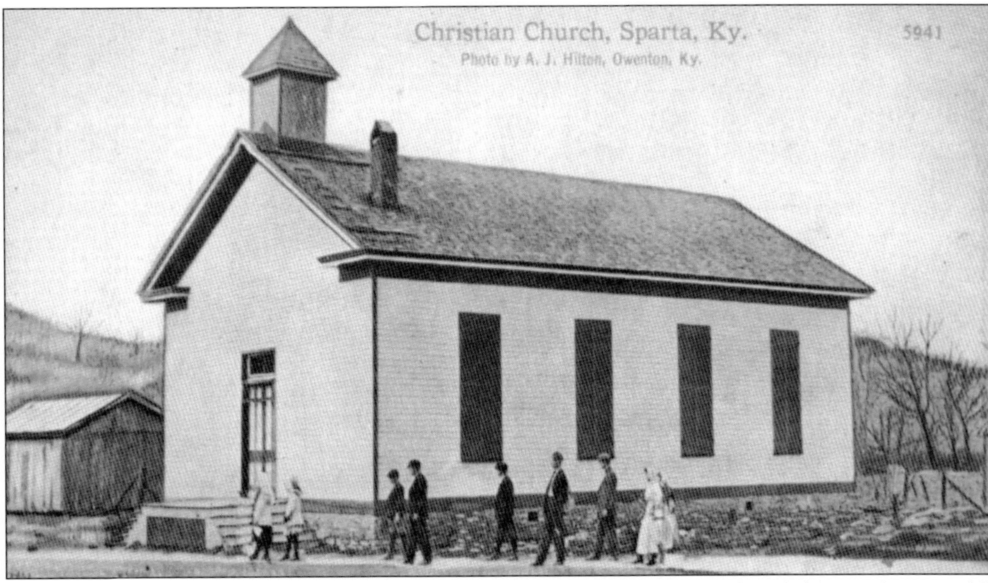

SPARTA CHRISTIAN CHURCH. The congregation of Sparta Christian Church began their weekly meetings at the schoolhouse in 1868. The church formally organized in 1878 but did not build its own meeting house until 1890. Pictured here around 1900 is the one-room frame church that was located on the Owen County side (Old Sparta) of the Eagle Creek Bridge. A brick structure was built in 1921 on the Gallatin County side of Sparta. (Courtesy of Darrell Maines.)

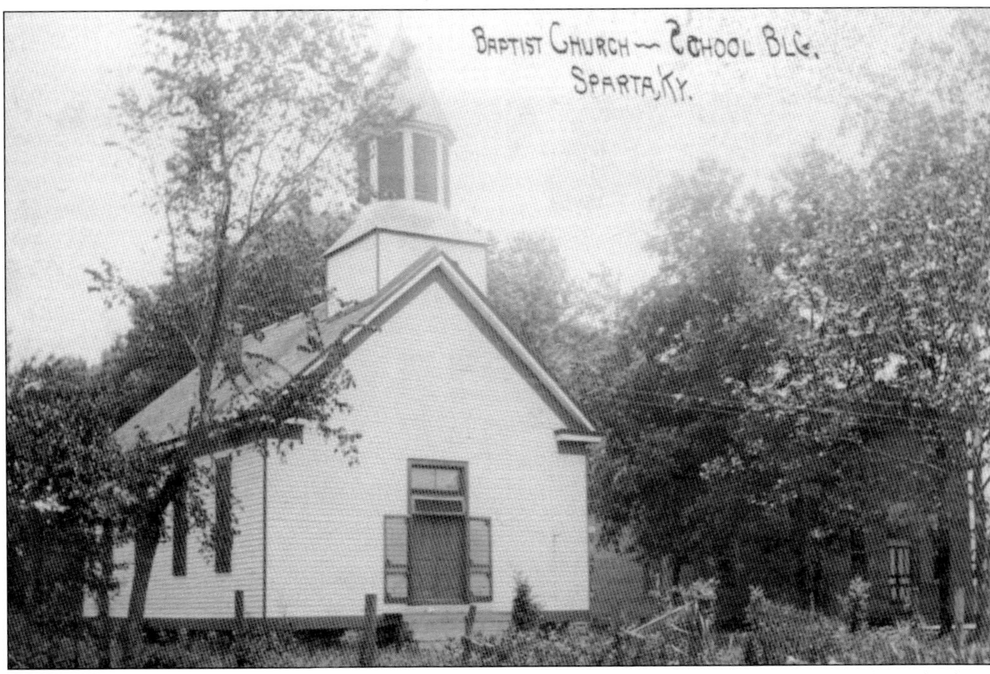

SPARTA BAPTIST CHURCH. Pictured here around 1890 is the old Sparta Baptist Church and school (on right). Sparta Baptist Church organized in 1881, meeting at the schoolhouse in Old Sparta. The congregation later built a one-room frame church next to the school. This building was used until a new church building was dedicated in 1976. This structure is located near US 35 at Eagle Creek. (Courtesy of Darrell Maines.)

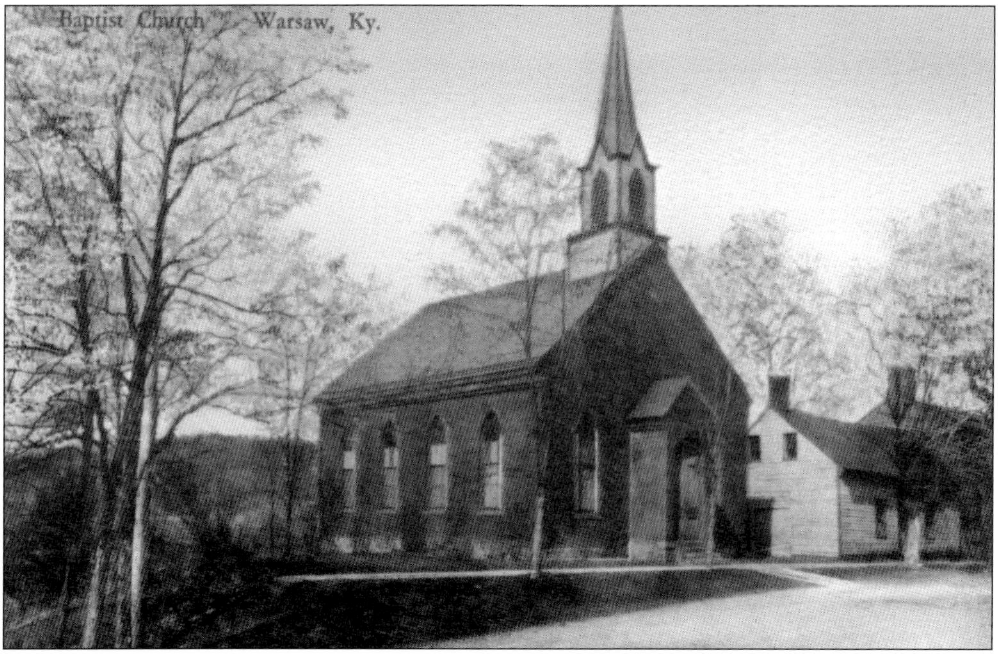

WARSAW BAPTIST CHURCH. The Warsaw Baptist congregation organized in 1843 and built a brick church on the northwest corner of Third and High Streets (Baptist Hill). In 1882, that building was replaced with the church pictured here around 1910. The church burned in 1973 and was rebuilt at the same site. (Courtesy of Darrell Maines.)

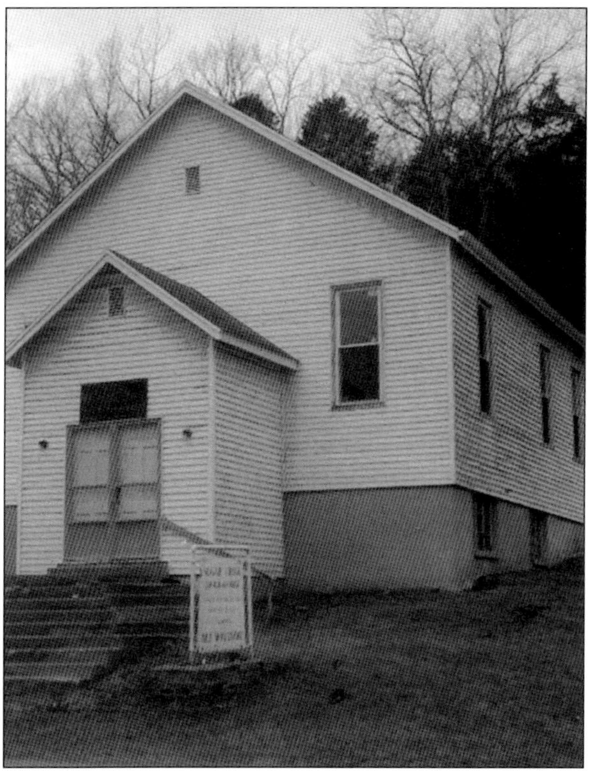

SUGAR CREEK CHURCH OF CHRIST. The first Sugar Creek Church was built in 1853, but the structure was replaced in 1870 as it was too close to the creek. The new church was built on the adjacent lot but on a slope to keep it from flooding. Though it was located off Tapering Point Road, (the main road from Sugar Creek to Glencoe until the highway system was created) it was not until 1949 that it was moved to a more accessible area on Highway 127. The old church was torn down, and all that remains of the original site is the old cemetery. (Photograph by Rebecca Riesenberg.)

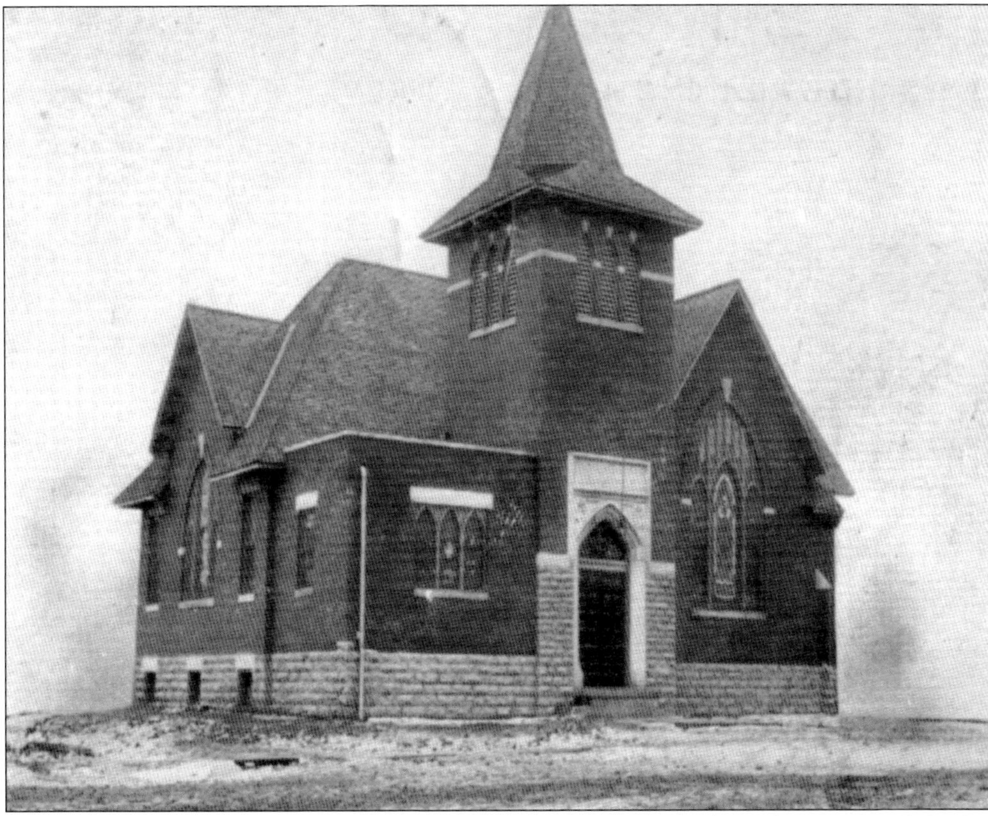

WARSAW CHRISTIAN CHURCH. The Christian church congregation formed in 1836, and the first building was erected on the southwest corner of First and Main Streets in 1868 (site of the present-day Methodist church). The second building, pictured above around 1900, was constructed on Fourth and High Streets, and is still in use today. The first pastor of the church was Benjamin Tiller. Reverend Tiller served the church from its inception in 1836 until his death in 1878. He was an influential figure in early Warsaw church history. He is buried in the old Warsaw Cemetery (below) with his wife, Zerelda. (Above, courtesy of Darrell Maines; below, photograph by Rebecca Riesenberg.)

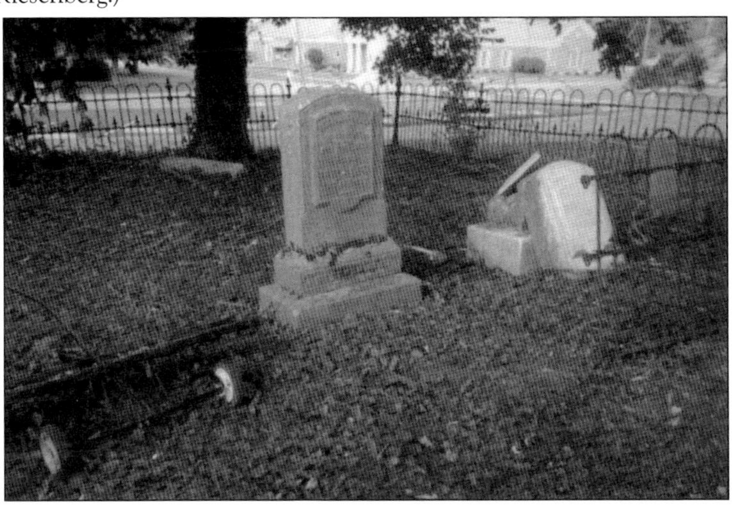

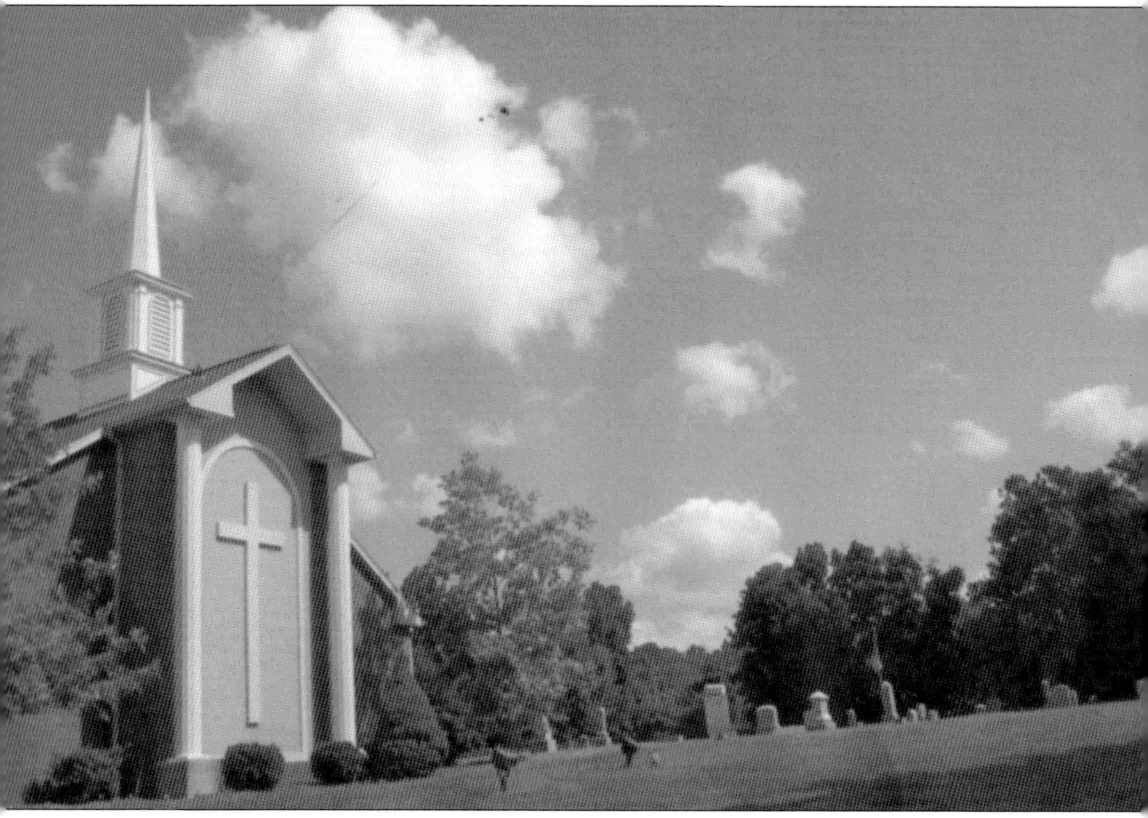

Paint Lick Baptist Church. The Paint Lick Church is believed to have been founded in the early 1860s. The church was a member of the Ten Mile Association and used a log building on the North Fork of Paint Lick Creek on the northeastern end of the county as its first meeting house. The church moved to its present location in 1886 and added a cemetery. In 1957, the church added another tract of land to expand the cemetery. By the 1990s, the building was in need of costly repairs, so it was torn down and replaced with the current brick building in 2001. The Paint Lick area received its name from the clay found there that the Indians used for war paint. (Photograph by Rebecca Riesenberg.)

Seven

People

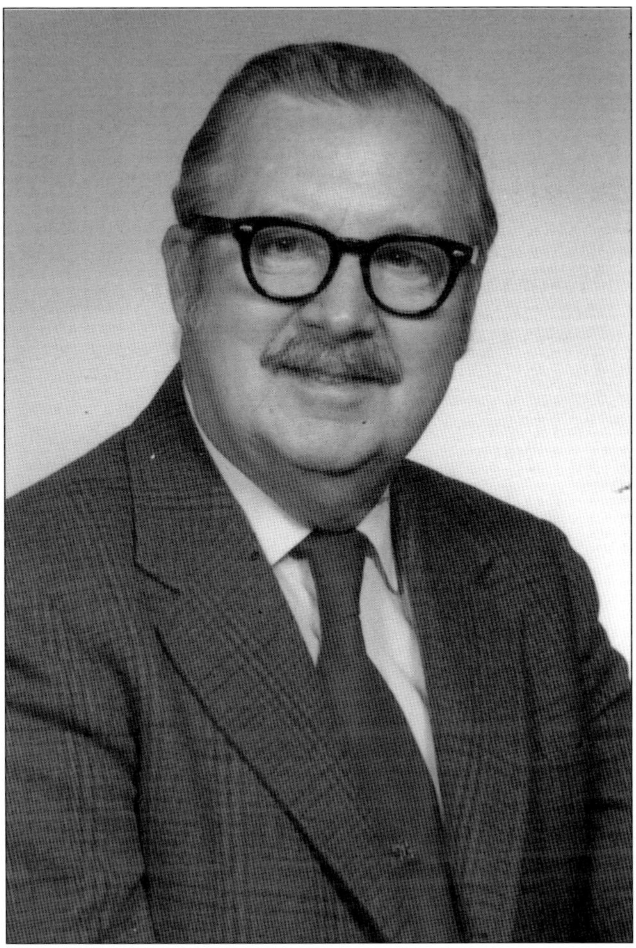

Local Historian. Dr. Carl Bogardus is well-known to Warsaw residents. "Dr. Carl," as he was called, was born in Warsaw in 1924, and his father, O.A. Bogardus, owned the Warsaw Furniture Company. Bogardus studied medicine at the University of Cincinnati and practiced in Indiana for over 40 years. After retirement, he came home to his beloved Gallatin County. As a prolific writer and dedicated local historian, he produced much of the written history of Warsaw and the county. He also had a love of the old steamboats and collected memorabilia and histories of the river. Dr. Bogardus died in 1995 and is buried in the Warsaw Cemetery. (Courtesy of the Gallatin County Free Public Library.)

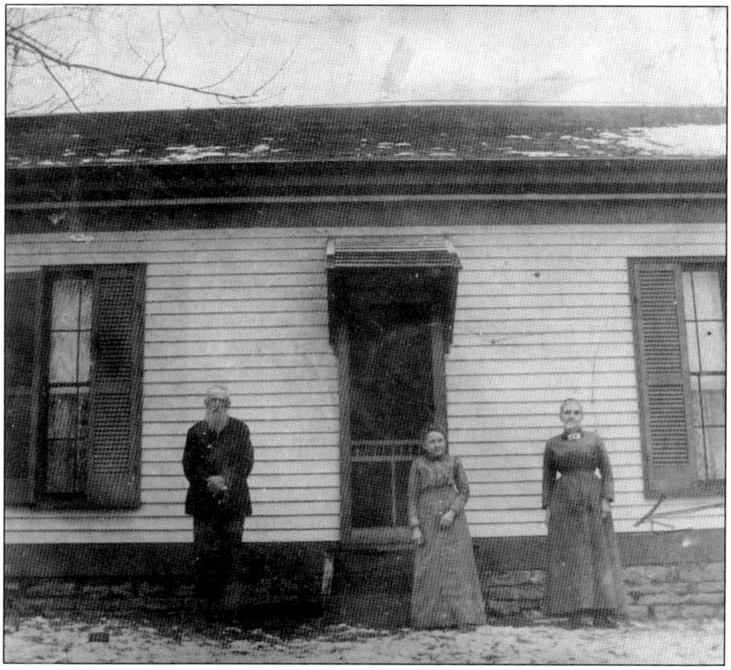

Glencoe Residents. Will Taylor, "Aunt" Benne, and Addie Greer stand in front of the Taylor home in Glencoe. All were lifelong residents of the Eagle Creek valley. (Courtesy of Dana Benne.)

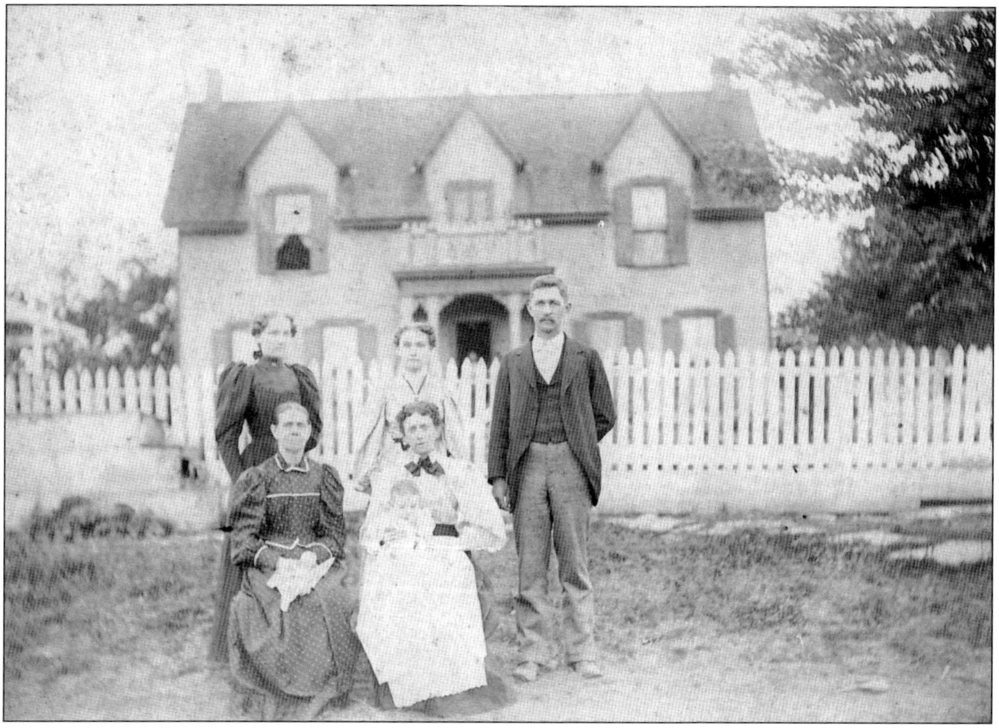

Generations. Three generations of the Ellis family pose for this 1890s photograph in front of the Carver home in Sparta. Pictured are, from left to right, (first row) Bettie Ellis and her daughter Kate Ellis Carver (holding daughter Ruth); (second row) Berta Ellis, Sally Ellis, and Harry Carver. Sadly, little Ruth Carver died shortly after this photograph was taken. (Courtesy of Dale Samuel.)

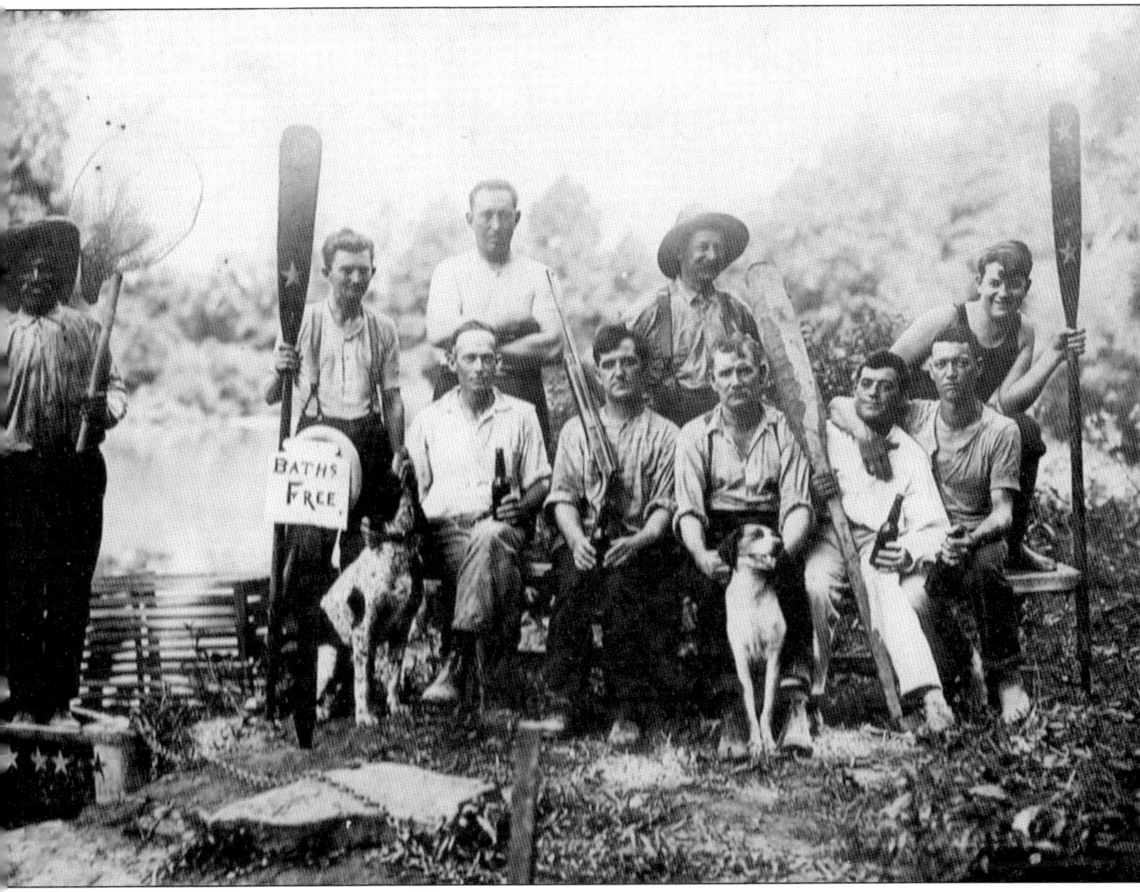

GOOD TIMES. A group of men gather for some fun at Eagle Creek near Sparta around 1900. On the left (holding the net) is Bill Gross, who lived near the creek in Old Sparta on the Owen County side. He had been a slave until the age of 12. Seated on the front left is Elbert Brock, and in the back row on the left is Elzie Wilson. The other men are unidentified but are believed to have traveled from northern Kentucky to the camp. (Courtesy of Dale Samuel.)

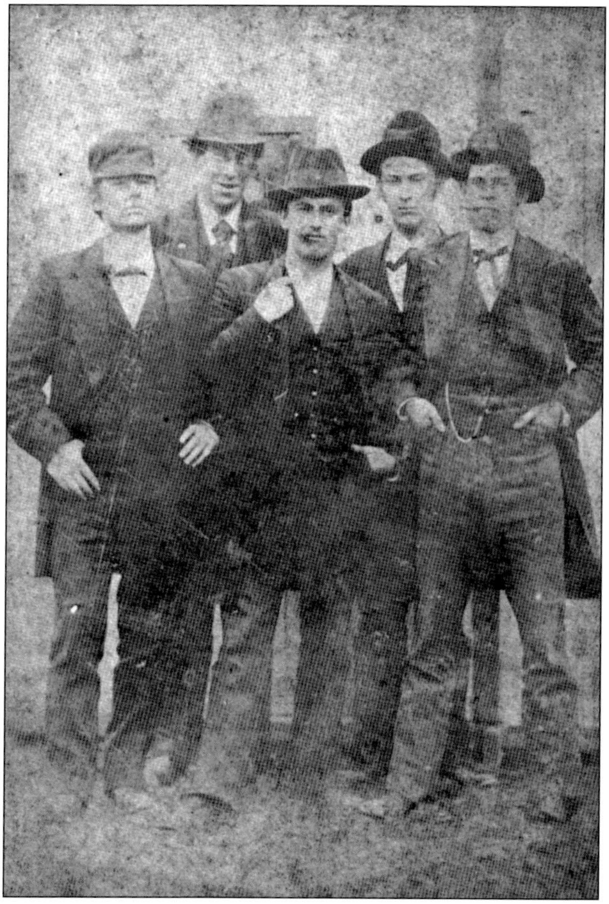

Handsome Men. Five dapper gentlemen from Warsaw take a moment to pose for the camera in this faded 1874 photograph. They are identified as Maurie Turpin, Dr. Robinson, Walter Pulliam, Turp Chambers, and Mr. Kirby, in no particular order. (Courtesy of Robert and Alexandra Weldon.)

The Undertaker. Joseph K. Nesbit served as the undertaker in Warsaw; he is pictured here taking a break from his business around 1910. The building stood on Main Street (US 42) west of the courthouse. Nesbit was a lifelong bachelor and Warsaw resident. (Courtesy of Darrell Maines.)

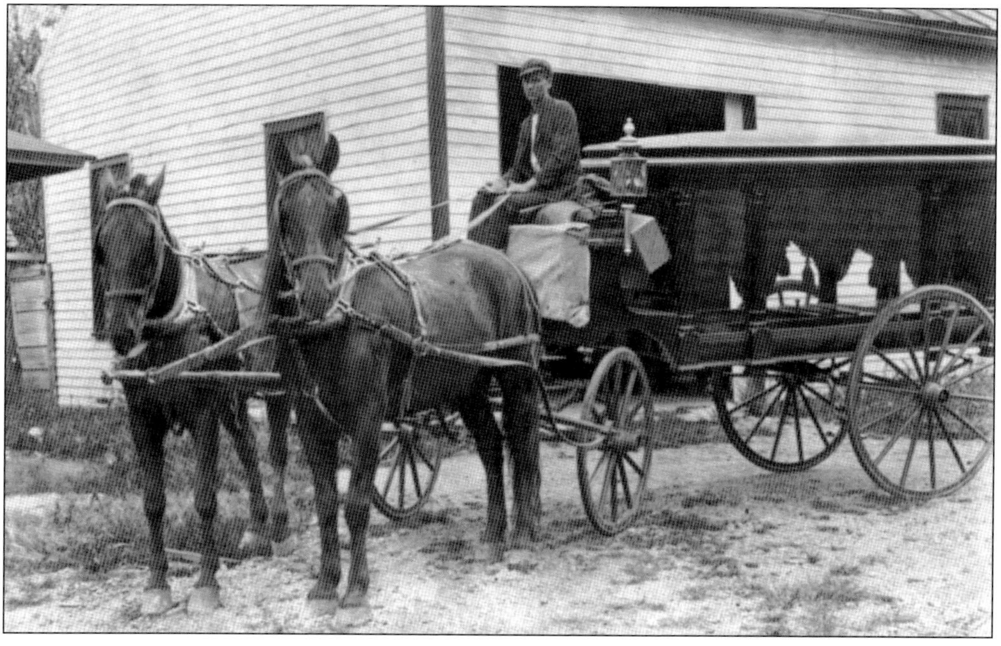

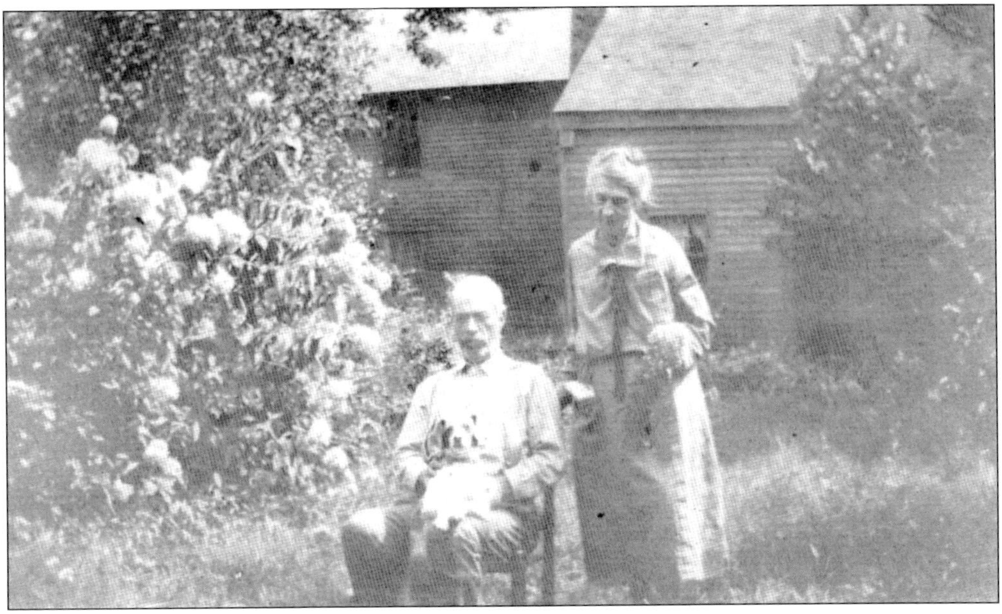

Sparta Couple. Will and Alma Riblin pose by some flower bushes around 1930. Their farm was located on the hill above Sparta, and Will was a cousin of Rea Gano, a local historian and poet. (Courtesy of Dale Samuel.)

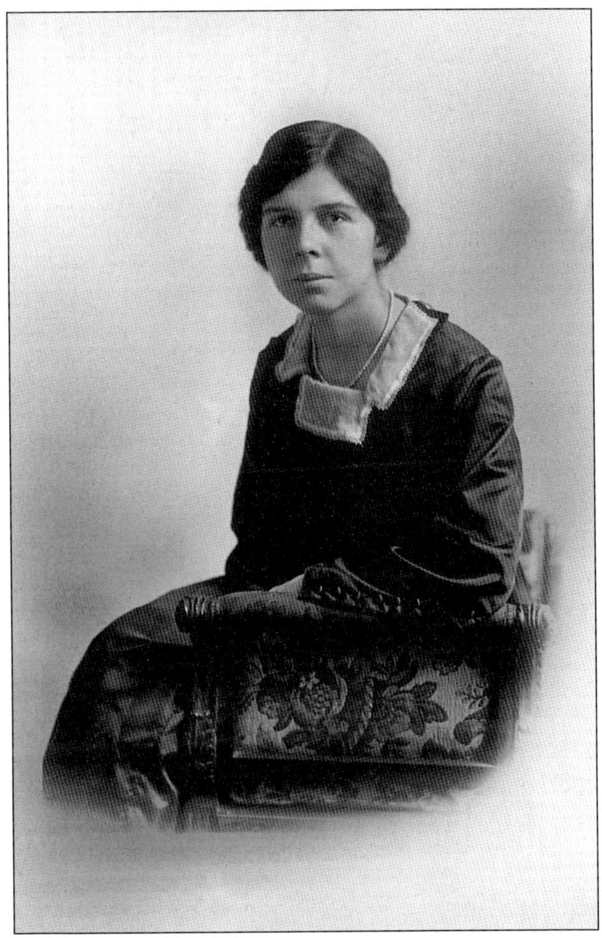

Miss Rea. In 1889, Sydney Rebecca Gano, "Miss Rea" (pronounced "Ree"), was born in Sparta. The Gano family has lived in Sparta for several generations, and Rea never married and remained in the family home until her death in 1952. She was well known in the area for her poetry and detailed written history of Sparta. This photograph was likely taken around 1930. (Courtesy of Dale Samuel.)

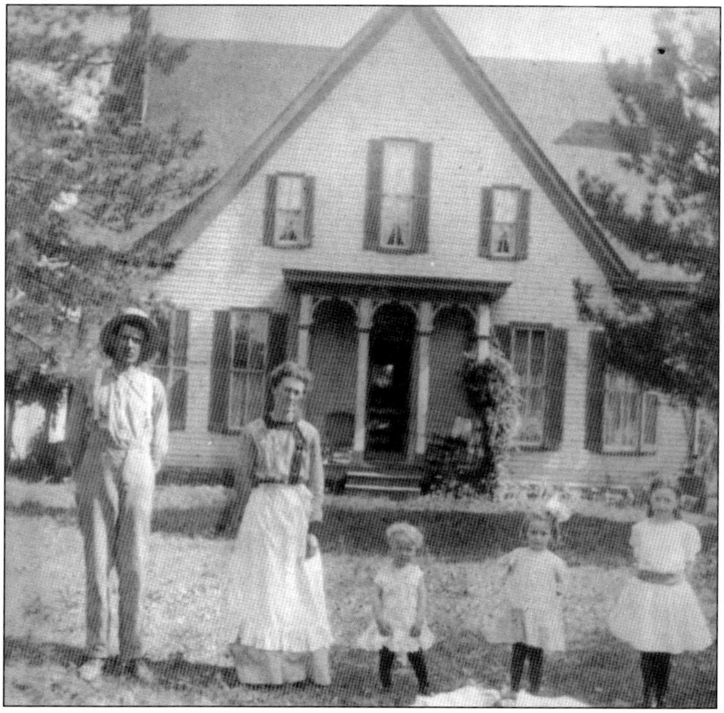

CROUCH/HOWARD FARM. The young Crouch family stands in front of their lovely home around 1913. From left to right are William Prior Crouch, Carrie Chapman Crouch, Joy Chapman Crouch, Evelyn Crouch, and Clifford Prior Crouch. Their farm was located on Johnson Road outside Warsaw (currently Heritage Hills). The family later moved to Glencoe to operate the Crouch Lumber Yard. (Courtesy of Dana Benne.)

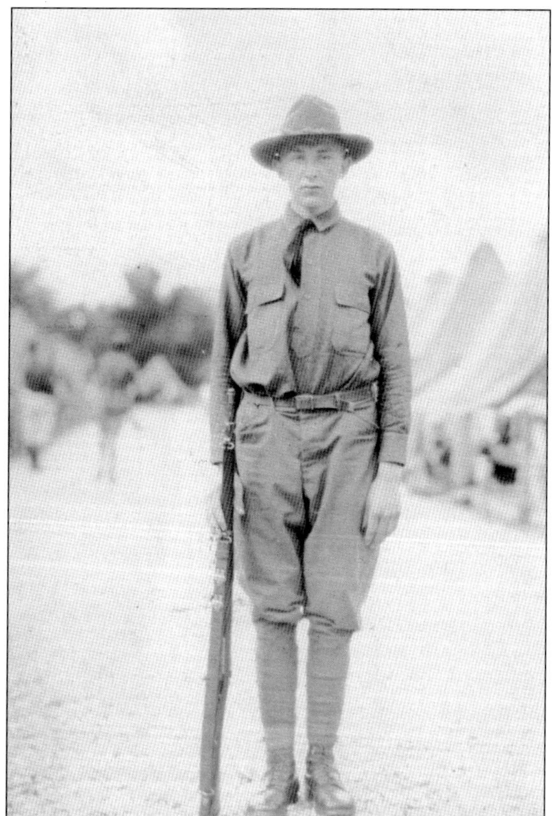

ROTC. Young Clifford Prior Crouch stands at attention for this photograph, taken about 1920. Crouch, an ROTC member, was stationed at the barracks in Fort Thomas, Kentucky. He later returned to Gallatin County and opened Crouch's Gas Service in Glencoe. (Courtesy of Dana Benne.)

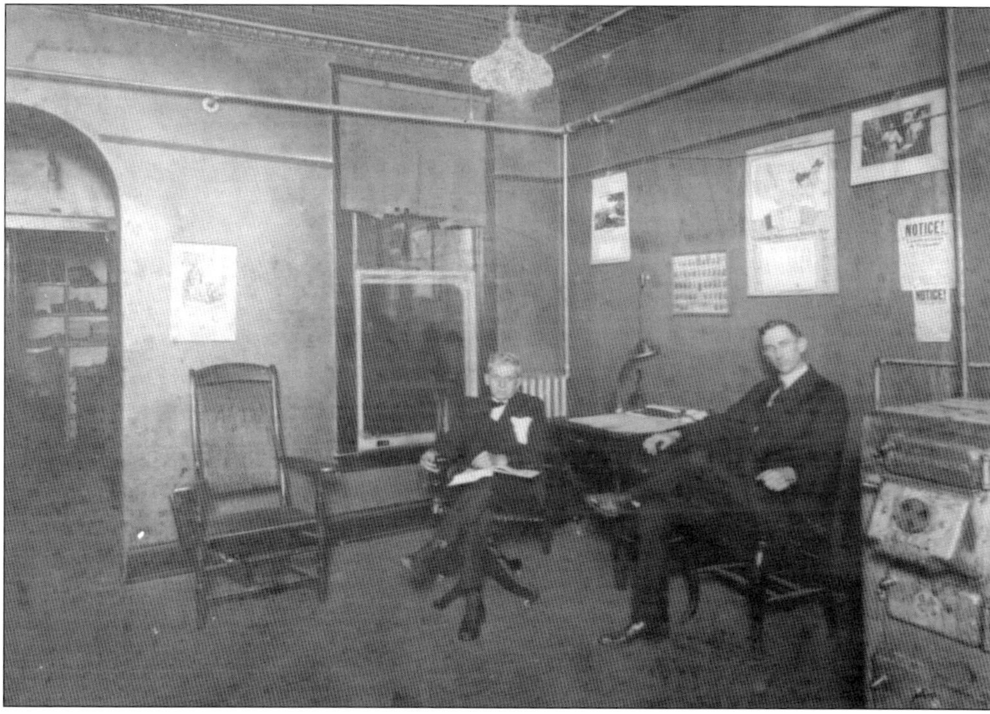

Law Men. Robert B. Brown (left) and Frank B. Connely relax in their law office around 1930. The office was located on Main Cross on the first floor of the building west of the Brown Hotel. Connely was Brown's son-in-law and owned the old Payne home known as Seven Pines, at the end of Fifth Street in Warsaw. (Courtesy of Robert and Alexandra Weldon.)

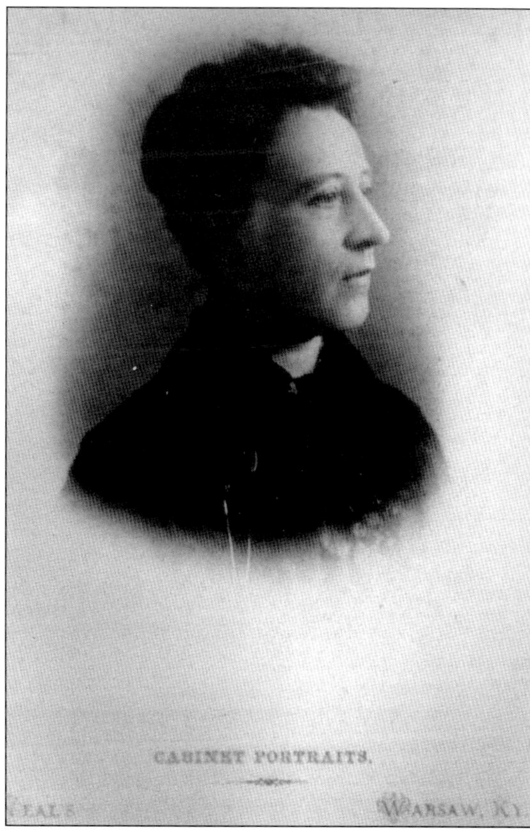

First Female Dentist. Dr. Lucy DuPuy Montz is widely recognized as the first female dentist in the commonwealth of Kentucky. Born in Warsaw in 1842, she first became a schoolteacher before deciding to enroll in the Cincinnati College of Dental Surgery. She served as a faculty member after graduation but returned to Warsaw at age 51 to open a dental practice in her home on West High Street in Warsaw. She practiced there until just before her death in 1922. The home still stands and is listed in the National Register of Historic Places. (Courtesy of Darrell Maines.)

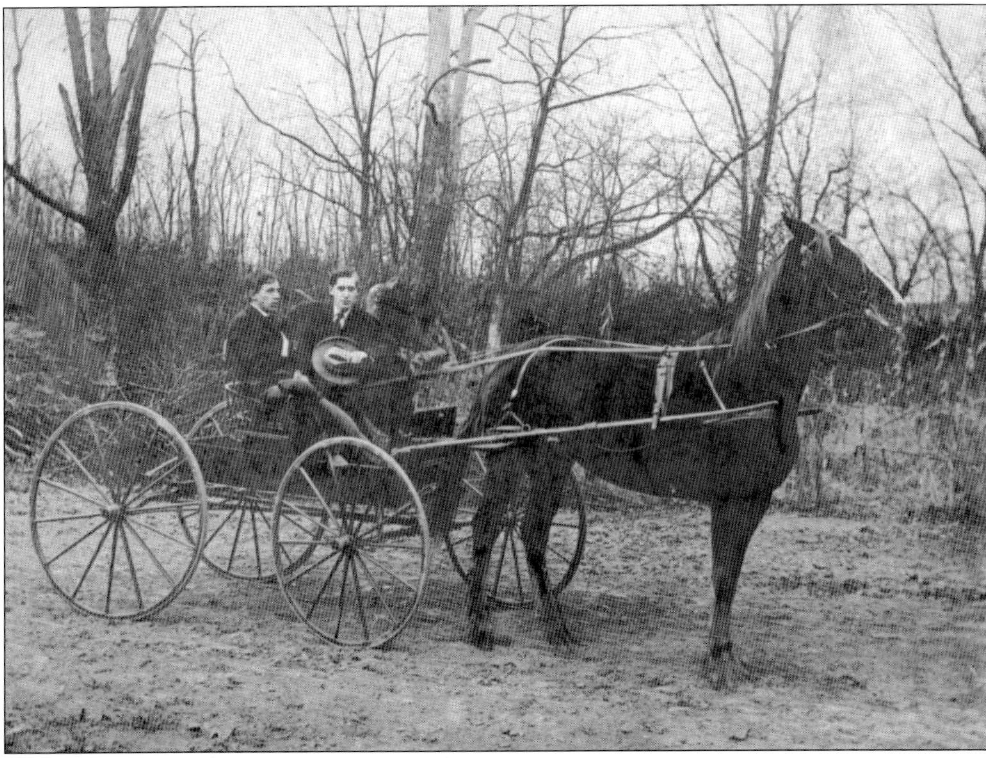

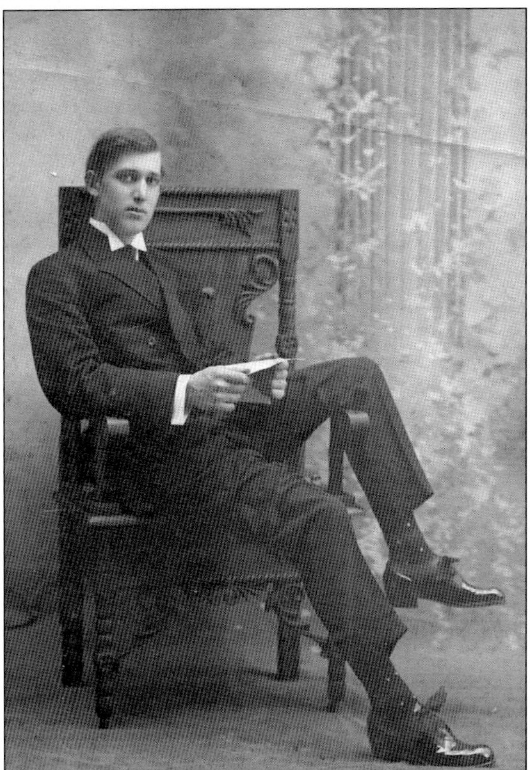

Out for a Ride. Harold Brown (left) and Whitney Payne enjoy a carriage ride near Warsaw around 1910. Harold Brown died in 1918 during the Spanish flu epidemic. The Payne family owned Seven Pines, which was later sold to Brown's family. (Courtesy of Robert and Alexandra Weldon.)

Dashing Young Man. Whitney Payne cuts a fine figure in this photograph taken around 1910. Payne was the son of Robert and Ella Payne, who owned large properties at both the eastern and western ends of Warsaw. Whitney died in 1932 at the age of 41. (Courtesy of Robert and Alexandra Weldon.)

Fancy Party. Harold Brown Connely twirls a fancy umbrella while attending a Chautauqua meeting at the Payne residency about 1922. She was the daughter of Nannie and Frank Connely and was named Harold after her uncle, Harold Brown, who died young during the 1918 Spanish flu outbreak. The Chatauqua visited Warsaw every summer in the early 1900s, setting up in tents on the grounds of Seven Pines. (Courtesy of Robert and Alexandra Weldon.)

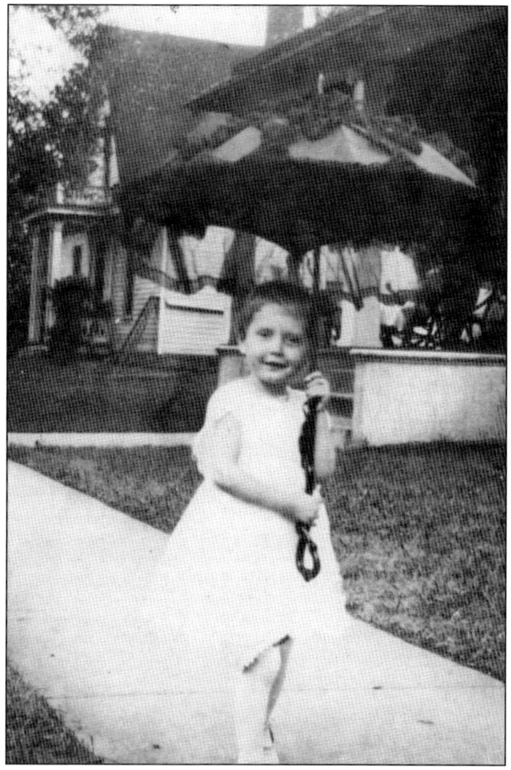

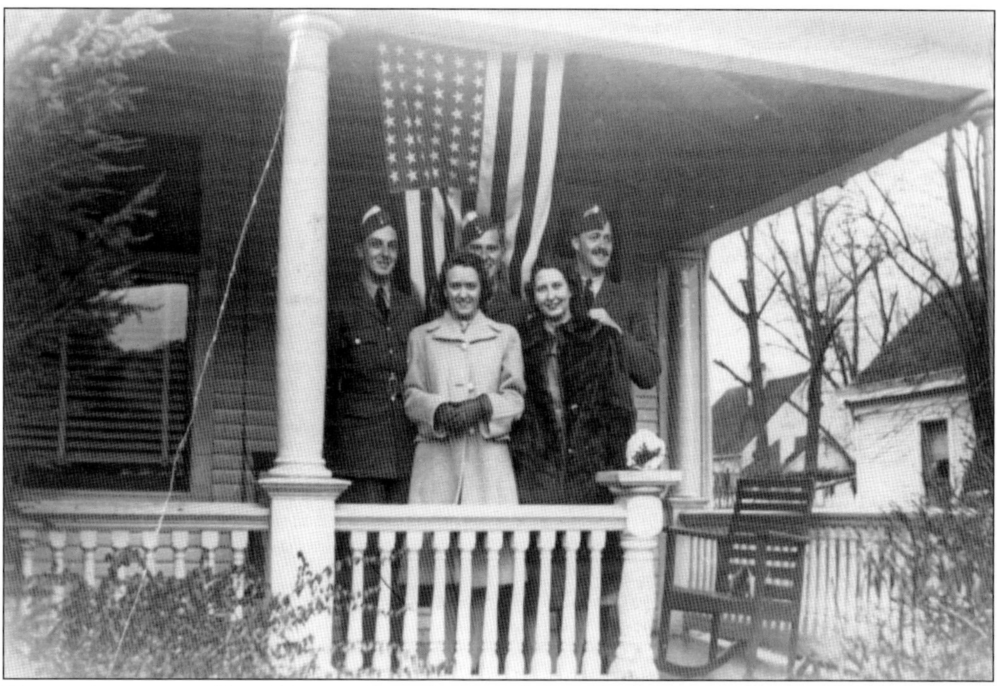

Young Americans. Harold Brown Connely (front left) poses with unidentified friends in Warsaw during World War II. Brown served in the Women's Army Corps during the war. (Courtesy of Robert and Alexandra Weldon.)

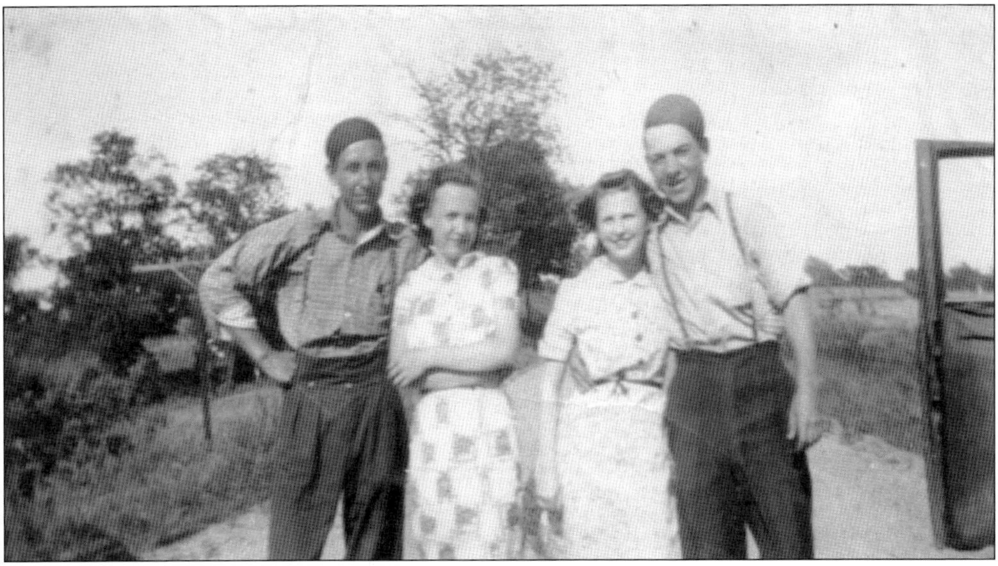

Cruising the Country Road. Two young couples take a break from an afternoon drive in the 1940s. They are standing on Route 16 near Napoleon. From left to right are JC Noel, Mary-Evelyn Spencer (later Noel), Agnes Lilliard, and Mono Lilliard. (Courtesy of JC and Mary-Evelyn Noel.)

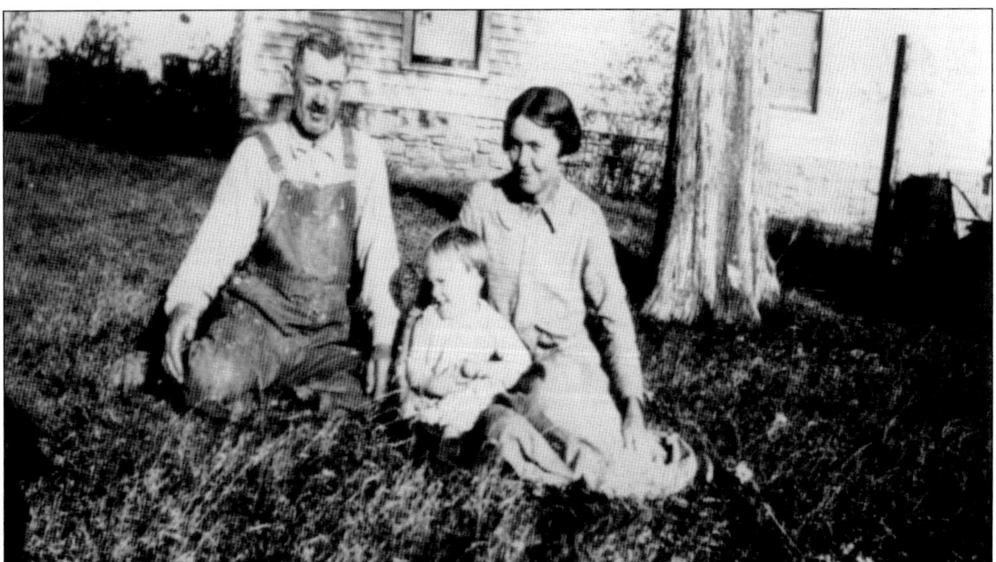

Young Family. Floyd and Nina Peak sit on the grass with their one-year-old daughter Mary-Evelyn in this 1926 photograph. Behind them is the Oakland Baptist Church, located on Johnson Road (Highway 455) outside Warsaw. (Courtesy of JC and Mary-Evelyn Noel.)

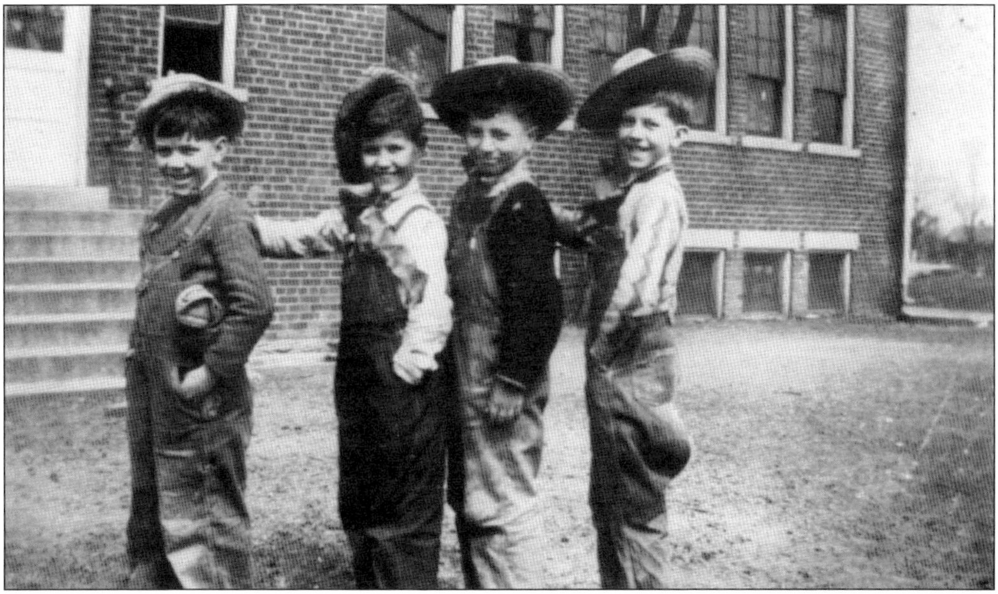

Cute Children. Four young friends strike a pose around 1929. From left to right are William Hill, James Furnish, Wayne Closser, and Robert Allphin. The boys were in the fourth grade at the Warsaw school. (Courtesy of Darrell Maines.)

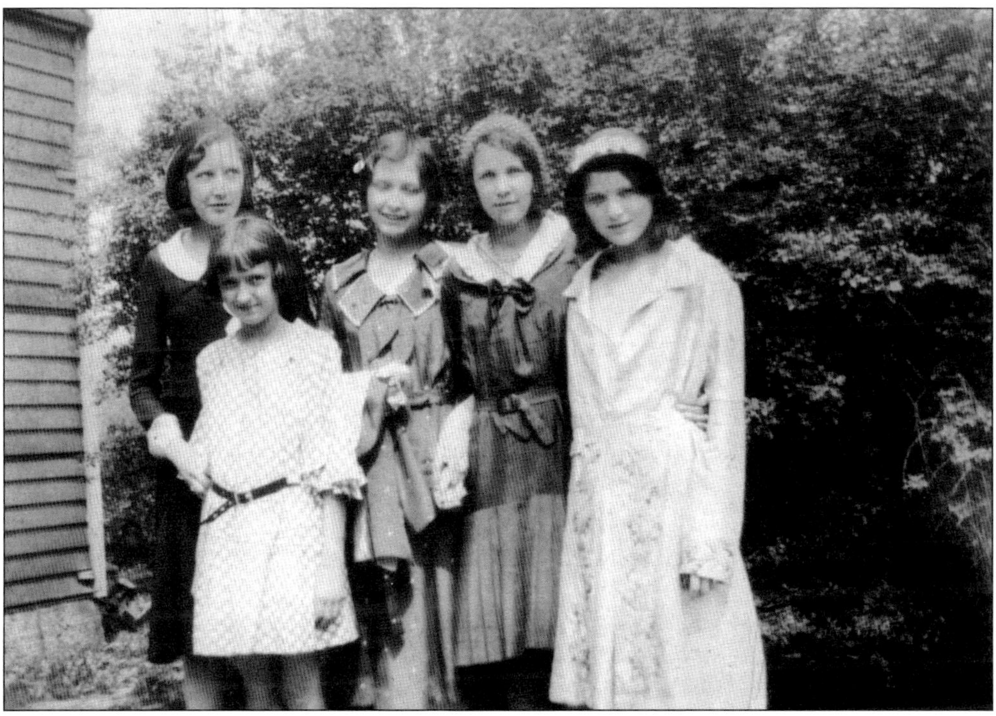

Pretty Girls. Five young girls flash pretty smiles while posing for the camera. The location is unknown but likely in Warsaw. From left to right are unidentified, Maybelle Connely, Harold Brown Connely, and two unidentified. (Courtesy of Robert and Alexandra Weldon.)

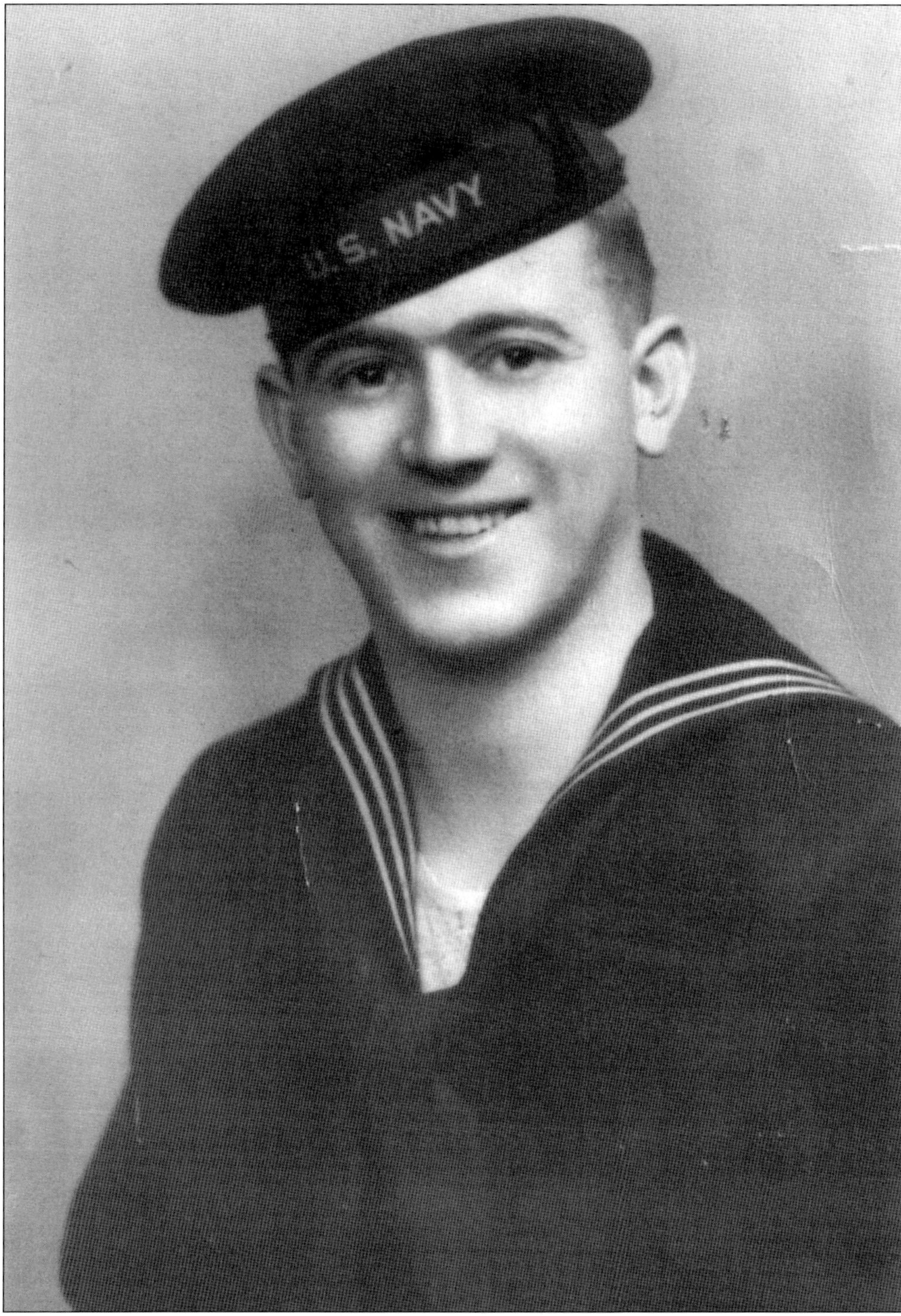

Not Just a Veteran. A lifelong resident of Warsaw, Russell Hall was a local riverboat and airplane pilot, self-taught barber, horse trader, restaurant owner, and ferryboat operator. He served as a Navy gunner in the Pacific theater during World War II. (Courtesy of Russell Hall.)

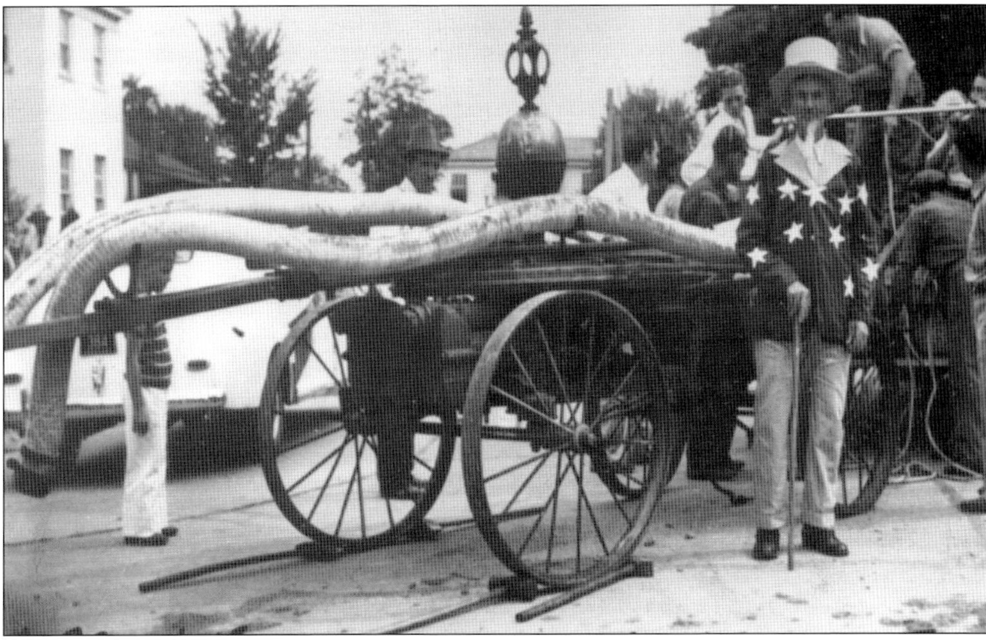

Old Fire Engine. Jess Miller displays his patriotic spirit dressed as Uncle Sam. He is standing beside the old 1890 fire engine from Warsaw that was donated for scrap during the 1942 World War II Scrap for Victory drive. (Courtesy of Darrell Maines.)

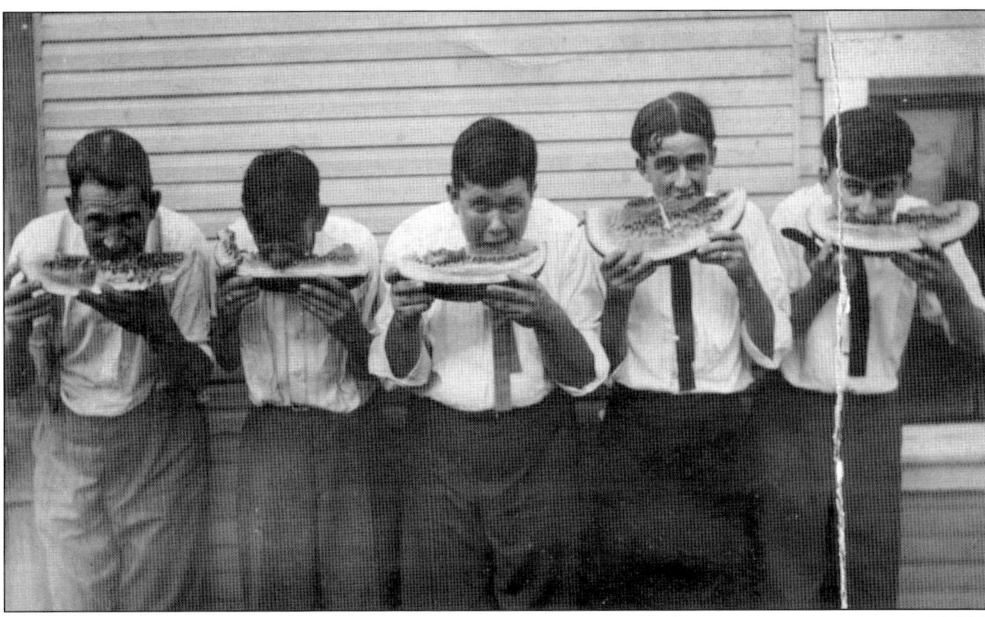

Watermelon Contest. Five young men participate in a watermelon-eating contest around 1940. Pictured are, from left to right, George Snyder, Robert Abbott, Dilver Scudder, Tom Weldon, and Perry Weldon. (Courtesy of Darrell Maines.)

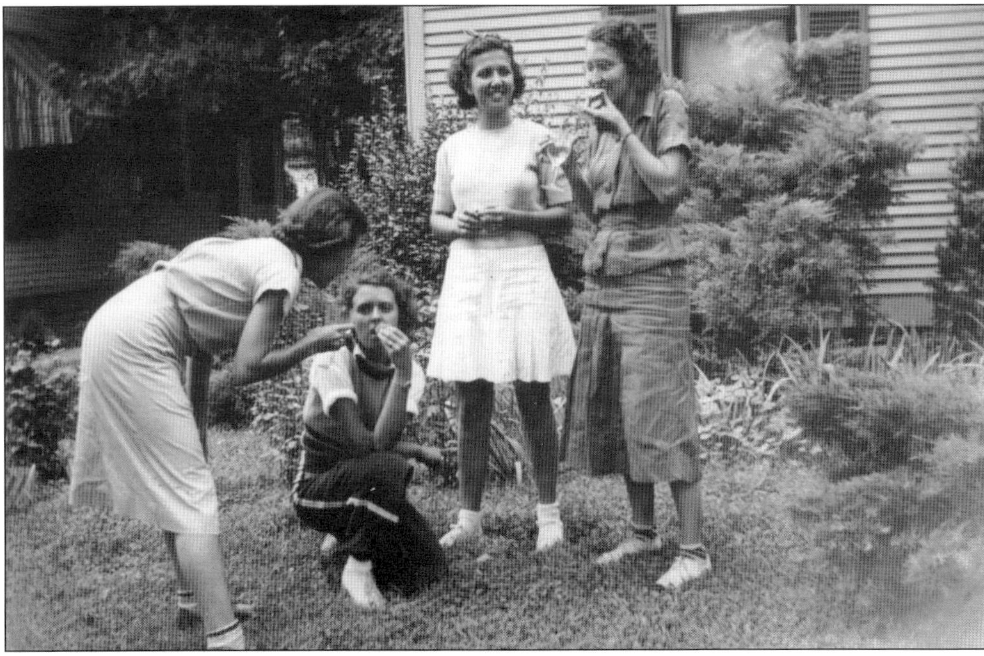

Snack Time. Four young women take a break for a snack around 1935. From left to right are Peggy Williams, Maybelle Connely, Maria Williams, and Harold Brown Connely. (Courtesy of Robert and Alexandra Weldon.)

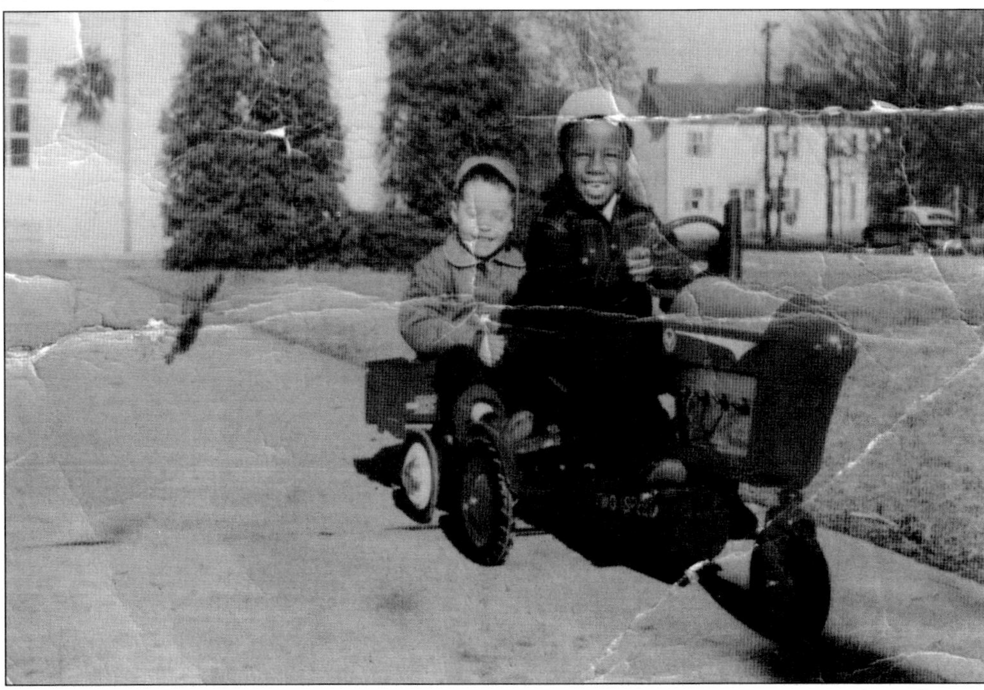

Playtime. Young buddies Tom Weldon (left), and Connelly Green enjoy a pretty day riding on their toy tractor. This photograph was taken on the front sidewalk of the courthouse about 1957. Tom Weldon is the son of Dr. Thomas and Harold Brown Weldon. (Courtesy of Robert and Alexandra Weldon.)

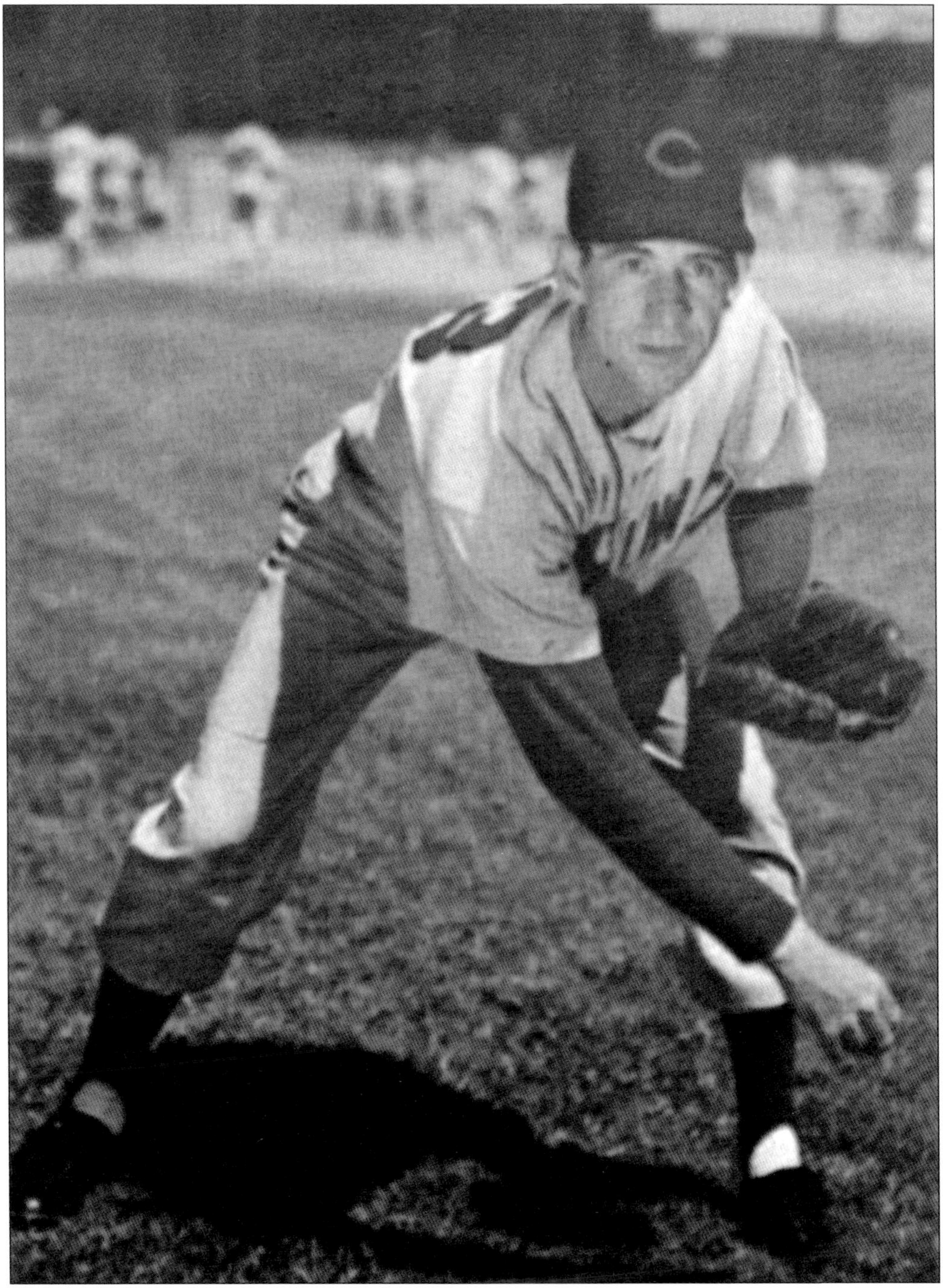

Major League. James "Jim" Blackburn was born in Warsaw in 1924. He served with the Army in Europe during World War II and was taken prisoner. Later freed, he returned to the United States, was signed by the Cincinnati Reds in 1946, and assigned to their Columbia farm team. He debuted as a pitcher for the Reds in July 1948, appearing in 18 games between 1948 and 1951 and earning an 0–2 record. He died in Cincinnati in 1969 and is buried in the city's Spring Grove Cemetery. (Courtesy of Michael Riesenberg.)

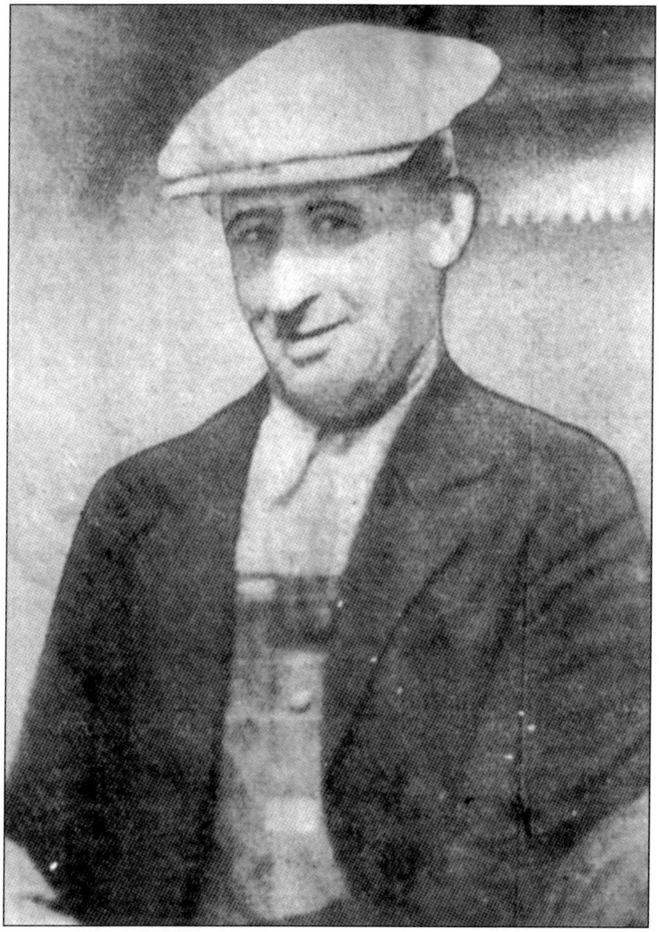

Mystery. In June 1954, the body of Gallatin County sheriff James Hubbard "Hub" Ferguson (left) was found floating in the Eagle Creek at Sparta. He was shot in the head and had a 22-pound cast-iron plate and wire around his neck. His car was found abandoned and his gun missing from the glove compartment three days prior to the discovery. Hundreds of residents searched the countryside for him to no avail, until a horse shied away from the creek, leading to the grim discovery. Ferguson was divorced, lived alone, and had no known enemies. His killer was never found. The map below shows the location of Ferguson's body at the creek. (Both, courtesy of the Gallatin County Free Public Library.)

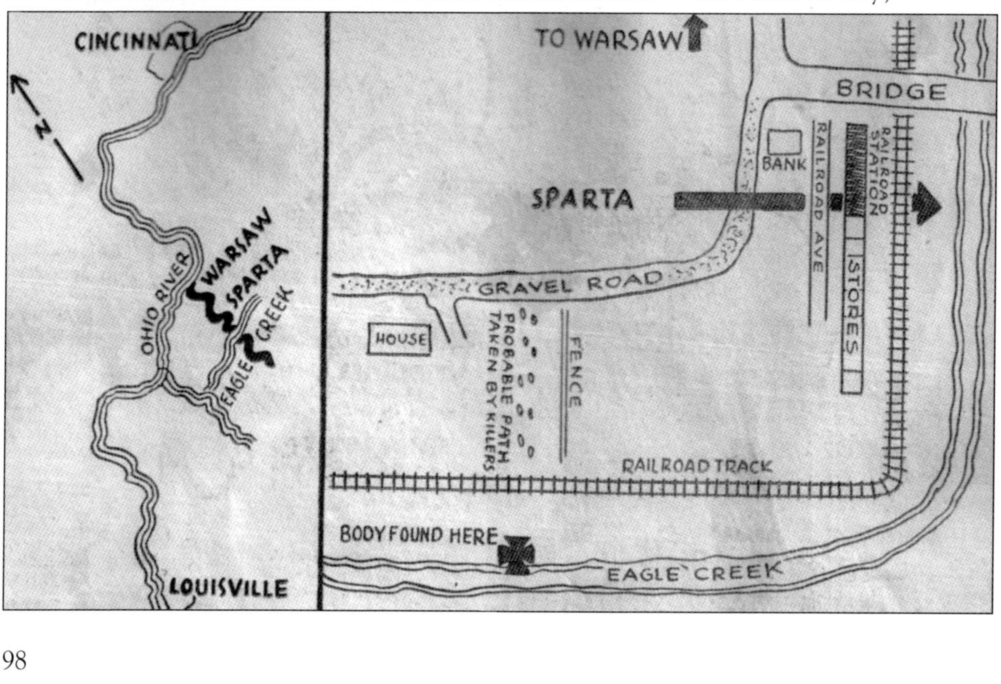

Eight

Around the County

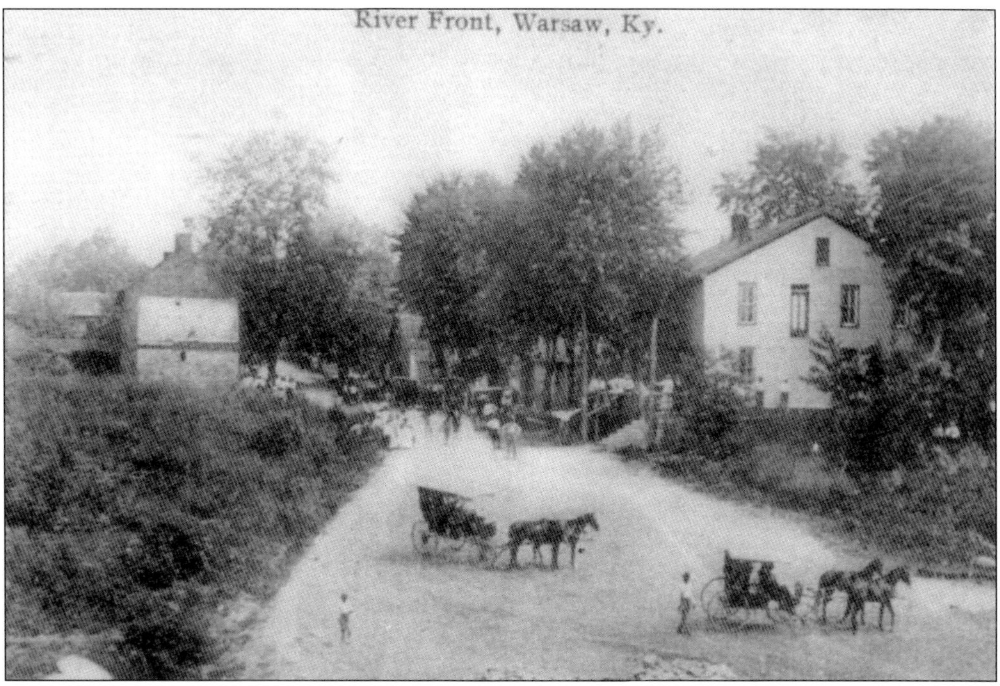

Riverfront, Warsaw. As the only river bottom area in Gallatin County, the riverfront in Warsaw was a bustling hub of activity. After the construction of the Lock and Dam No. 39 in 1916 and the Markland Dam in 1964, the topography of the riverfront was dramatically changed. This portion of Water Street now lies approximately 15 feet under the Ohio River. (Courtesy of Darrell Maines.)

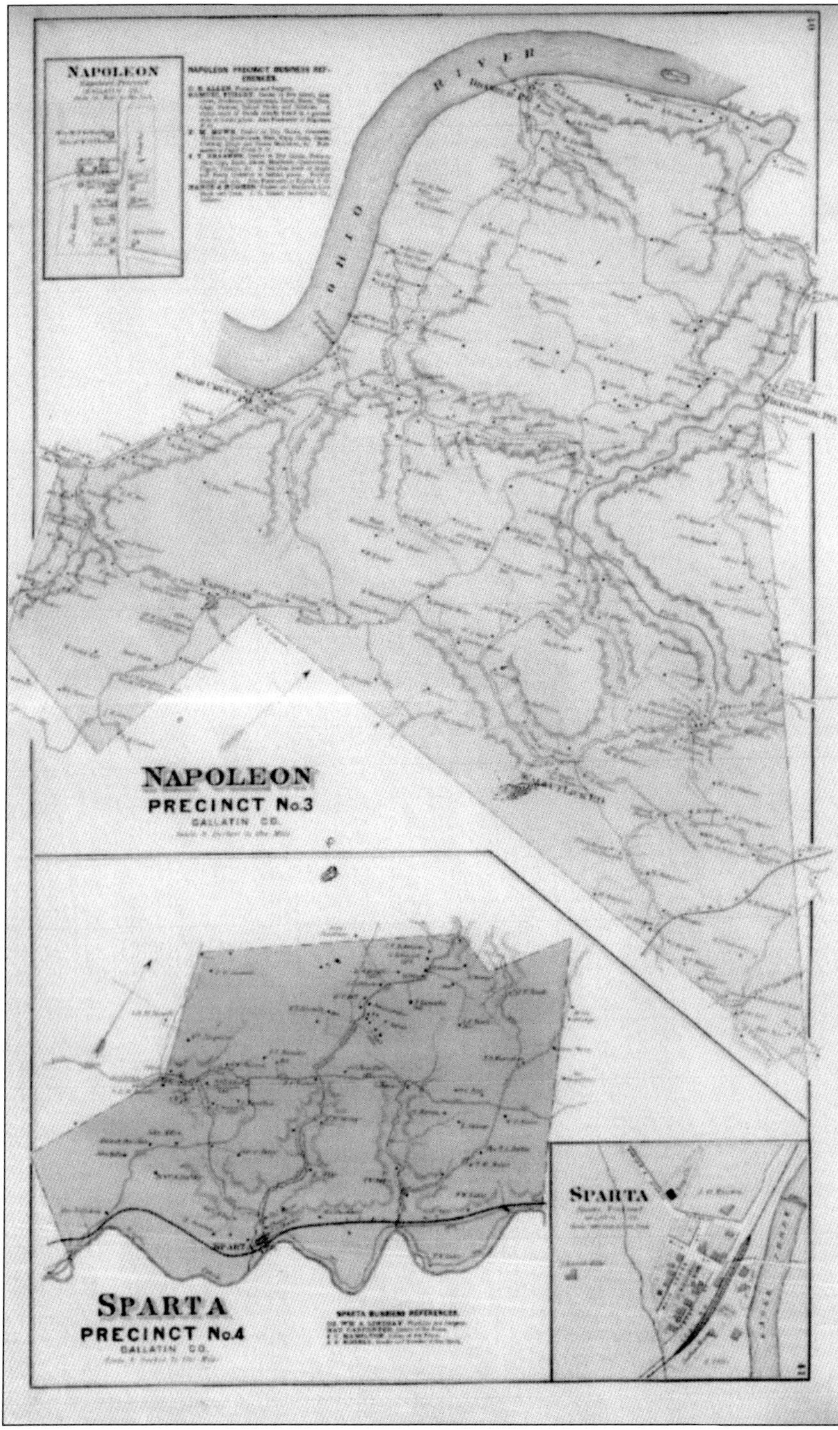

NAPOLEON PRECINCT. This 1883 atlas image shows the Napoleon precinct of Gallatin County. On the eastern side of the county, the village of Napoleon is located only three miles from both the Ohio River and the L&N Railroad. The precinct also includes Sparta, Sugar Creek, and the Paint Lick areas. (Courtesy of the Gallatin County Free Public Library.)

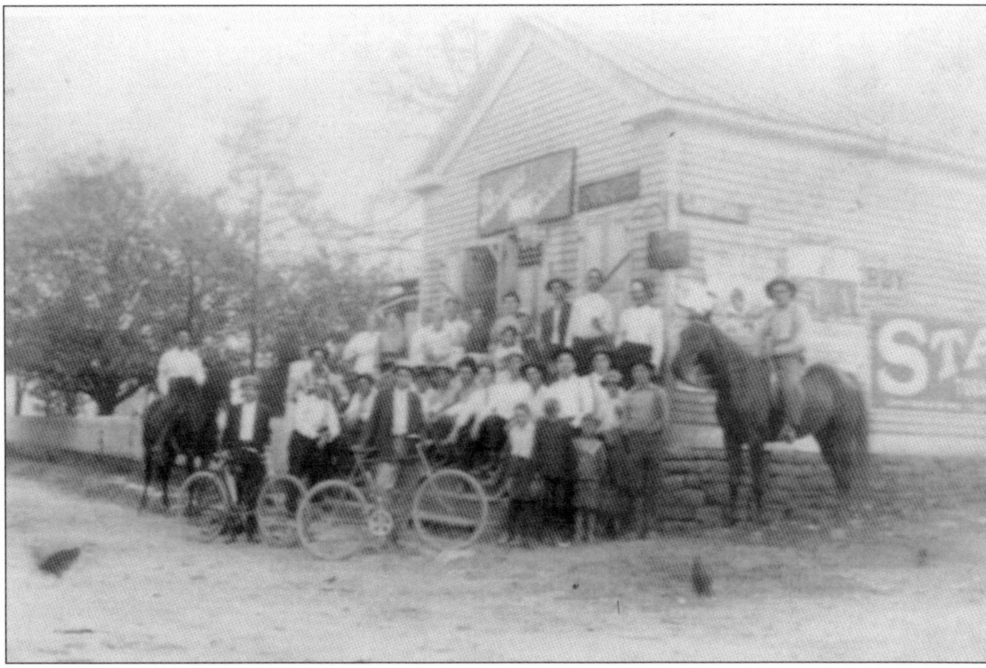

Napoleon General Store. On the eastern side of the county lays the tiny hamlet of Napoleon. Pictured here around 1890 is the general store, which provided essential goods and a gathering place for local residents. The general store still stands at the junction of what is now Route 16 and Tapering Point Road. (Courtesy of Darrell Maines.)

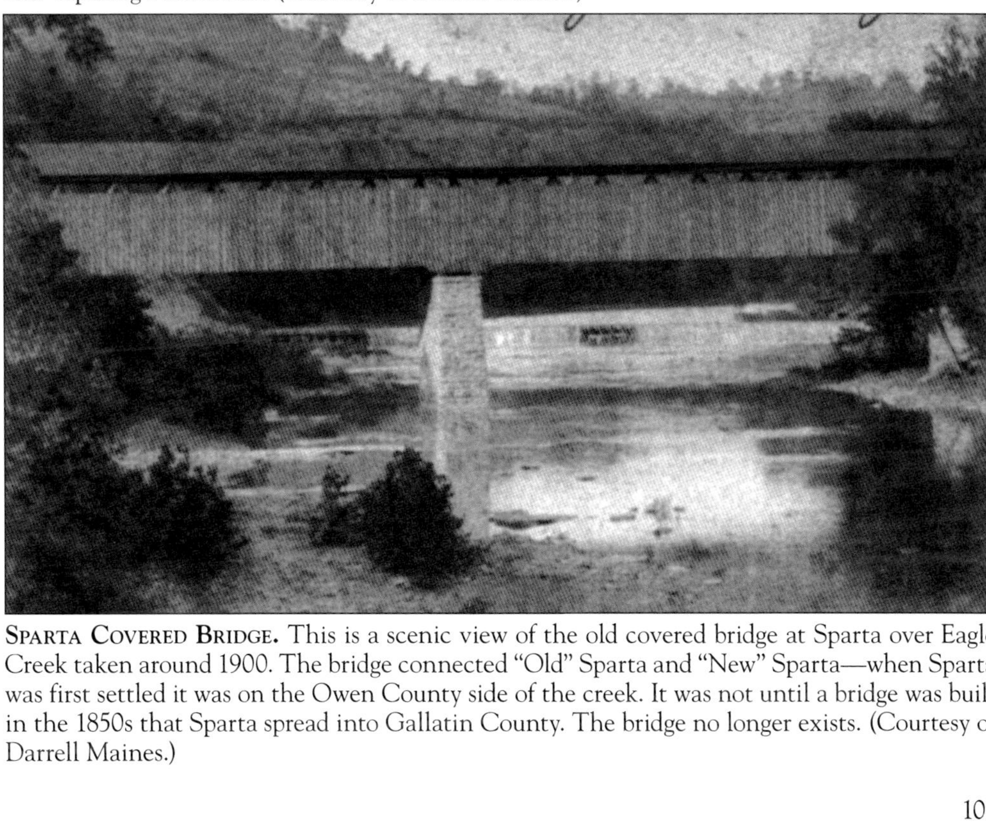

Sparta Covered Bridge. This is a scenic view of the old covered bridge at Sparta over Eagle Creek taken around 1900. The bridge connected "Old" Sparta and "New" Sparta—when Sparta was first settled it was on the Owen County side of the creek. It was not until a bridge was built in the 1850s that Sparta spread into Gallatin County. The bridge no longer exists. (Courtesy of Darrell Maines.)

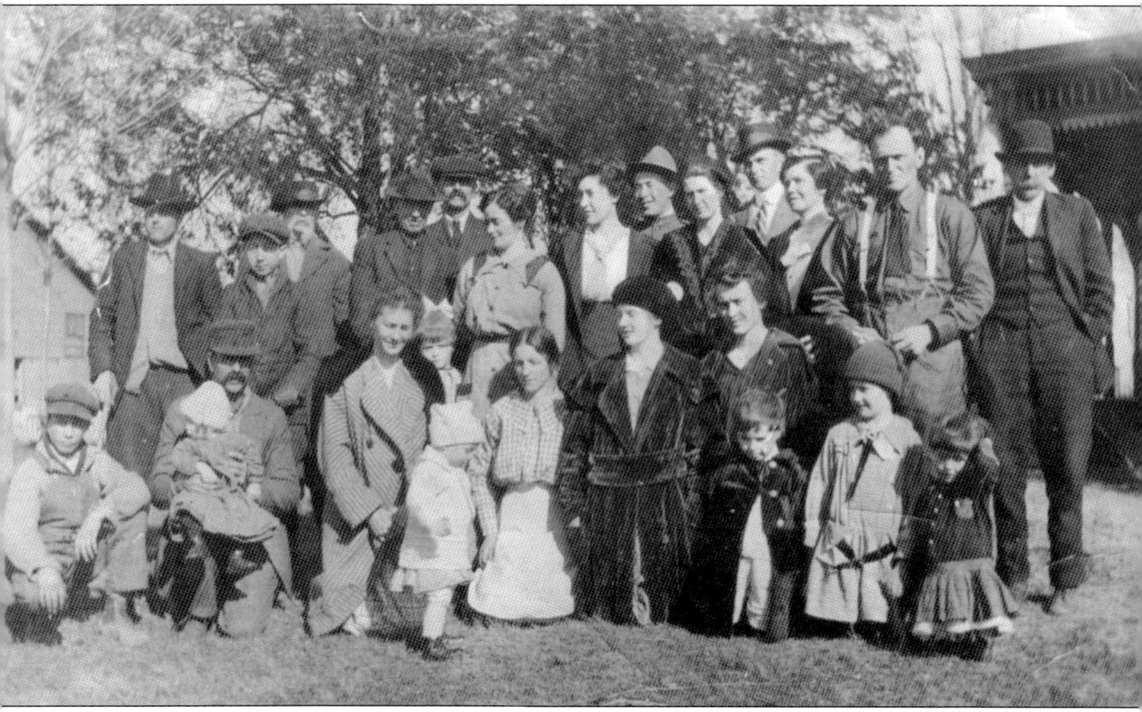

Family Reunion. The Chapman and Crouch families gather for a reunion around 1918. Pictured are, from left to right, (first row) Clifford Prior Crouch, Tony Chapman, Carrie Chapman Crouch, Margie Crouch, Evalyn Crouch, Joy Chapman Crouch, unidentified child, Elizabeth Chapman, and another unidentified child; (second row) four unidentified, Evie Chapman, four unidentified, and William Chapman; (third row) unidentified, William Prior Crouch, and two unidentified. (Courtesy of Dana Benne.)

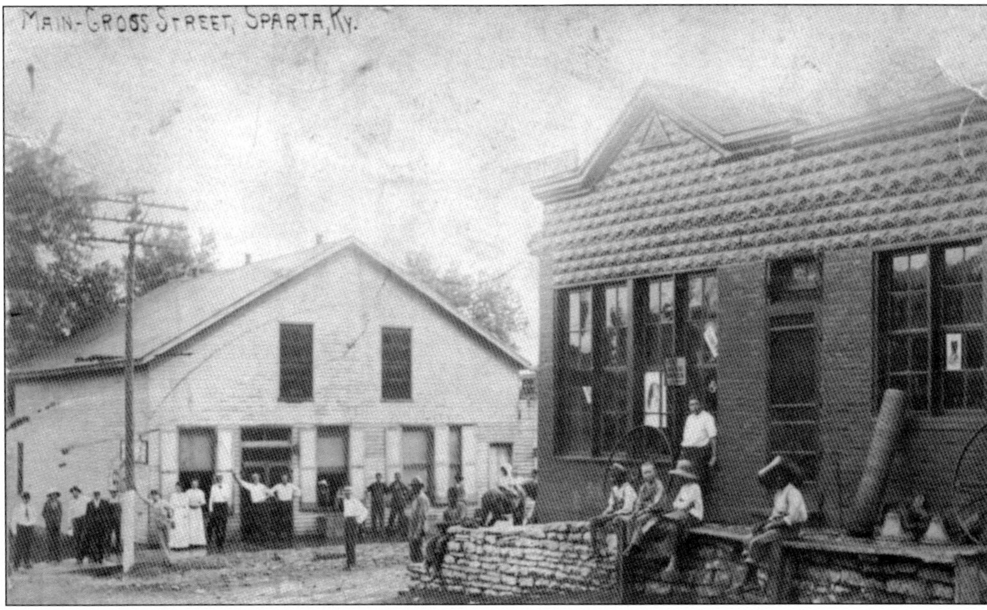

MAIN STREET, SPARTA. Incorporated in 1852, Sparta is a sleepy little village located along Eagle Creek in the southwest corner of Gallatin County. Residents gather around the businesses on Main Cross Street in the photograph above from around 1900. In another view below, a group of residents have gathered outside the Sparta Deposit Bank. Looking south, the L&N Railroad is just out of view. In 1969, the Kentucky leg of Interstate 71 was completed and became the major travel route between Cincinnati and Louisville. Although the interstate bisected the entire county, the local landscape remained largely unchanged until 2000, when the Kentucky Speedway opened outside Sparta. Downtown Sparta has remained the sleepy little village through the influx of race fans to the track and the excitement of hosting the NASCAR Sprint Series Quaker State 400. (Both, courtesy of Darrell Maines.)

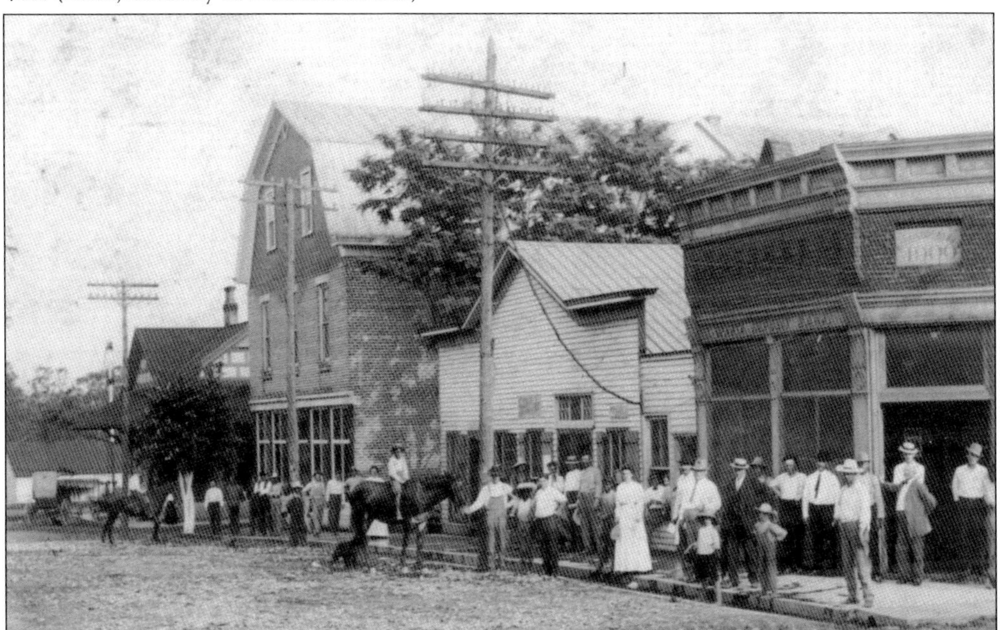

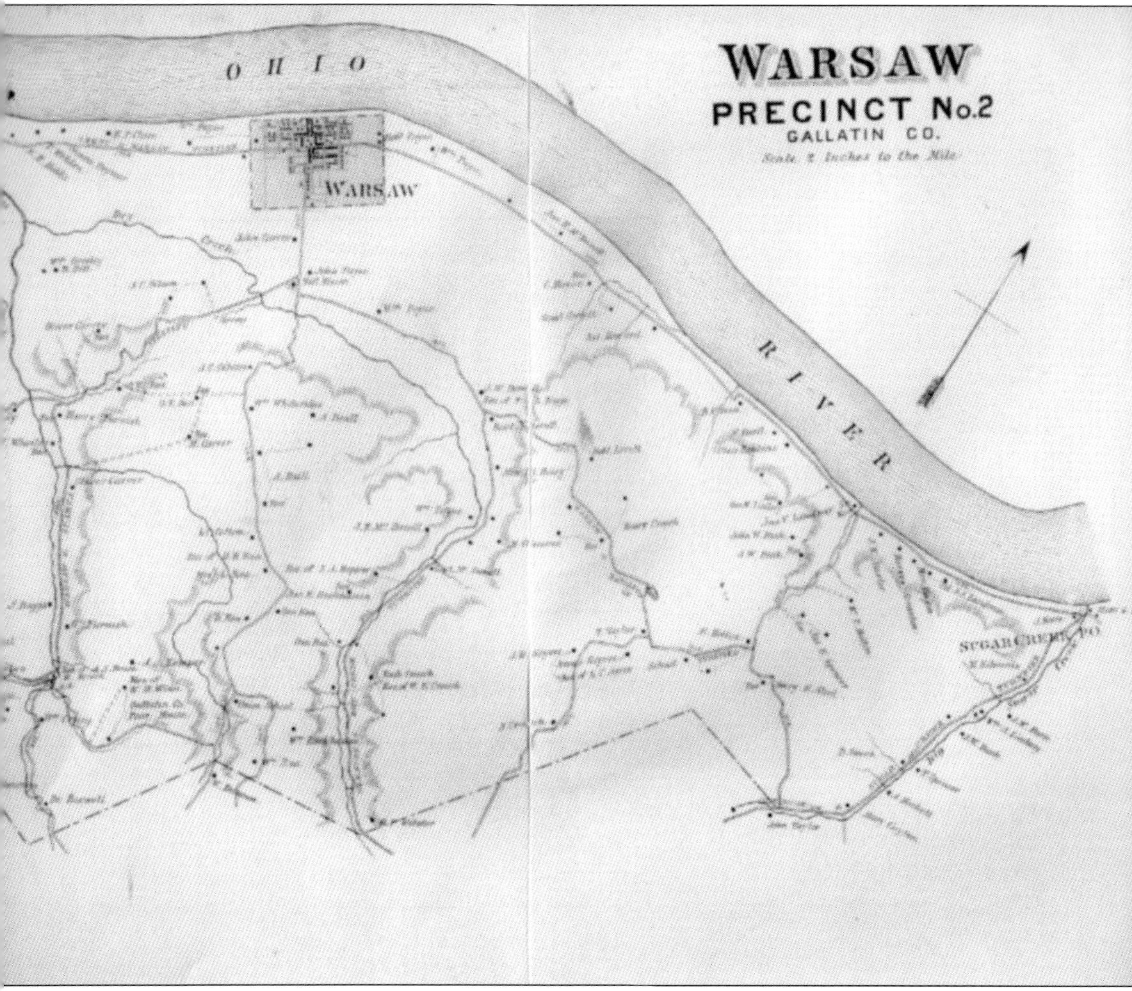

PRECINCT NO. 2 WARSAW. The 1883 atlas shows Warsaw and surrounding area in its precinct. It encompassed the land south toward Glencoe and Sparta and east toward Sugar Creek. (Courtesy of the Gallatin County Free Public Library.)

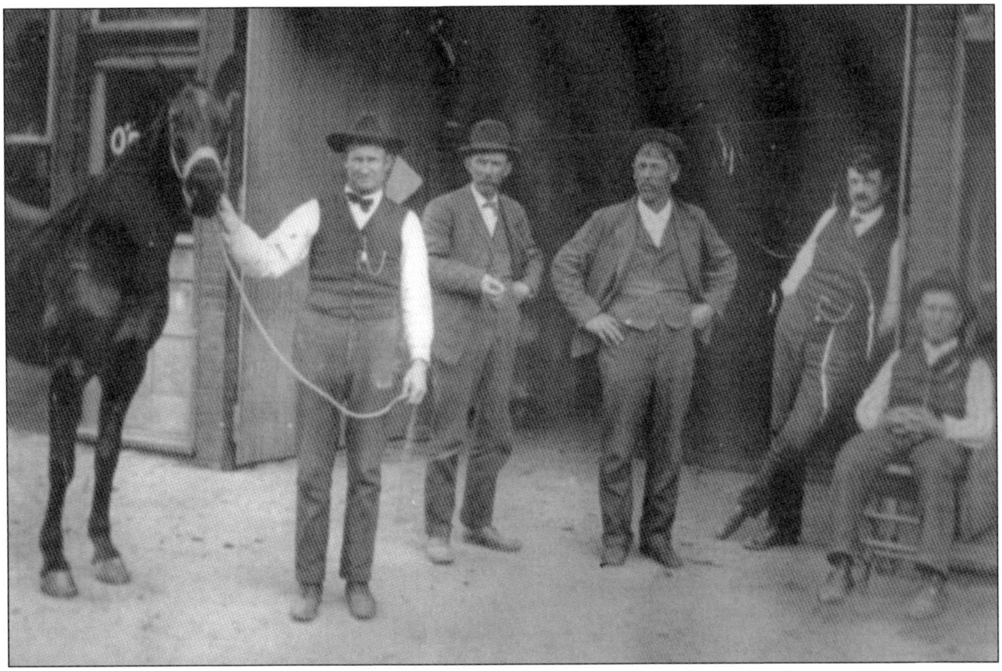

Livery Stable. Four gentlemen stand in front of one of the two livery stables in Warsaw. This livery stable was under the hill on the west side of Main Cross at Locust Street. It was owned and operated by John D. Pulliam in the 1880s. (Courtesy of Darrell Maines.)

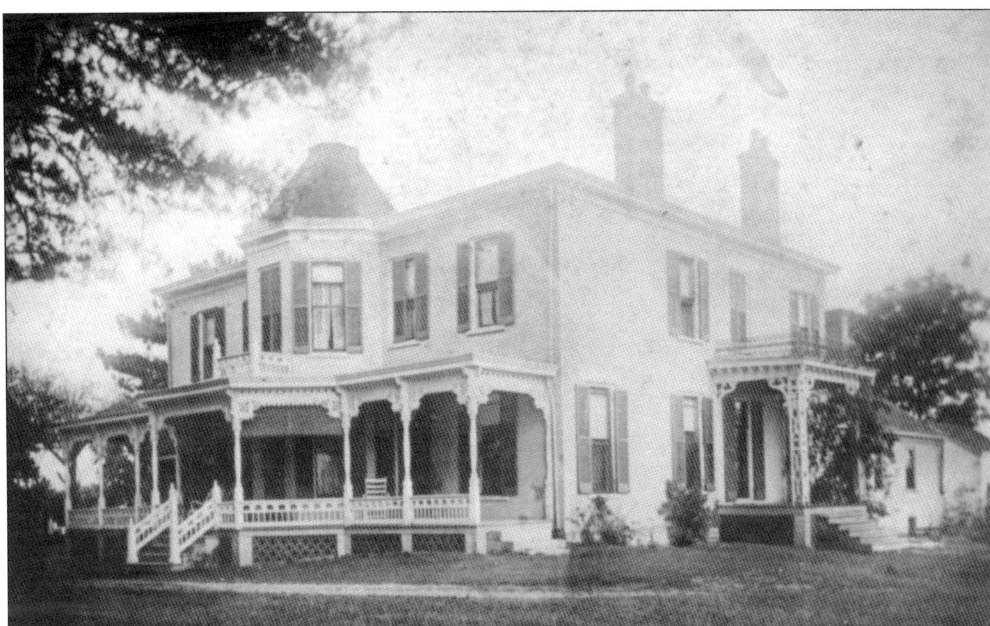

Payne/Connely House. Pictured here around 1895 is the Payne/Connely house, built about 1852 by William Payne. There have only been three families to live in the house. Now owned by Robert and Alexandra Weldon, it is known as Seven Pines. The house has been in the Weldon family since 1934. (Courtesy of Robert and Alexandra Weldon.)

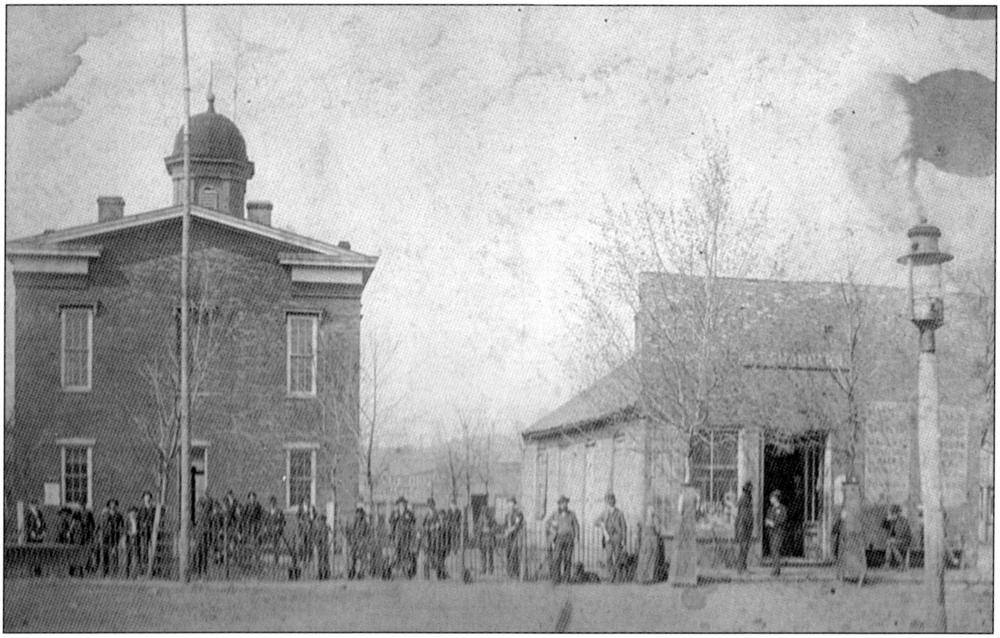

Courthouse Square. The view above of the courthouse from about 1880 shows the original configuration facing the river. The photographer would have been standing on the south side of Main Street looking toward the river. The H.T. Chambers Drug Store is on the southeast corner of the square. On the southwest corner of the square sat a public privy (below). This octagon-shaped structure sat at the site of the jail before it was moved to Main Cross and Pearl Street. (Both, courtesy of Darrell Maines.)

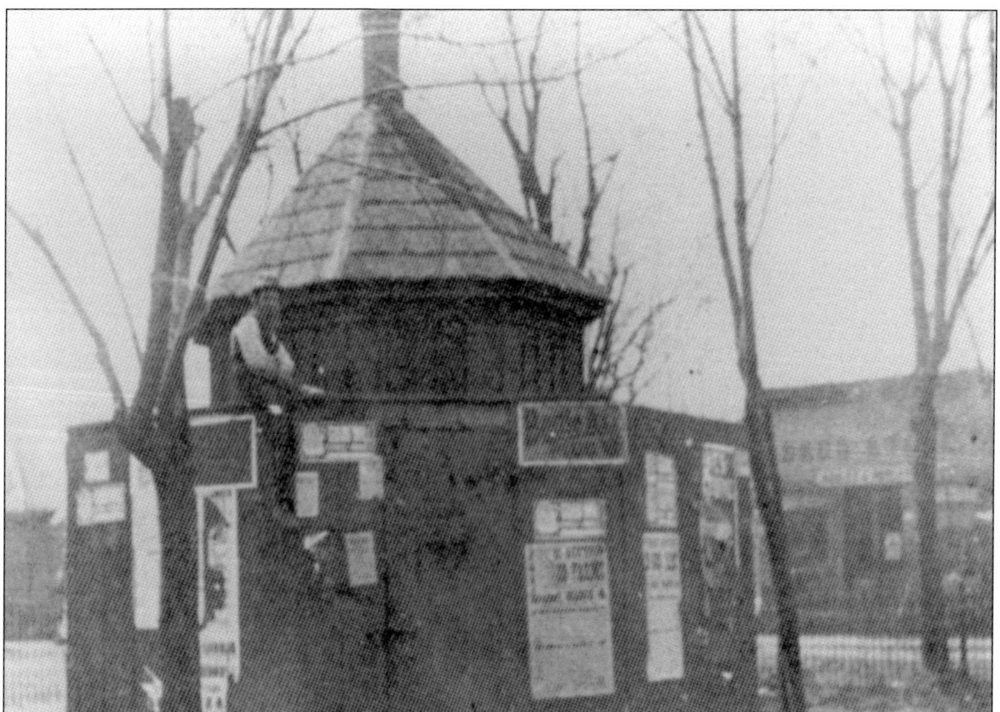

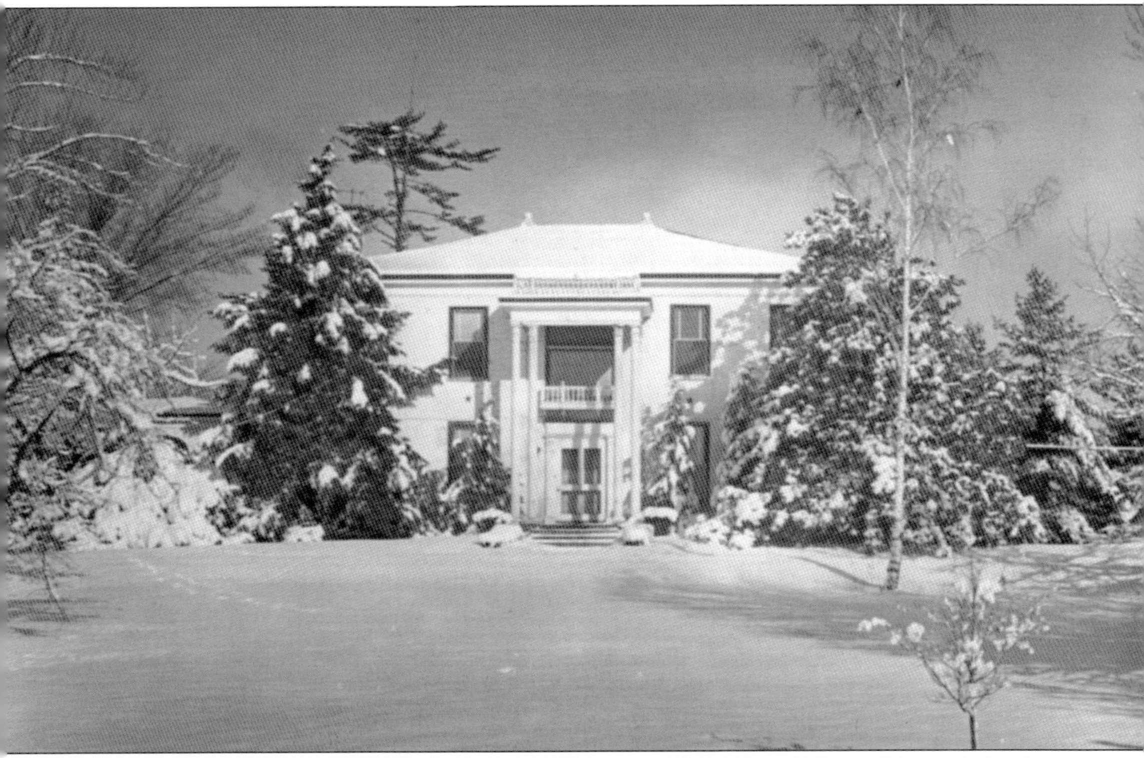

Heritage Hall. This house was built in 1865 by James H. McDanell Sr. and housed the three generations of the McDanell family. It was known to local residents as Heritage Hall. Acquired in 1950 by nurseryman William H. Hill, the house and grounds are noted for their beauty. Before reconstruction in 2011 into a bed-and-breakfast, many referred to the house as the Marie Roberts (daughter of William H. Hill) house. (Courtesy of Darrell Maines.)

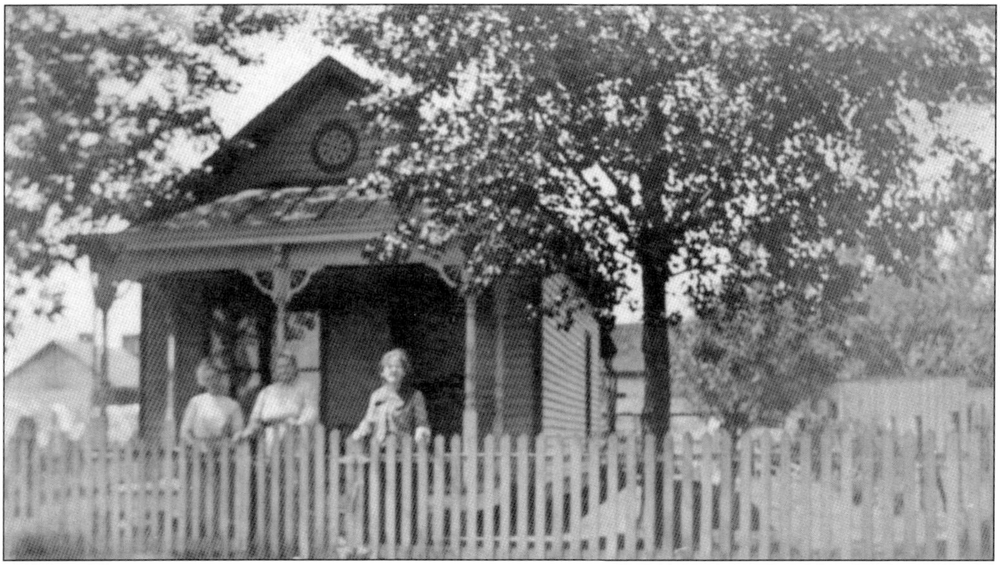

Tyson House. The Tyson family lived in this house in the community of Gex in 1915. Gex was a tiny hamlet on US 42 in western Gallatin County near the current site of Nucor Gallatin Steel. (Courtesy of Darrell Maines.)

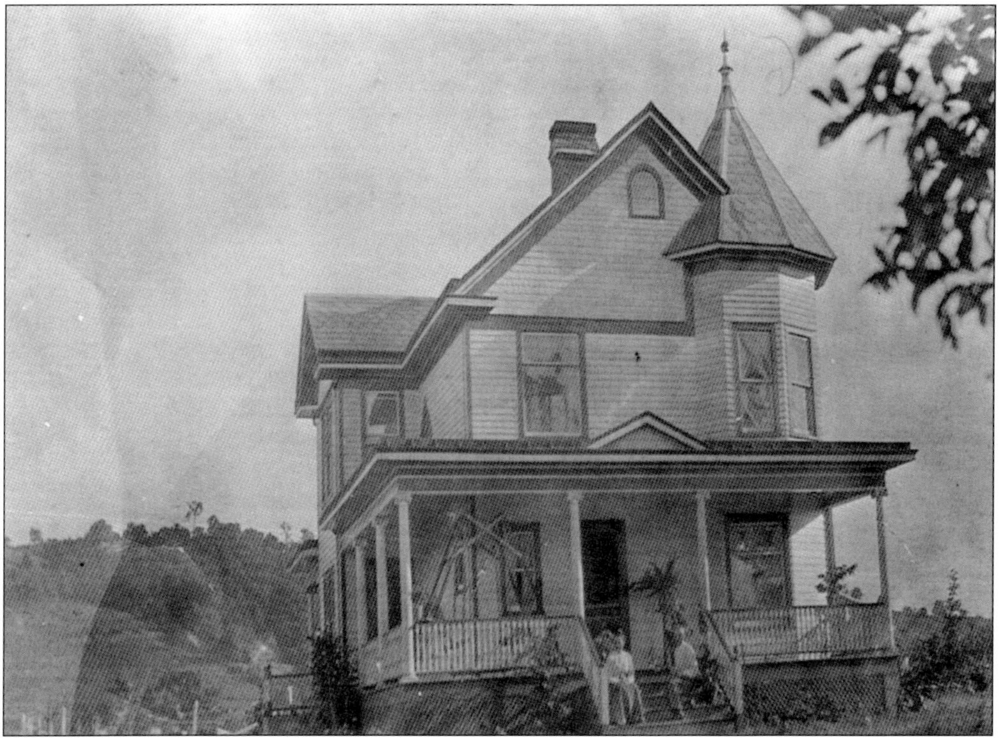

Long-Standing Home. This photograph shows John and Lizzie Peak seated on the steps of their home around 1910. The house was located on the corner of Sparta Pike and Dry Creek Road. The house is still standing and now belongs to the Bingham family. (Courtesy of JC and Mary-Evelyn Noel.)

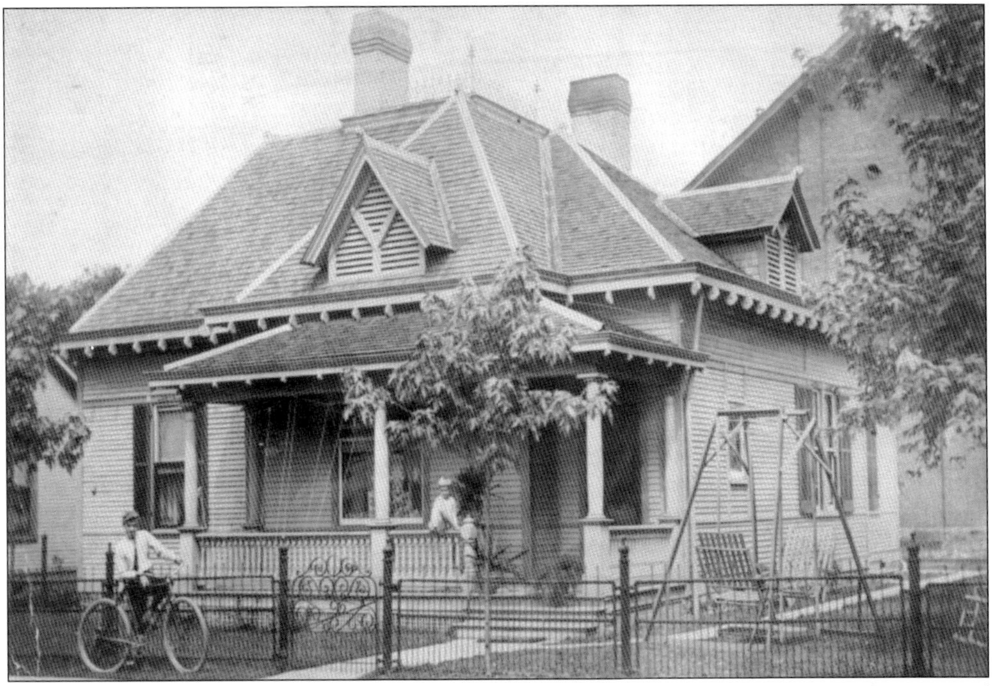

Winn-Payne House. This house was built around 1900 by George Marshon. It was later owned by Everett Winn and his wife, Alice Montgomery Winn. It faced Main Street near Fourth Street, and the Christian church can be seen behind it. Winn had the unfortunate honor of being the first person killed in an automobile accident in Gallatin County. His widow married into the Payne family and remained in the house. (Courtesy of Darrell Maines.)

The Opera House. Most small towns had what was called an opera house, which usually hosted traveling shows and other entertainment. This building also housed the International Order of Odd Fellows and was located on West High Street. It was damaged in the 1940s. (Courtesy of Darrell Maines.)

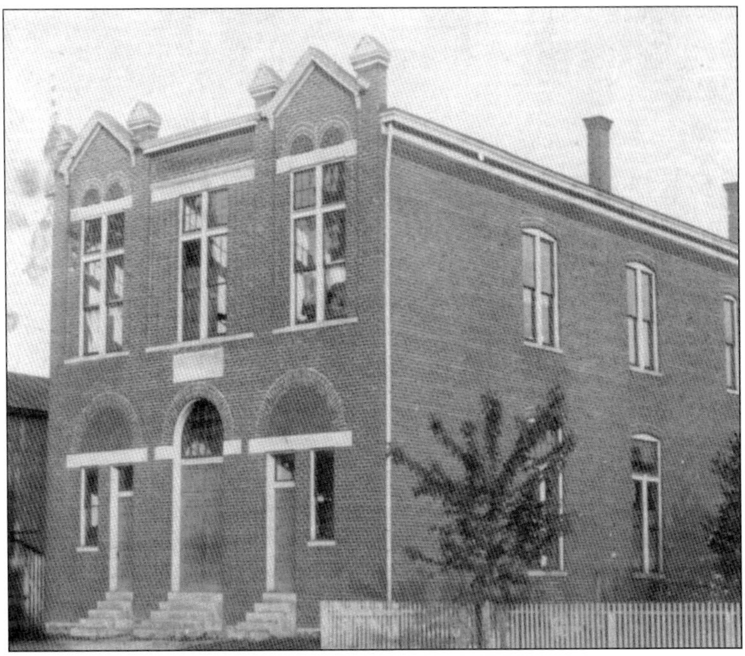

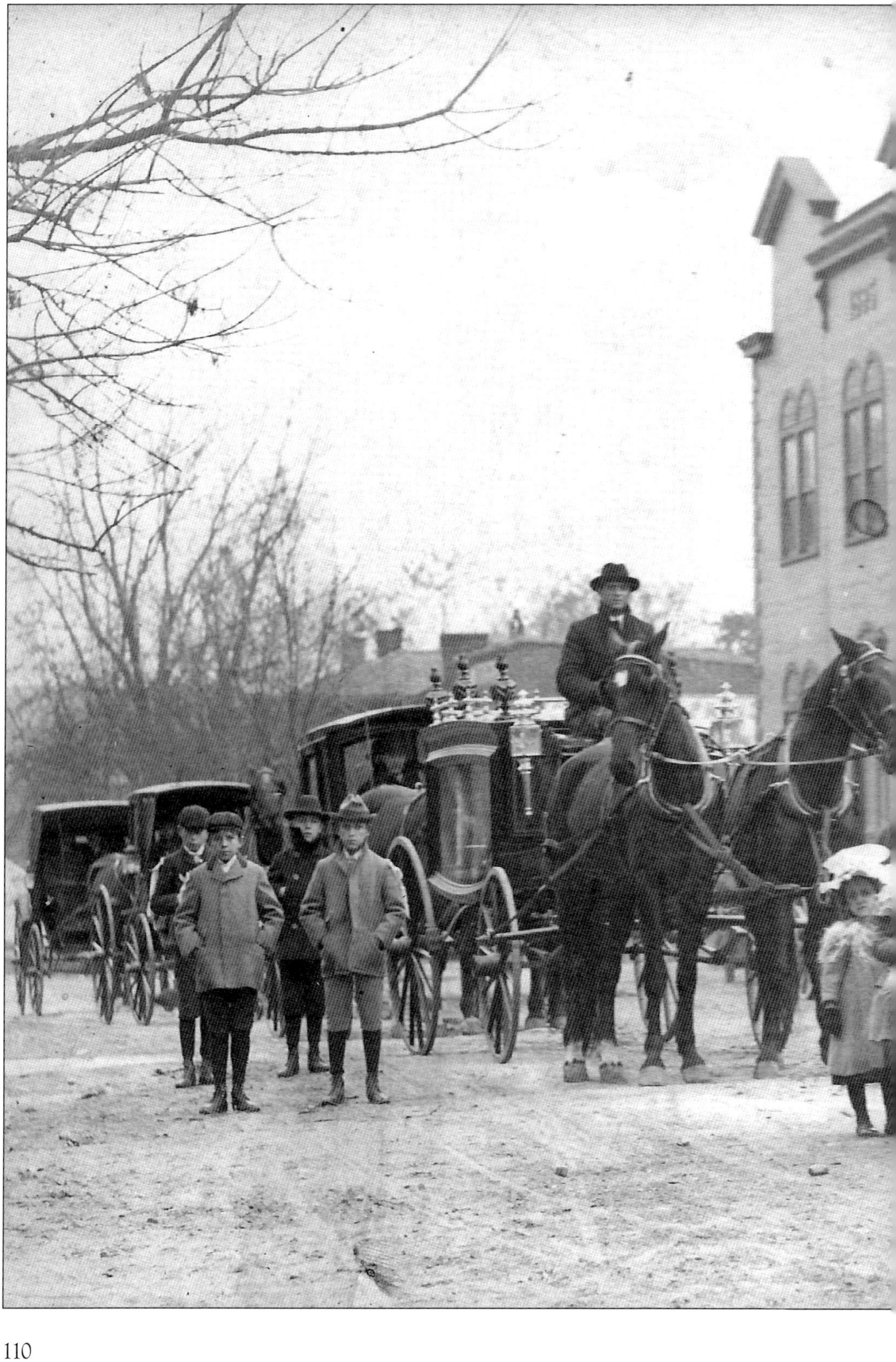

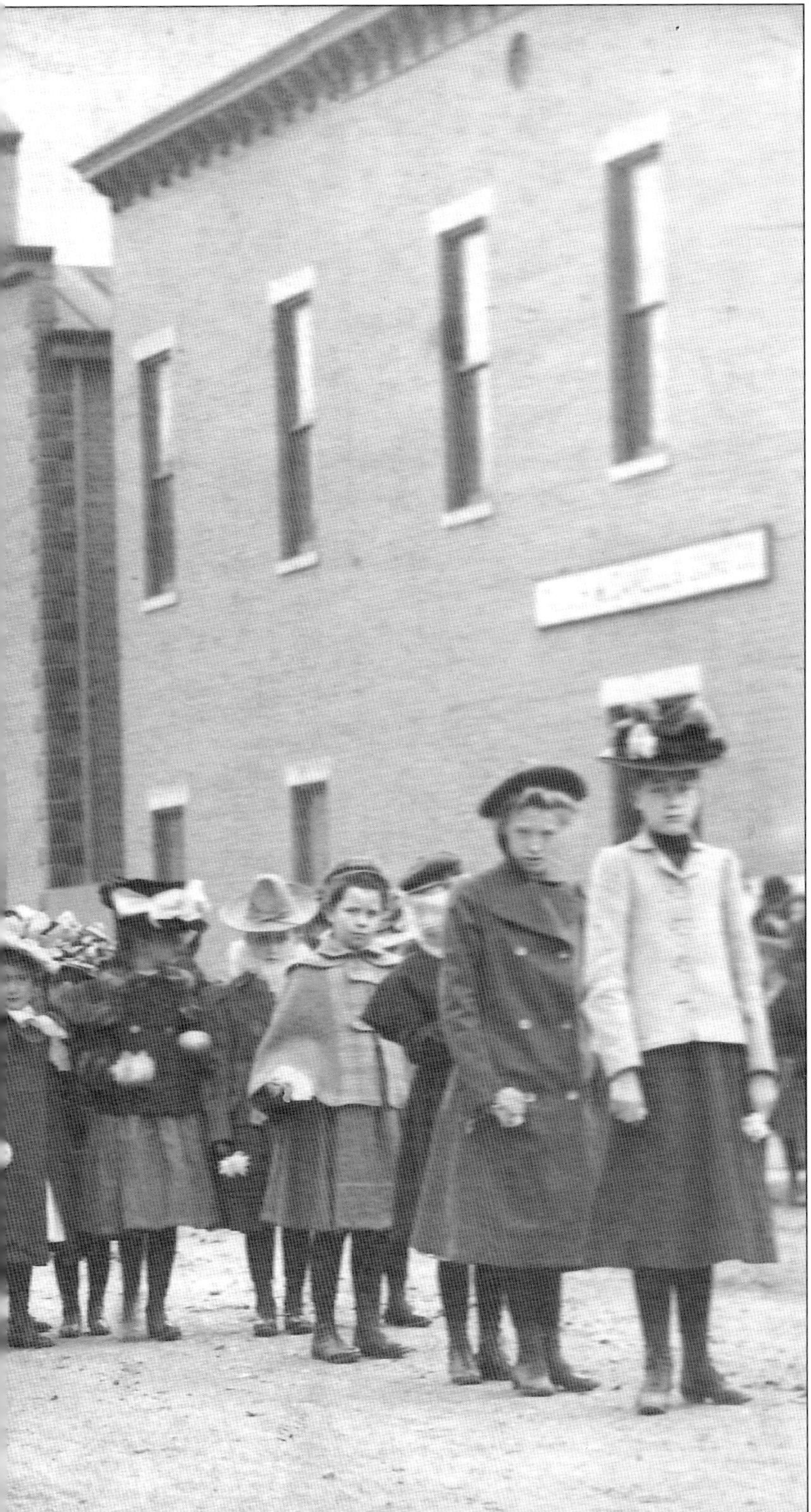

Funeral Procession. A funeral procession for one-year-old Harry Hanson makes its way down Main Cross south toward Market Street. The buildings in the background are the opera house (left) and McDanell's General Store. John Mylor is driving the horse. Pall bearers are Harold Brown, Whitney Payne, Emerson Abbott, and Walter Simpson. The group of girls at the front are, in no particular order, Mary Snyder, Agnes Orr, Leah Taaffe, Jessie Lee Montgomery, Bess Abott, Eunice Conrad, Florence Abbott, Myrtly Carver, Lavinia McDanell, Mary Louise Herrick, Florence Morton, and Ruth Graham. (Courtesy of Darrell Maines.)

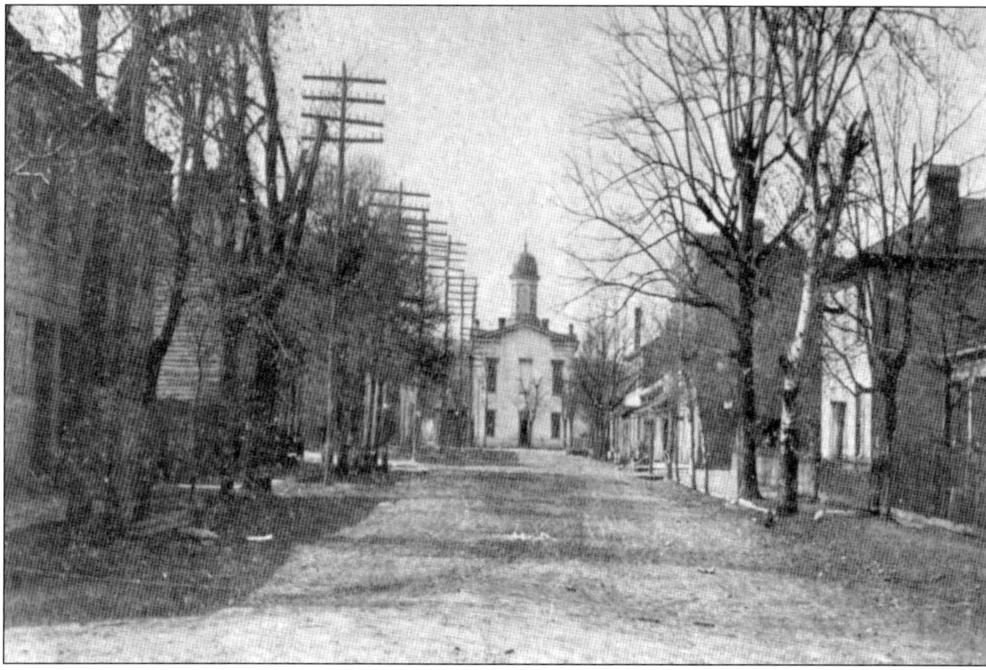

A View from Below. In the early years, the county courthouse faced the river since most visitors arrived by boat, and the town was clustered around the riverfront. Looking south from Main Cross, one can see the courthouse in the distance from the shore in this image from around 1900. The Lindell Hotel (left) and livery stable buildings were both destroyed in the 1937 flood. (Courtesy of Darrell Maines.)

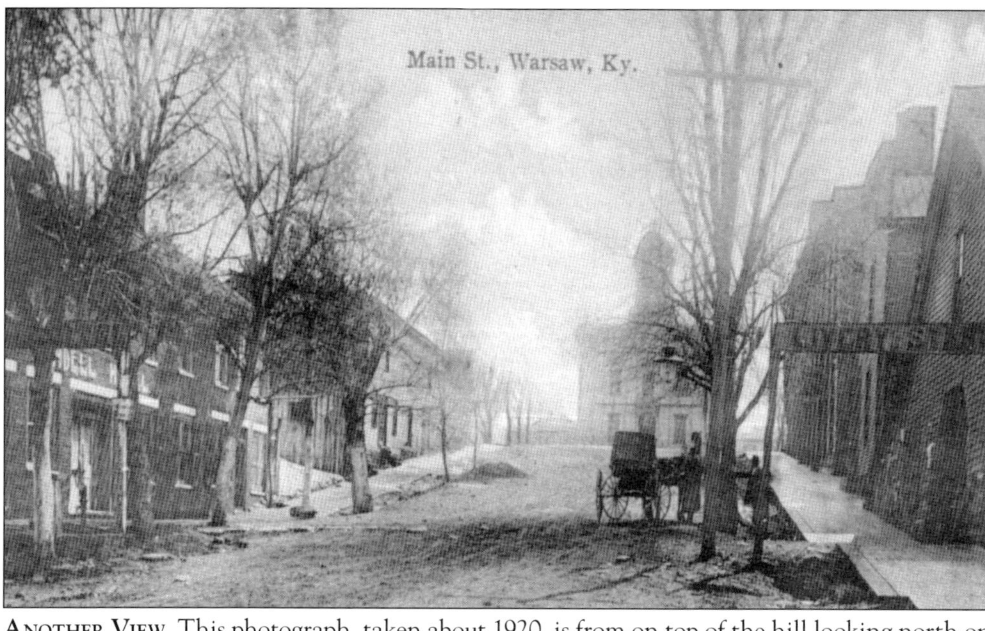

Another View. This photograph, taken about 1920, is from on top of the hill looking north on Main Cross toward the back of the courthouse. The building on the right in the far background, hidden behind the trees, is the second livery stable. The Brown Hotel was directly across from the stable on the corner. (Courtesy of Darrell Maines.)

GLENCOE PRECINCT. On this 1883 atlas page of the Glencoe precinct, the southern boundary of the county is Eagle Creek. The L&N Railroad runs parallel to the creek through Glencoe. (Courtesy of the Gallatin County Free Library.)

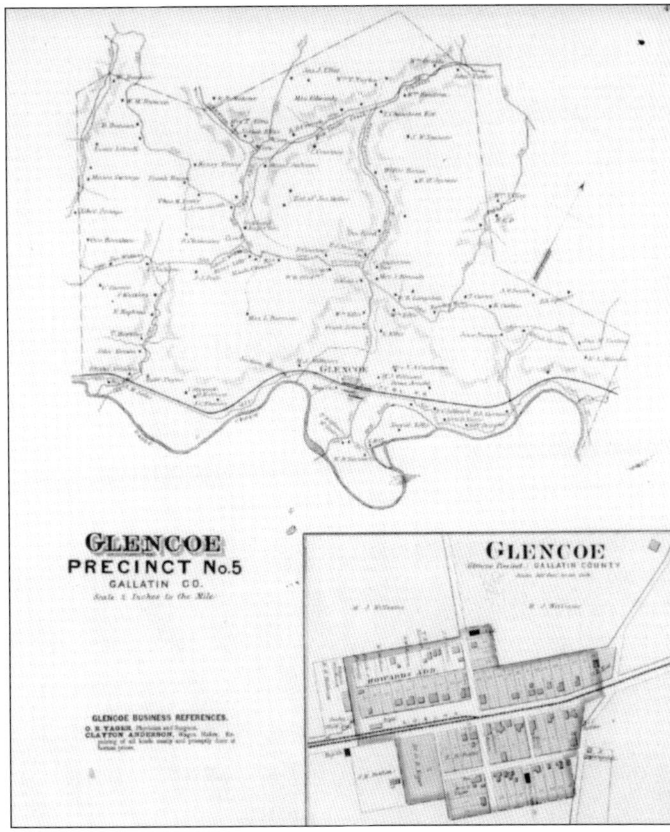

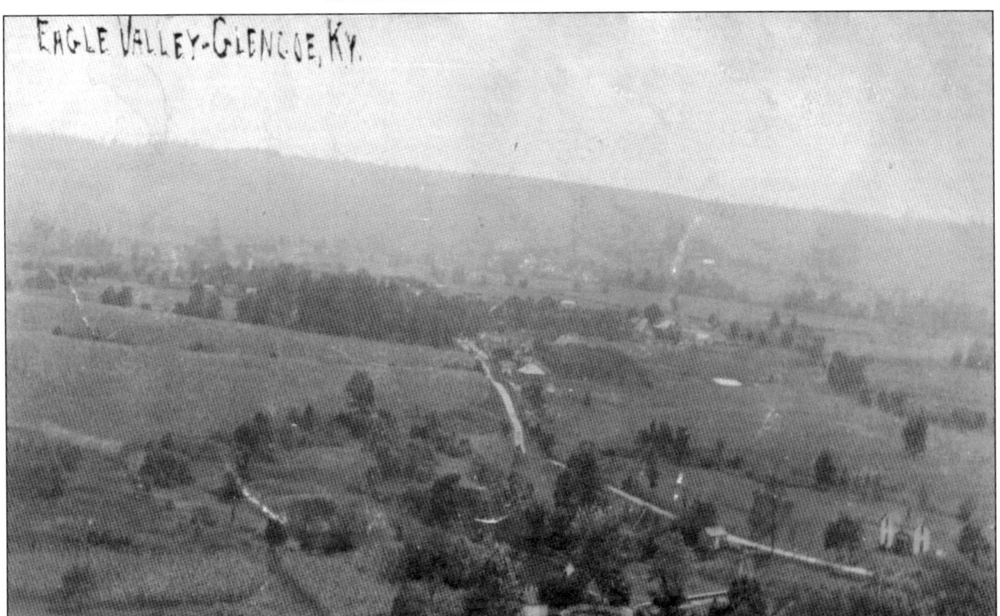

BEAUTIFUL VALLEY. This view of the Eagle Creek Valley near Glencoe from about 1920 shows its beauty. The area has remained largely rural despite Interstate 71 cutting through the county near Glencoe. (Courtesy of Darrell Maines.)

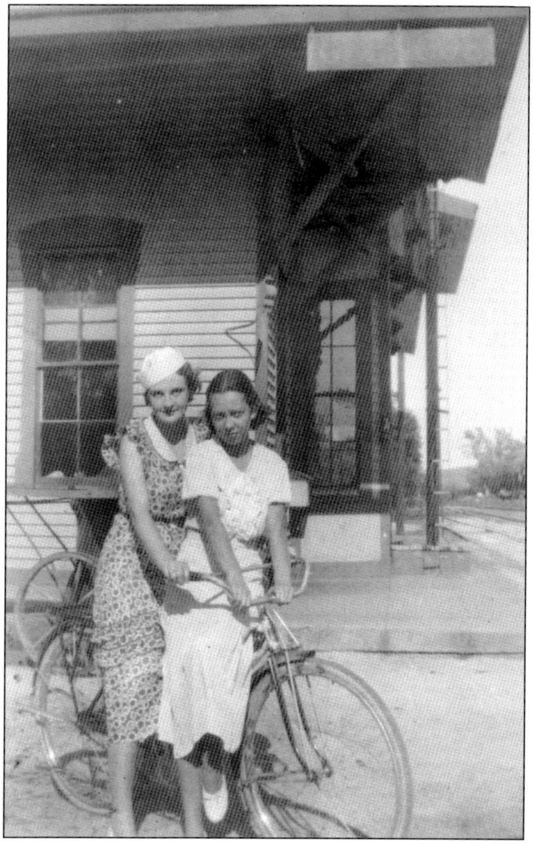

Bicycle Riding. Two girls pause for a moment by the Glencoe Depot while out riding their bicycles around 1930. The girl on the left is identified only as Gladys; the girl on the right is unidentified. (Courtesy of Dana Benne.)

Road Gang. Pictured here around 1900, William Prior Crouch (left foreground) works with a crew to build a road near Sparta. Crouch was the engineer who oversaw the construction. (Courtesy of Dana Benne.)

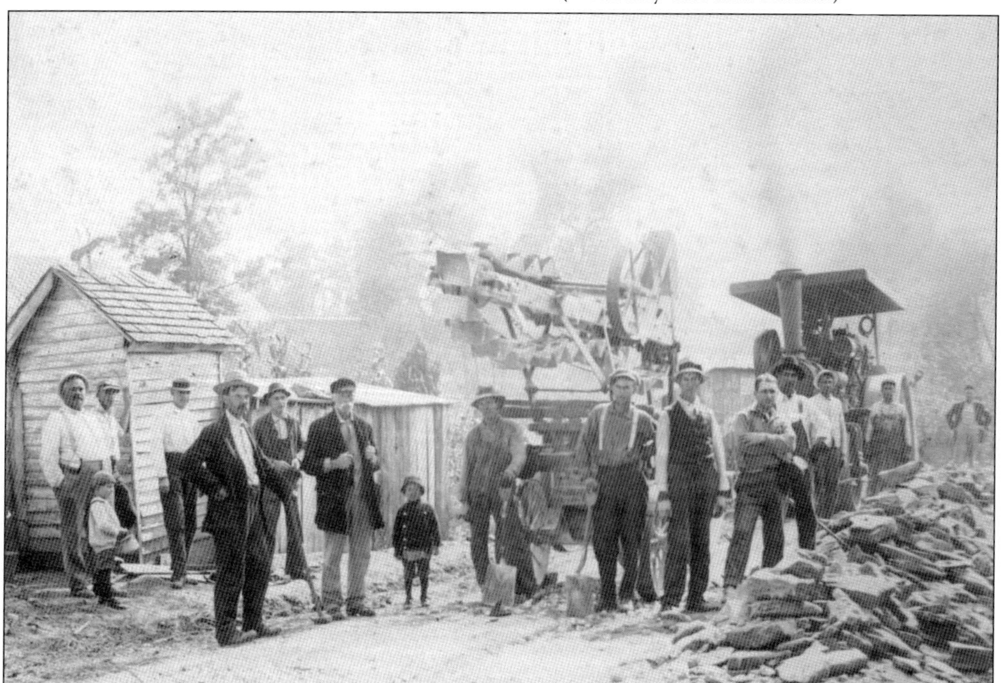

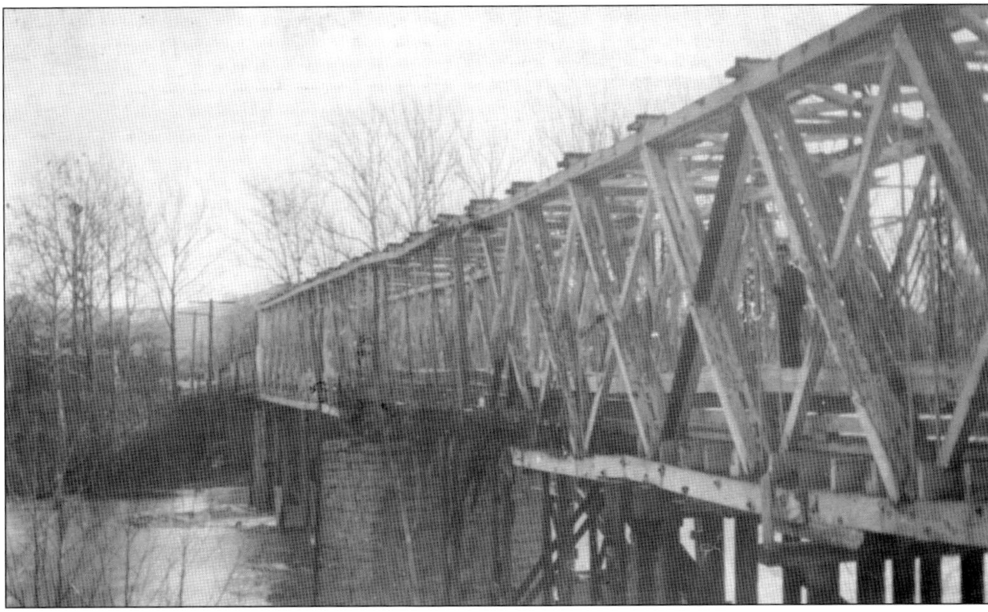

Eagle Creek Bridge. This early 1900s photograph shows the old Eagle Creek Bridge near Sparta as it is being refurbished. At this point, it was close to 50 years old and in need of extensive repair. (Courtesy of Darrell Maines.)

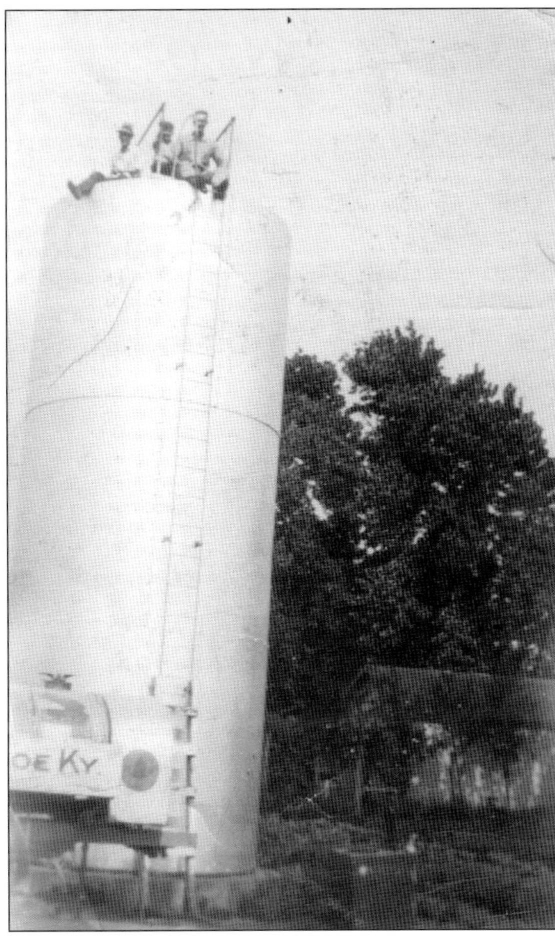

Water Tower. Three unidentified young men decided to climb the Glencoe water tower around 1940. The back of the water truck can be seen on the left. (Courtesy of Dana Benne.)

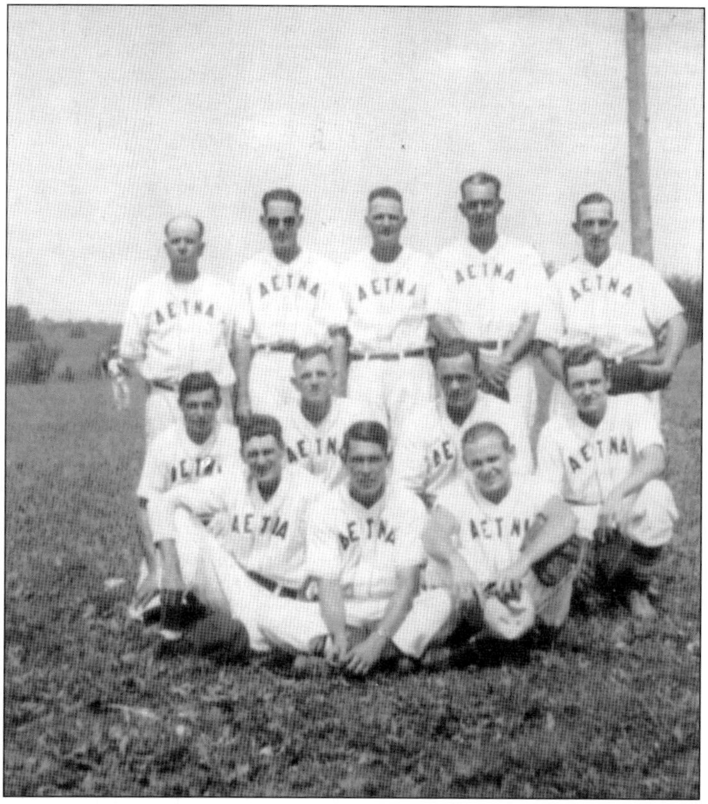

Team Sport. Aetna Gas Company operated three locations—Warsaw, Glencoe, and Carrollton in Carroll County. The company also sponsored a baseball team, shown here in the 1950s. (Courtesy of Dana Benne.)

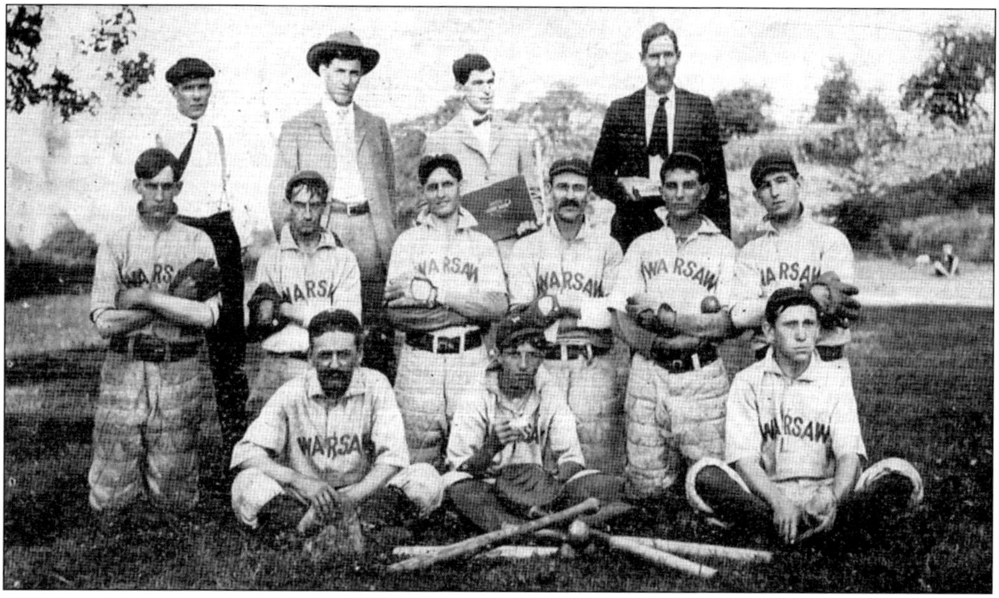

Warsaw Team. Most small towns in the early 20th century had their own baseball teams. This 1905 team from Warsaw won 15 games and lost three that year. Pictured are, from left to right, (first row) H. Davis, H. Brown, and L. Brinley; (second row) G. Winters, B. Abbott, C. Keisel, C. Otter, and G. Downey; (third row) Ed Winters, Jim Connelly, Roy Clore, and H. Gibson. (Courtesy of Darrell Maines.)

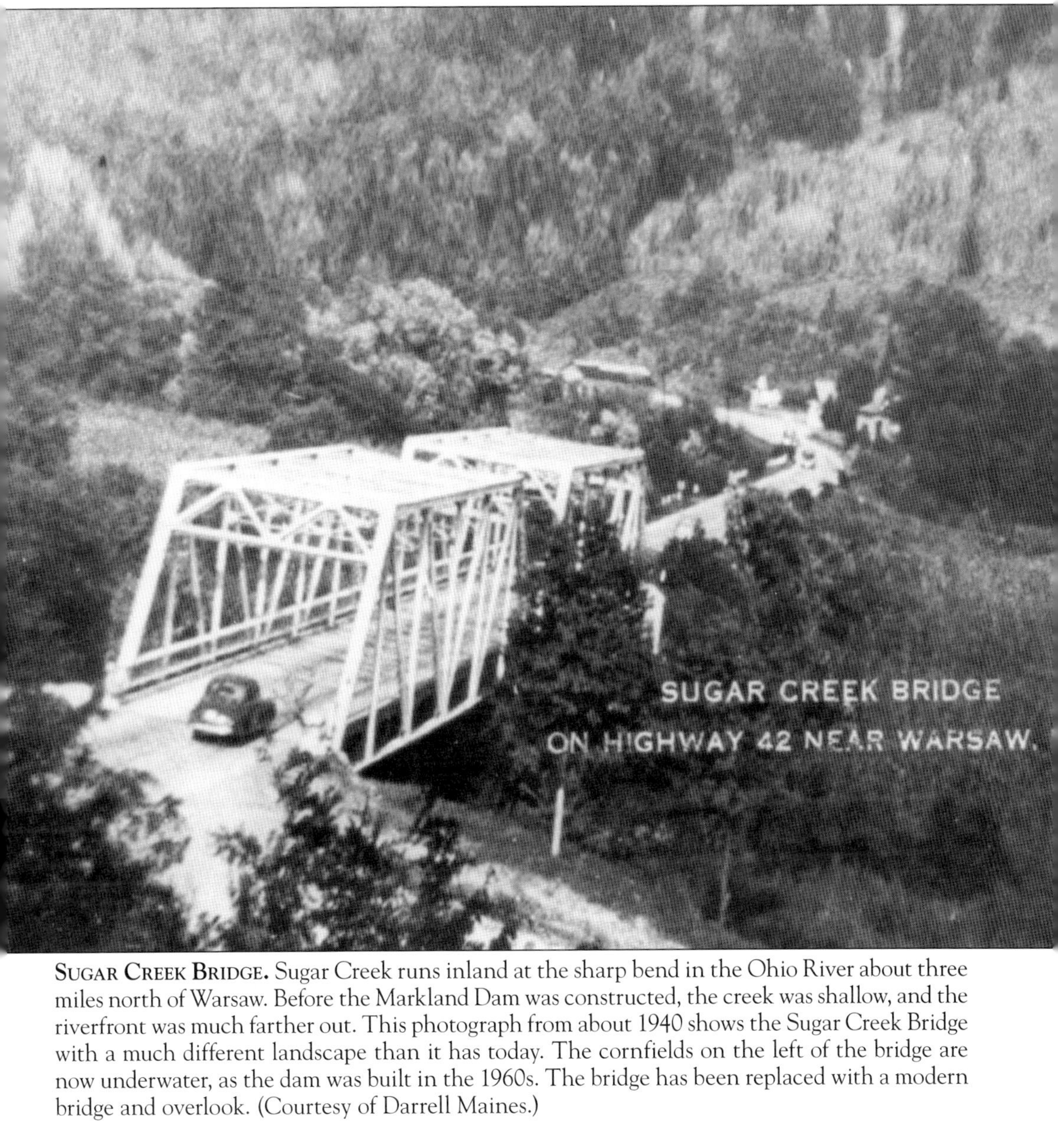

SUGAR CREEK BRIDGE. Sugar Creek runs inland at the sharp bend in the Ohio River about three miles north of Warsaw. Before the Markland Dam was constructed, the creek was shallow, and the riverfront was much farther out. This photograph from about 1940 shows the Sugar Creek Bridge with a much different landscape than it has today. The cornfields on the left of the bridge are now underwater, as the dam was built in the 1960s. The bridge has been replaced with a modern bridge and overlook. (Courtesy of Darrell Maines.)

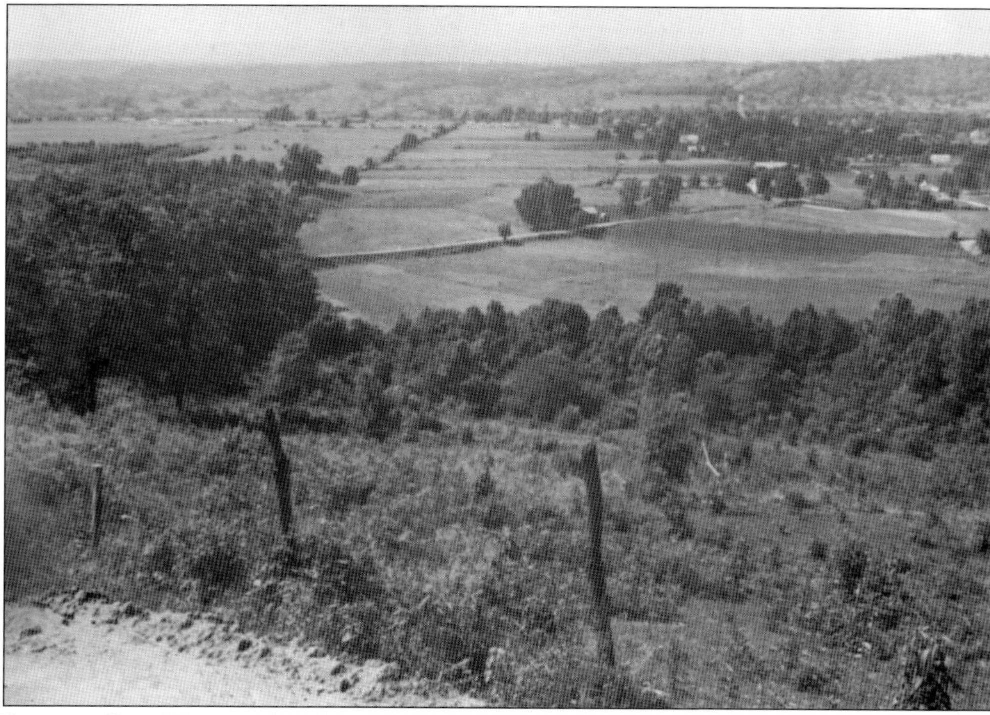

Johnson Hill. Warsaw's founding father, Col. Robert Johnson, mapped out a road leading from the riverfront to Georgetown, near Lexington, Kentucky. That road is now known as Highway 127 and routes through Glencoe. Local residents still know it as Johnson Road. The road winds through the countryside and up the hill, giving the traveler a spectacular view of the valley. These photographs offer two different views from the hill overlooking Warsaw around 1930. (Courtesy of Darrell Maines.)

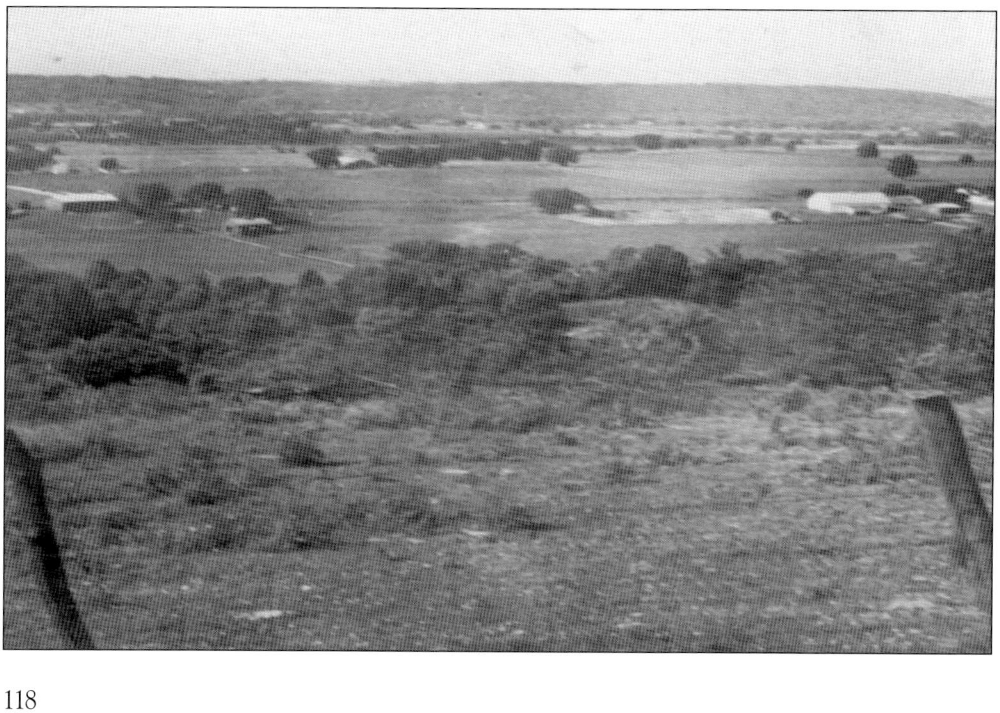

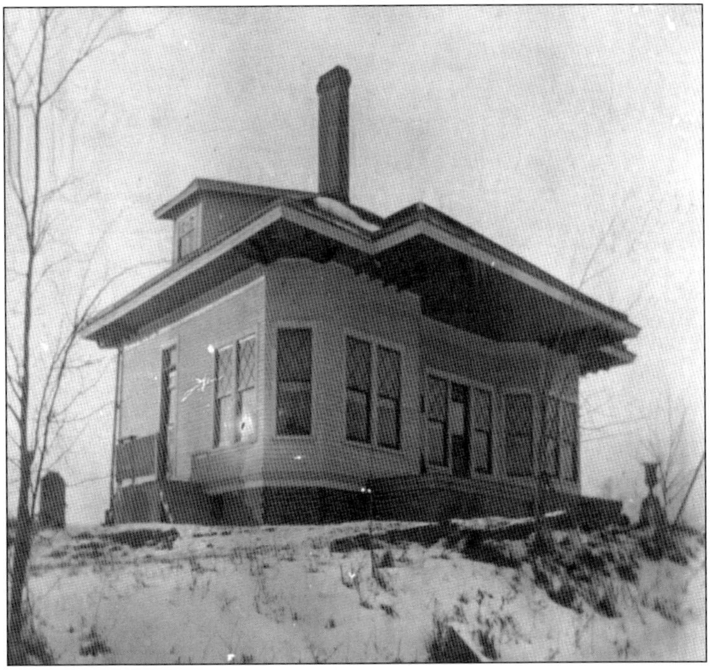

GARVEY HOME. This was the home of former postmistress Julia W. Garvey in Sparta. It was next to the Exchange Hotel, on the west side of Main Street. (Courtesy of Darrell Maines.)

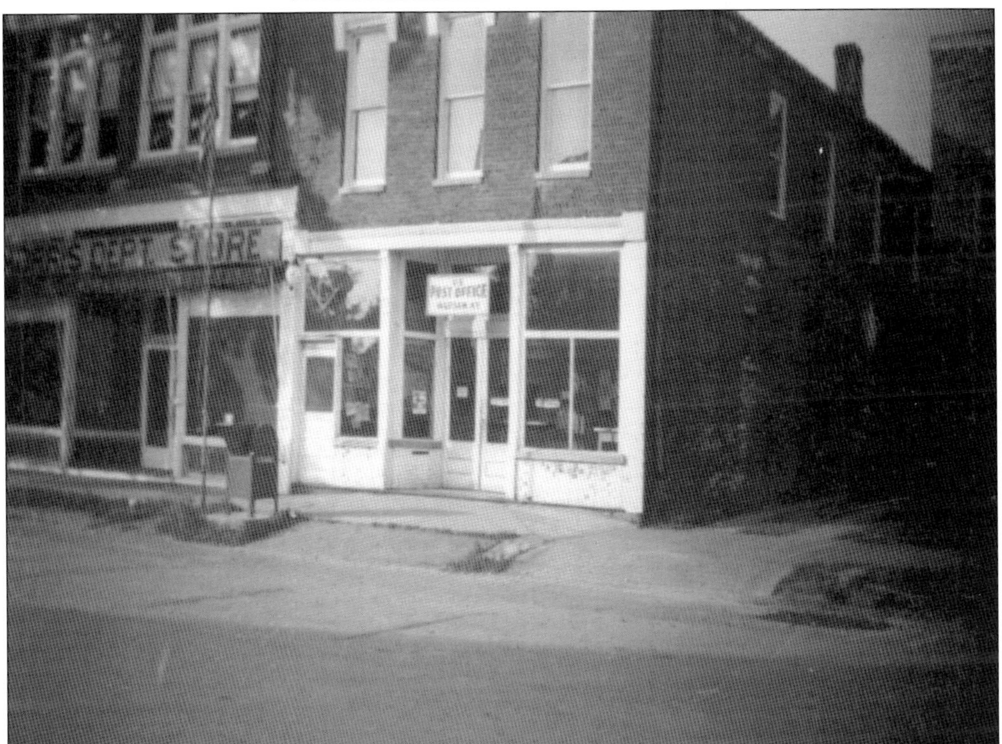

OLD POST OFFICE. The post office was located on the courthouse square, with Morris Hardware next door. At one time, it was the Mountjoy and White store, later bought by Perry Maines who located his store, Maines Hardware, there. Maines moved to a newer location on Market Street, but the building is still owned by the Maines family. (Courtesy of Darrell Maines.)

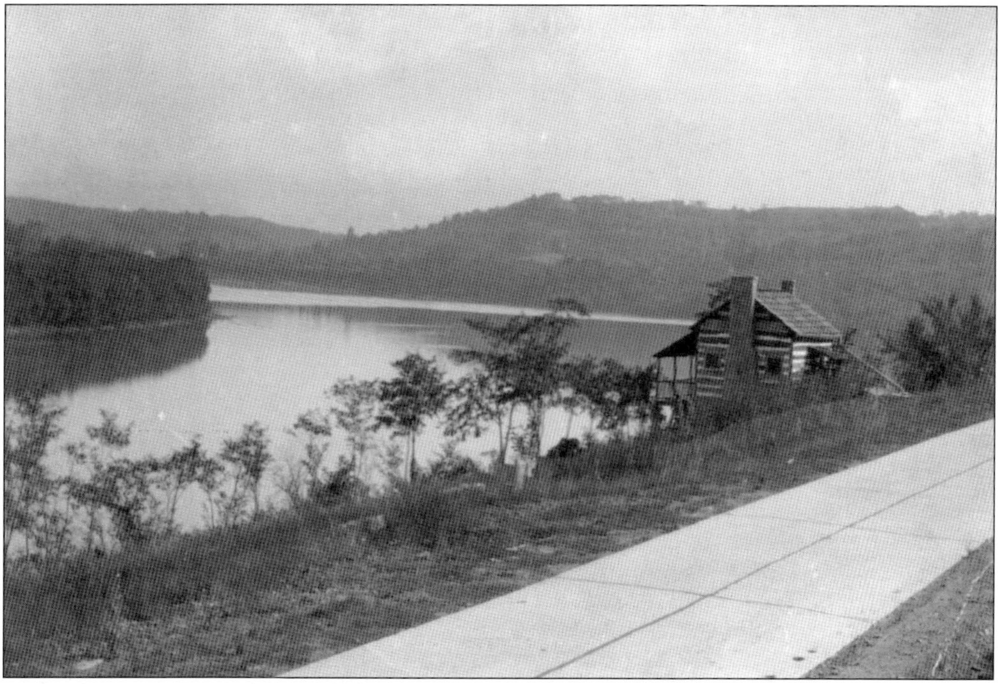

Log Cabin, US 42. This small log cabin with a big view is located on US 42, near Sugar Creek, and overlooks the Ohio River and Indiana. The cabin still stands today. (Courtesy of Darrell Maines.)

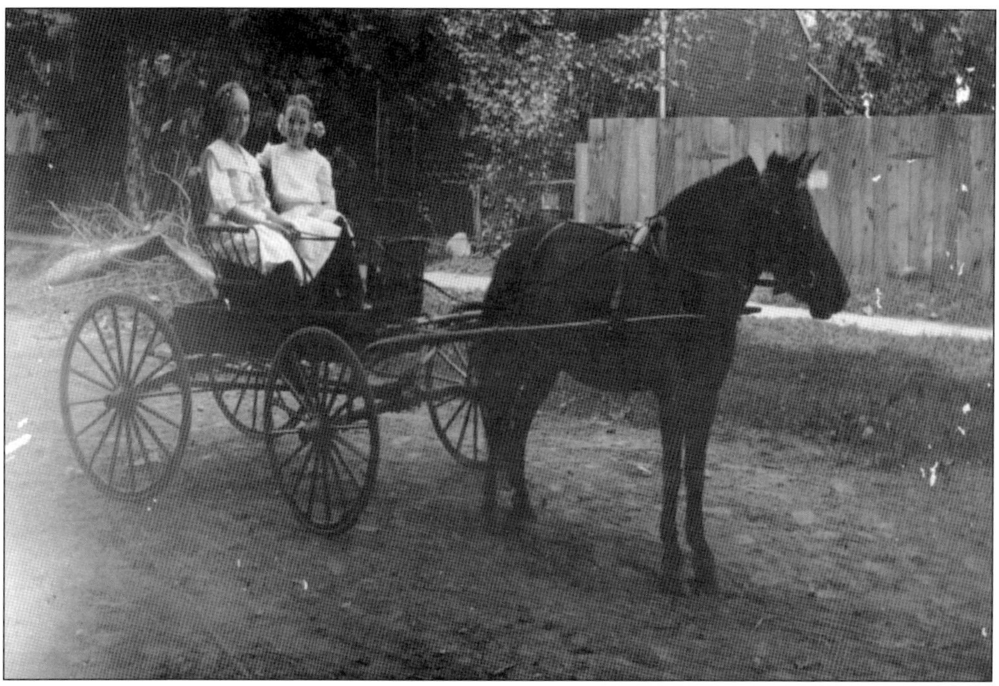

Riding Around. Marjorie Bogardus (left), and Winnie Beall Spencer take a ride around Warsaw in a carriage around 1920. Marjorie was the daughter of O.A. Bogardus, owner of the Bogardus Furniture Factory. (Courtesy of Darrell Maines.)

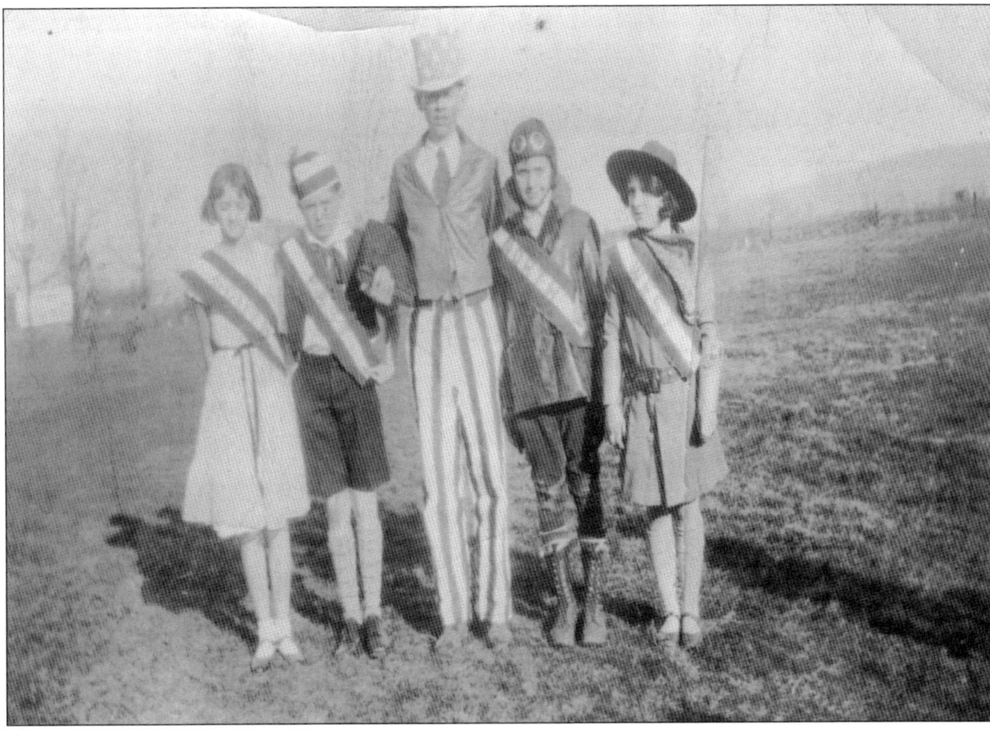

FOURTH OF JULY. Some Gallatin youngsters are dressed to represent the four directions (north, east, south, west) at a 1950s Fourth of July celebration. The boy in the center is dressed as Uncle Sam. On the right is Maybelle Connely. (Courtesy of Robert and Alexandra Weldon.)

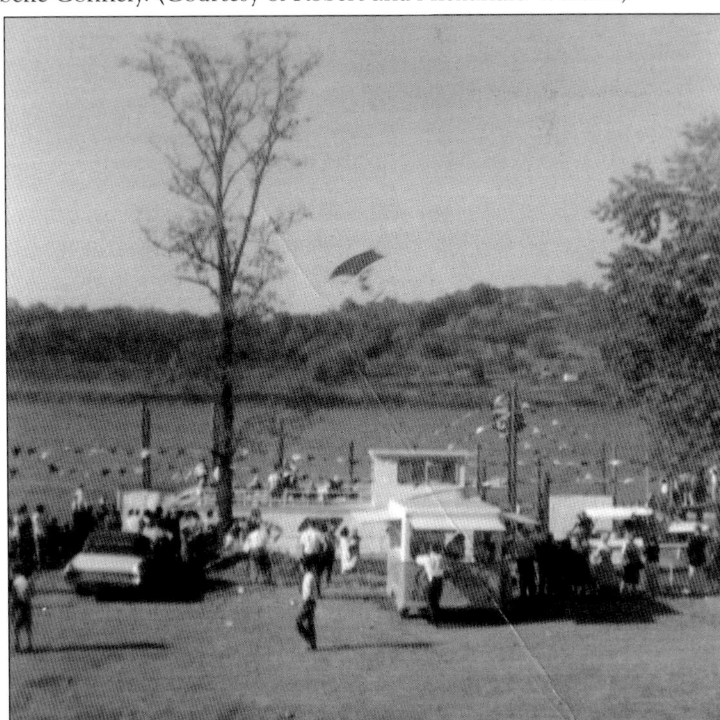

SUMMER FUN. Visitors enjoy the riverfront in this 1960s photograph. The county has a river festival every year at the landing in Warsaw to celebrate the river and its importance to the county. (Courtesy of Dana Benne.)

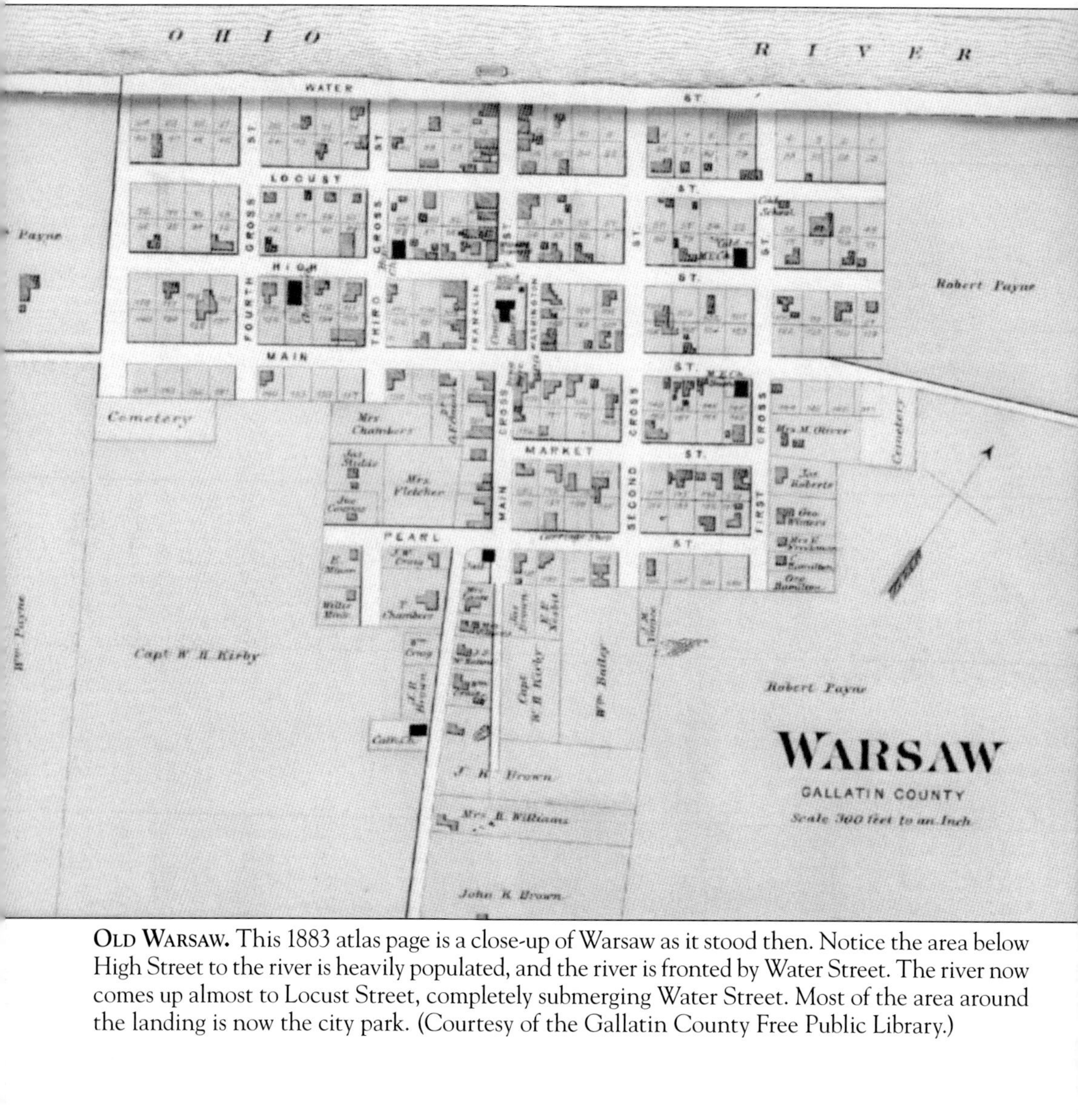

Old Warsaw. This 1883 atlas page is a close-up of Warsaw as it stood then. Notice the area below High Street to the river is heavily populated, and the river is fronted by Water Street. The river now comes up almost to Locust Street, completely submerging Water Street. Most of the area around the landing is now the city park. (Courtesy of the Gallatin County Free Public Library.)

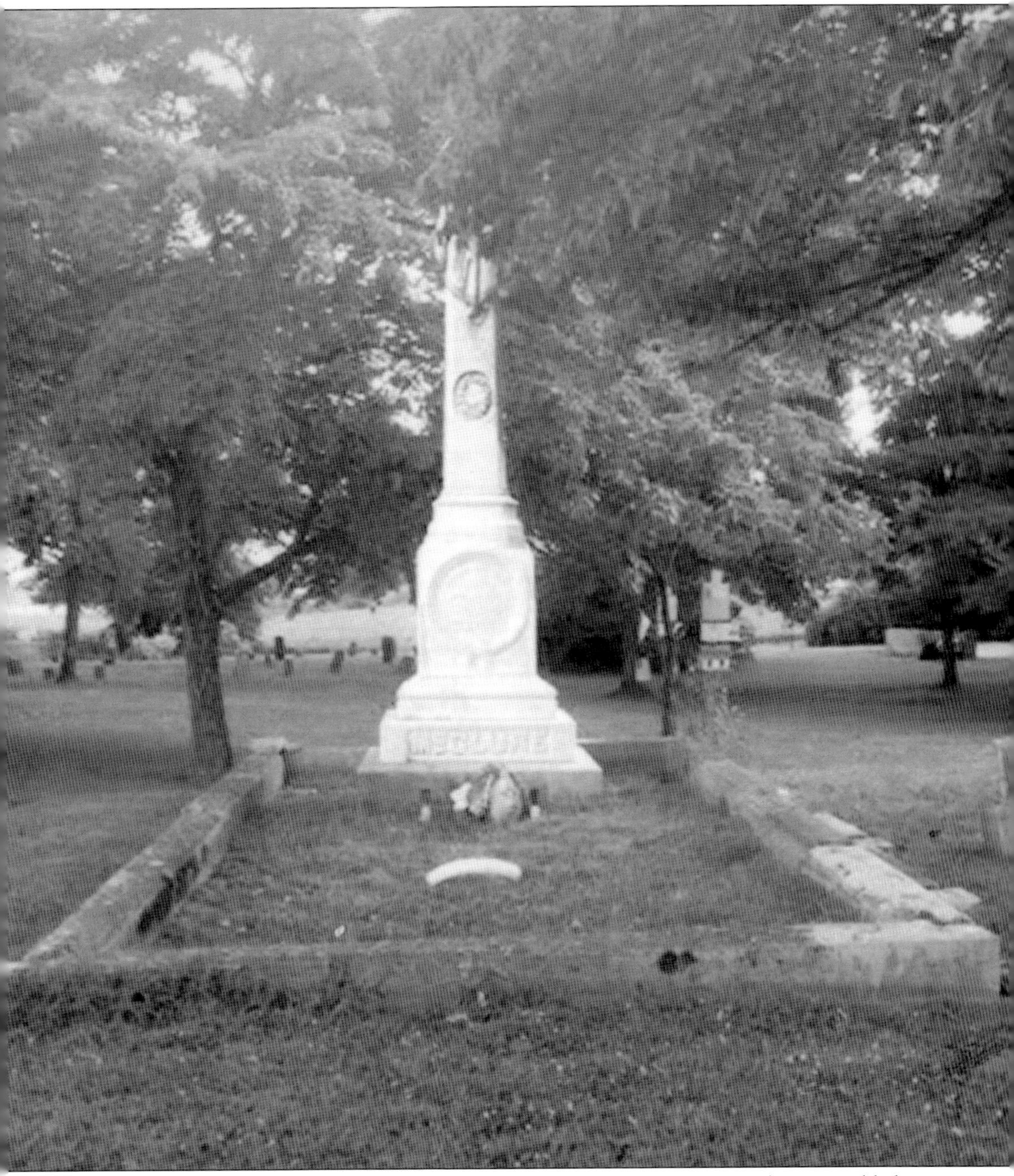

PIONEER CEMETERY. This cemetery was the early graveyard for Warsaw residents, so old that the original land records cannot be located. Active burials no longer take place here, as a new cemetery opened on the east side of town around 1860. Notable residents such as Rev. Benjamin Tiller are buried here. This beautiful headstone marks the grave of Dr. Victor McClure, a popular doctor in town. The rest of the cemetery is in disrepair through years of neglect and vandalism. It is located on Fourth Street, across from the library. (Photograph by Rebecca Riesenberg.)

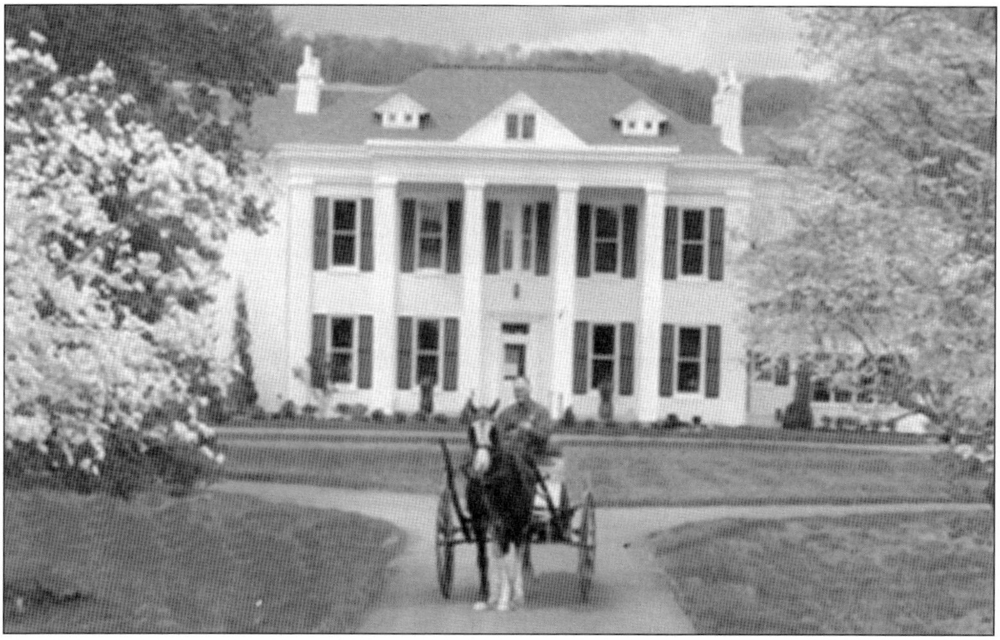

Riverside Inn. Built in 1865 by James McDanell, the renovation and expansion was completed in the spring of 2011 at a cost of over $1 million, making Riverside Inn one of Kentucky's newest and most luxurious bed-and-breakfasts. (Courtesy of Riverside Bed and Breakfast.)

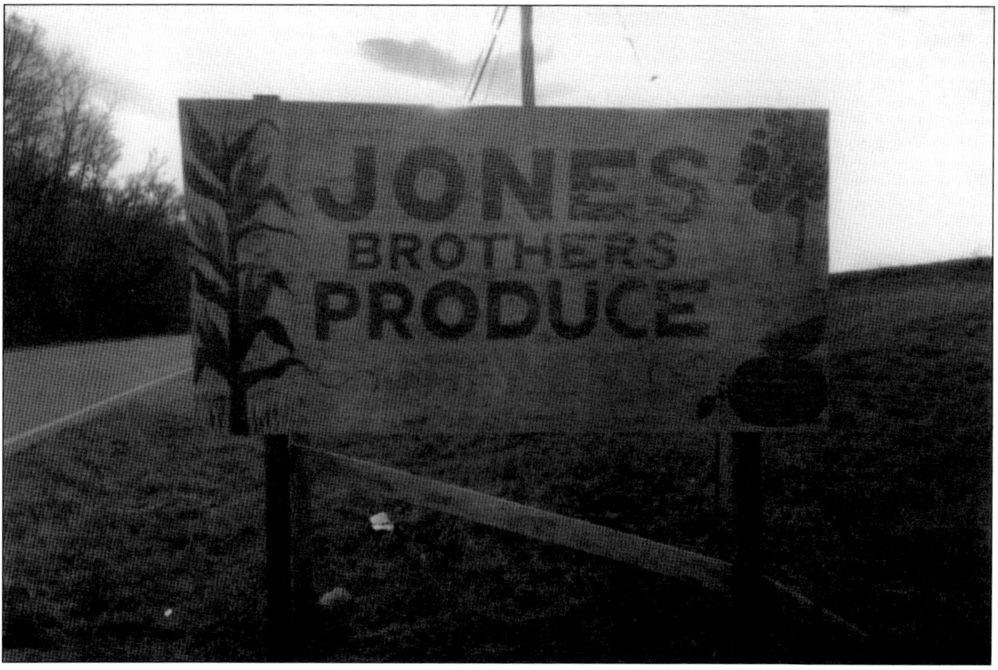

A New Business. Jones Brothers Produce was established in 2012, offering locally grown and distributed produce owned and operated by local brothers Taylor and Zachary Jones. The young brothers grew up in Gallatin County and studied agriculture and business at the University of Kentucky. The two returned to their hometown of Warsaw after college to start the business. (Courtesy of Taylor Jones, Jones Brothers Produce.)

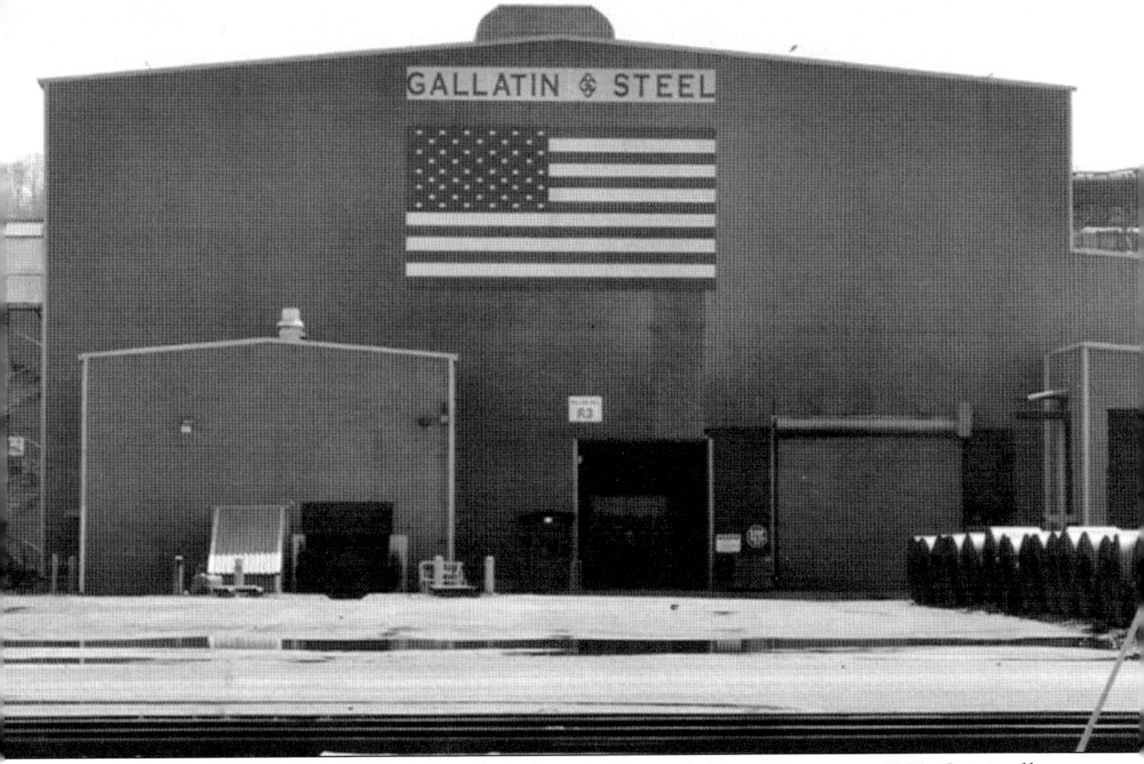

Nucor Steel Gallatin. This major steel producer came to Gallatin County in 1993. Originally called Gallatin Steel, it was purchased by Nucor in 2014 and now uses both names. It is located on US 42 on the border of Gallatin and Carroll Counties. (Courtesy of Gallatin Steel.)

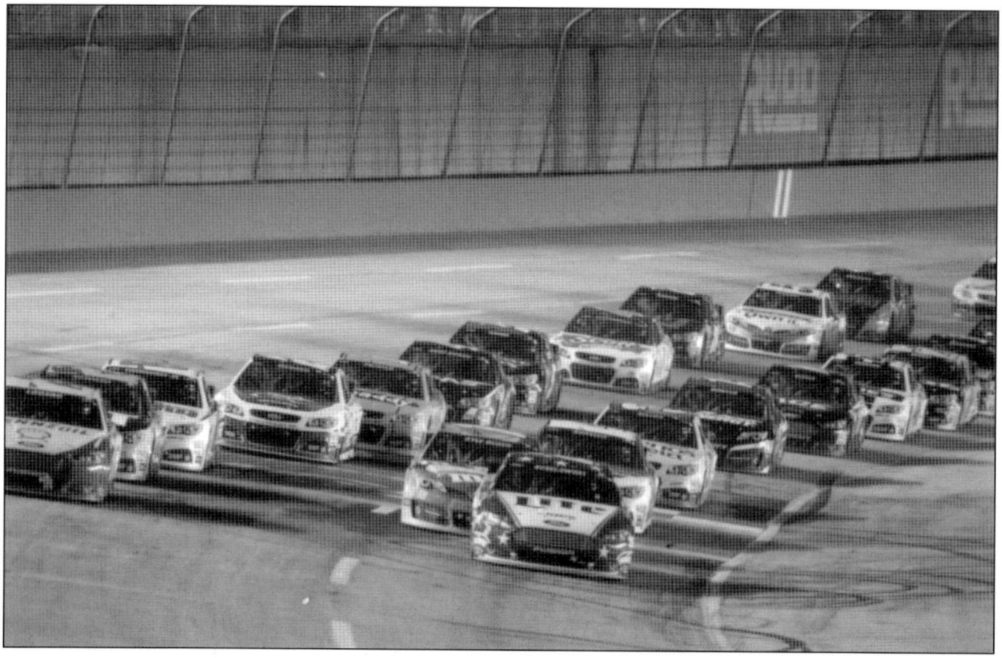

Kentucky Speedway. The track is a 1.5-mile (2.4 kilometers) tri-oval speedway, which has hosted ARCA, NASCAR, and Indy Racing League racing annually since it opened in 2000. The track is currently owned and operated by Speedway Motorsports Inc. and Jerry Carroll, who, along with four other investors, owned Kentucky Speedway until 2008. The speedway has a grandstand capacity of 117,000. (Both, courtesy of the Kentucky Speedway.)

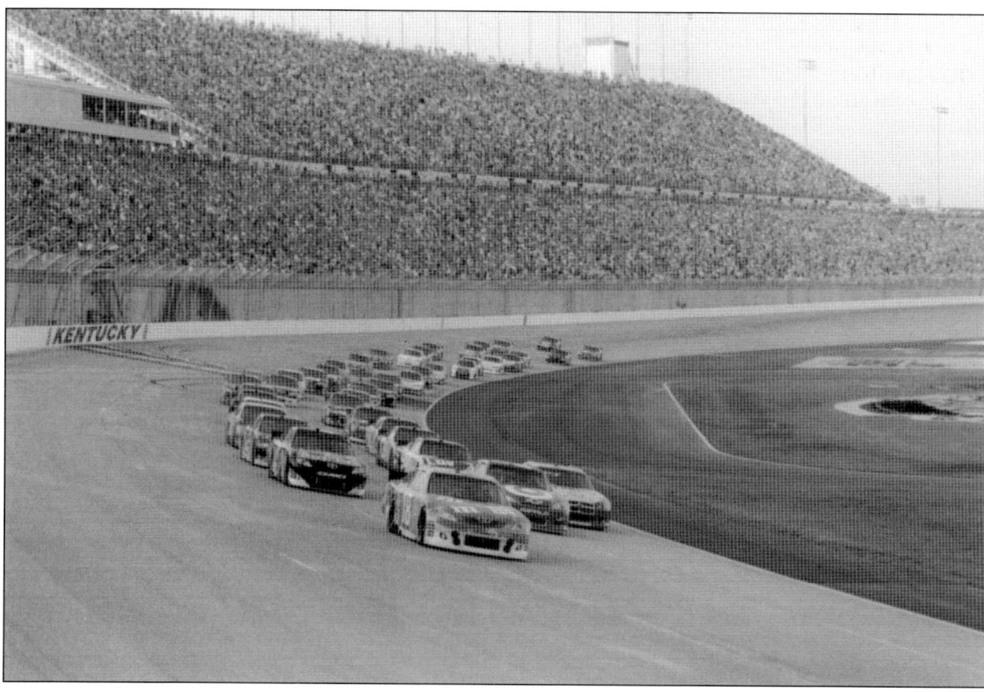

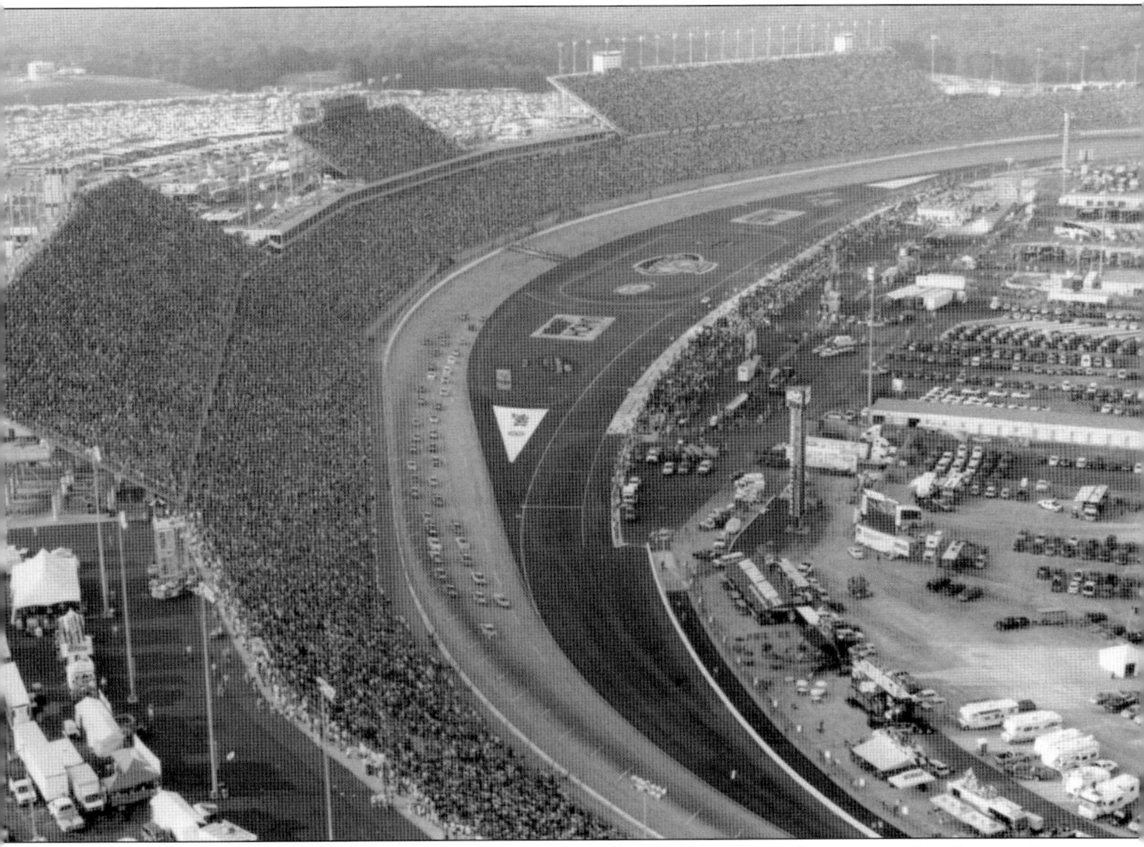

Roar of the Engines. Construction of the speedway began in 1998 and was completed in mid-2000. The speedway has hosted the Camping World Truck Series, Nationwide Series, IndyCar Series, Firestone Indy Lights Series, and most recently, the Sprint Cup Series, which began in 2011. (Courtesy of the Kentucky Speedway.)

Consistent with our mission to preserve history on a local level, this book was printed in South Carolina on American-made paper and manufactured entirely in the United States. Products carrying the accredited Forest Stewardship Council (FSC) label are printed on 100 percent FSC-certified paper.